What's *New* for Parents

What's *New* for Parents

Irene Franck

David Brownstone

Prentice Hall General Reference
New York   London   Toronto   Sydney   Tokyo   Singapore

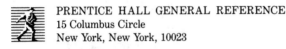 PRENTICE HALL GENERAL REFERENCE
15 Columbus Circle
New York, New York, 10023

Library of Congress Cataloging in Publication data

Franck, Irene M.
  What's new for parents : the essential resource to products and
services, programs and information, new for the '90s / Irene Franck,
David Brownstone.
      p.   cm.
  Includes bibliographical references and index.
  ISBN 0-671-85036-9
  1. Child rearing—United States—Handbooks, manuals, etc.
2. Parenting—United States—Handbooks, manuals, etc. 3. Children—
United States—Handbooks, manuals, etc. 4. Children—Health and
hygiene—United States—Handbooks, manuals, etc. 5. Child
development—United States—Handbooks, manuals, etc.
I. Brownstone, David M. II. Title.
HQ769.F718 1993
649'.1—dc20   92-39944
                                                         CIP

Designed by Irving Perkins Associates Inc.
Manufactured in the United States of America
  10 9 8 7 6 5 4 3 2 1

First Edition

Contents

Preface

Every day brings news reports of discoveries, approaches, recommendations, controversies, services, and products of vital interest to parents. But parents generally come across them only on a catch-as-catch-can basis, through brief, partial, and ephemeral summaries in newspapers and popular periodicals. As we found in the course of doing *The Parent's Desk Reference* (Prentice Hall, 1990), parents have no single, handy source summarizing the key news and innovations that affect them and their children. That is what *What's New for Parents* intends to do. The book is intended for parents of all ages—from those whose children are still the proverbial "twinkle in their eyes" to those whose "babies" are off to college.

This is, of course, a selective book—and we hope the first of many—to help keep parents up-to-date on information affecting their children. And the focus is on the *new*, specifically featuring the innovations of the 90s. In each case, we offer a brief overview of the discovery, product, report, or recommendation, and provide follow-up information where appropriate, such as numbers to call, organizations to contact, sources for products, and articles to read. We have not, however, included addresses and phone numbers for large, well-known publishers, whose books would generally be purchased through bookstores or borrowed from libraries. Articles are arranged in four general sections: What's New in Fun and Games, What's New in Family Health and Safety, What's New in Learning and Education, and What's New in Parenting Resources. The index at the back of the book provides alphabetical access to the contents.

As always, we wish to thank many people: our editors Kate Kelly, and then Susan Lauzau; the staff at the Chappaqua Library, our research mainstay, including director Mark Hasskarl; the expert reference staff, including Martha Alcott, Carolyn Jones, Elizabeth Peyraud, Paula Peyraud, Mary Platt, and Carolyn Reznick, and Marilyn Coleman, Lois Siwicki, Jane McKean, and the rest of the circulation staff. We also thank the dozens of people in firms and organizations around the country who so kindly provided us with information. They are too numerous to mention by name, but were all unfailingly generous and helpful.

Irene Franck
David Brownstone
Chappaqua, New York

What's *New* in Fun and Games

Children's Magazines—New and Booming

It's boom time in children's magazine publishing. According to the American Library Association, over 120 magazines are currently being published for children ages 2 to 14. Many of the old favorites—such as *Highlights for Children, Sesame Street Magazine, National Geographic World,* and *Cricket*—have soaring circulations. And in the last few years, several new children's publications have been launched, some so new they haven't even made it into the reference books below. So parents looking for *just* the right magazine for their children have a number of new offerings to choose from.

One of the most interesting is *Boomerang!*, not a print-on-paper publication, but an *audio* magazine for kids. Inspired by the publisher's own 8-year-old daughter's curiosity about the Berlin Wall, *Boomerang!*—described as "the children's audiomagazine about big ideas"—is designed to present complicated issues and ideas in ways that children can understand. In fact, many of the stories are read, acted, and reported by 9- to 13-year-old Kid Reporters, working with adult advisers. *Boomerang!* is a monthly 70-minute cassette tape for children 7 to 12, structured in typical magazine format, with letters to

Boomerang! (BOOMERANG!)

the editor, columns, and feature stories, interspersed with jokes and odd bits of miscellany. Some reviewers have compared it to the best of National Public Radio's *All Things Considered* and Garrison Keillor combined.

Boomerang!'s feature segments range from 2 to 15 minutes long and vary somewhat from issue to issue, but typically include topics such as:

• **The Big Idea.** *Boomerang!*'s cover story, exploring current and often controversial issues—such as the recession, the First Amendment, or rain forests—from a child's perspective, and in a child's language.

• **Money.** Information on how the economy works, often demonstrated by 9-year-old Freddie Baxter's Rhubarb and Banana Sandwich Roadside Stand.

• **Turning Points.** "Interviews" with historical figures, such as Rosa Parks and Louis Braille.

• **Big Talk.** A letters-to-the-editor feature about the strange things grown-ups do.

• **Natural Wonders.** A reporter's musings about the natural world, from dolphins to volcanoes to raindrops.

* **Mystery.** A humorous detective story, starring ace gumshoe Tucker Jones.
* **American Journey.** A young girl's reports from places visited on her cross-country journeys with her grandfather, such as Gloucester, MA, or Oshkosh, WI.
* **Book Beat.** Interviews with and readings by children's authors.
* **Green Tip.** Ecological advice.
* **Weird Words.** Quick quizzes involving unusual words.
* **Power Up.** An "empowering personal experience."
* **The Count.** A lesson in counting to 10 in a foreign language, such as Mandarin or Greek.
* **Schmave's Elevator.** Stories about childhood, from the elevator man in the *Boomerang!* building.
* **The Census.** Live interviews with subscribers who have sent in their phone numbers on topics such as their favorite hiding place or what makes a good friend.

Not a translation from the printed page, *Boomerang!* is created as an audio magazine, and includes appropriate background music and sound effects. It is designed to be played the way a magazine is read—in short, bite-sized chunks, with natural breaks. One big difference: Parents will be pleased to know that *Boomerang!* accepts no advertising. Each tape is accompanied by a four-color insert, containing program information, games, maps, and reading suggestions, to reinforce the audio material. In addition to the one-year subscription for 12 monthly issues, parents have the option of a trial subscription of three issues or the purchase of individual cassettes, including both current and back issues. (For more information, contact: Boomerang!, 123 Townsend Street, Suite 636, San Francisco, CA 94107; 800-333-7858.)

Among the many new print-on-paper magazines for children, parents may well want to take a look at:

* ***Ladybug: The Magazine for Young Children.*** A monthly magazine of stories, songs, and poems for children 2 to 7 years old. Each issue includes an activities insert and a section for parents, which discusses the issue's contents and recommends additional activities; it is the counterpart of *Cricket*, the magazine for kids 7 to 12. (For more information, contact: Carus Publishing Co., 315 Fifth Street, Peru, IL 61354; 815-223-1500 or 800-284-7257.)
* ***Spark!: The Magazine of Creative Fun for Kids.*** A magazine for children ages 3 to 11, published nine times a year. It offers "kid-tested

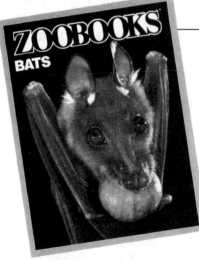

Ladybug (CARUS PUBLISHING)

Disney Adventures (WALT DISNEY MAGAZINE PUBLISHING GROUP)

Spark! (F & W PUBLICATIONS)

Sports Illustrated for Kids (TIME, INC.)

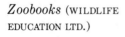

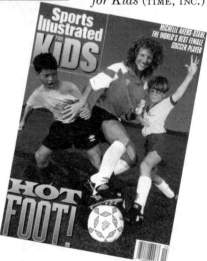

Zoobooks (WILDLIFE EDUCATION LTD.)

and parent-approved" projects and activities "to challenge children's imaginations and develop creative skills." (For more information, contact: F&W Publications, Inc., 1507 Dana Avenue, Cincinnati, OH 45207; 513-531-2222.)

◆ *Disney Adventures: The Magazine for Kids.* A monthly general-interest magazine for children 7 to 14 years old. It features adventures, music, movies, sports, science, comics, games, and more, designed to appeal to kids' imaginations. (For more information, contact: Walt Disney Magazine Publishing Group, 500 South Buena Vista, Burbank Center, Suite 101, Burbank, CA 91521; 818-973-4150; for subscriptions, 800-877-5396.)

◆ *Zoobooks.* A magazine designed for children 6 to 14 years old, and published 10 times a year. Each issue takes an in-depth look at one particular animal or group of animals. (For more information, contact: Wildlife Education Ltd., 3590 Kettner Boulevard, San Diego, CA 92101; 619-299-5034.)

◆ *Sports Illustrated for Kids.* A monthly for children 8 to 13 years old. This is spun off from the adult *Sports Illustrated*, and like the adult magazine, it features striking color photographs and action-oriented sports stories. (For more information, contact: Time, Inc., Magazine Co., Time and Life Building, Rockefeller Center, New York, NY 10020; 800-633-8628.)

◆ *KidSports.* A bimonthly for children 7 to 14 years old. This offers articles by or ascribed to sports stars on their techniques for success as well as inspirational or encouraging personal stories, and sidelights such as "My Worst Day" as an athlete. (For more information, contact: ProServ Publishing Corp., 1101 Wilson Boulevard, Suite 1800, Arlington, VA 22209; 703-276-3030.)

◆ *Sassy.* A monthly for teenage girls. This is a life-style magazine that also includes fiction and has won attention for its willingness to tackle controversial issues. (For more information, contact: Sassy Publications, 230 Park Avenue, New York, NY 10169; 212-551-9500.)

For a sample of the best from children's magazines, there is *Of Cabbages and Kings™: A Children's Magazine Guide®,* by Kimberly Olson Fakih, published by Bowker, an annual anthology of writing culled from children's magazines such as *Boy's Life, Calliope, Children's, Cricket, Current Events, Faces: The Magazine About People, Highlights for Children, Humpty Dumpty's Magazine, International Wildlife, Junior Scholastic, National Geographic, National Wildlife, Ranger Rick, Scholastic, Choices,* and *Sciencelands.* (For more

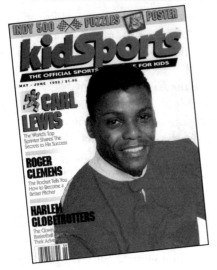

KidSports (PROSERV
PUBLISHING)

Sassy (SASSY PUBLICATIONS)

information, contact: R. R. Bowker Order Department, P.O. Box 31, New Providence, NJ 07974; 800-521-8110.)

For more information on magazines for children and young adults, parents may want to consult:

◆ ***Magazines for Children: A Guide for Parents, Teachers, and Librarians***, 2d ed., by Selma K. Richardson (ALA Books, 1991). An annotated reference book from the American Library Association on the subjects, contents, features, and graphics of selected publications, offering information important in evaluating them. (For more information, contact: ALA Books, 50 East Huron Street, Chicago, IL 60611; 800-545-2433.)

◆ ***Magazines for Young People***, 2d ed., by Bill Katz and Linda Sternberg Katz (Bowker, 1991). A standard reference work intended for librarians who choose magazines for children and young adults, but equally useful for parents looking for just the right magazine for the special interests and needs of their child. Also standard is their *Magazines for Libraries*, 7th ed. (Bowker, 1992), which includes children's magazines. (For more information, contact: R. R. Bowker Order Department, P.O. Box 31, New Providence, NJ 07974; 800-521-8110.)

Crayons: Something Old, Something New . . .

Crayola®, the grand old name in crayons, has somewhat surprisingly been in the news in the 1990s. First there was a brouhaha about eight "old-fashioned" colors that Crayola manufacturer Binney & Smith retired in 1990 to make room for some brighter, jazzier colors. After a startling outcry from parents who fondly remember their own childhoods with maize, raw umber, violet blue, blue gray, green blue, lemon yellow, orange red, and orange yellow, Binney & Smith relented—at least temporarily. They put together a "Classic" set of colors, including both the old and new, in a special metal box. For general purposes, however, the colors stayed retired, inducted into the "Crayola Hall of Fame."

Then, responding to requests from schoolteachers and children, the manufacturer in 1992 began packaging large-sized crayons in "skin-tone" colors—apricot, peach, tan, sepia, burnt sienna, mahogany, black, and white—in their own separate boxes, labeled "multicultural colors." These colors had been available all along in the 64–crayon pack for older children, but those crayons were too small for young children to hold. As of 1992, the Multicultural Crayons were not available from retail outlets, but only from educational supply outlets, through a Columbia, MD, school-supplies distributor, Chaselle (800-242-7355). In late 1992, Binney & Smith introduced My World Colors, sold in retail outlets, with 16 crayons for skin, hair, and eye colors.

But perhaps the most notable advance in crayon history came with the 1992 introduction of what Binney & Smith terms a "totally off-the-wall product": *washable* crayons. These have the potential for saving thousands, if not millions, of walls, floors, cabinets, and other household surfaces that have been the traditional "canvas" for budding Crayola Rembrandts and Van Goghs. Binney & Smith's first new formulation in nearly 90 years, these nontoxic washable crayons are made from special water-soluble polymers of the type found in many health and beauty aids. *Their* beauty is that they can be washed from "most walls, nonporous household surfaces, and nearly all children's clothing" simply with soap and water. The manufacturer notes that it is easiest to remove such crayon marks soon after they are made, but their tests have shown that washable crayon marks can be removed from walls and fabric even one to two months after being stained. Binney & Smith

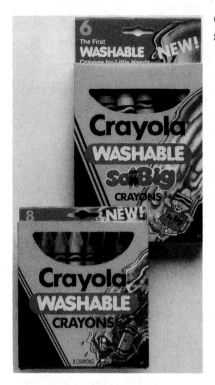

Crayola Washable Crayons (BINNEY & SMITH)

does caution that melted crayons may cause permanent heat-set stains, so parents should check pockets for crayons before placing clothing in a hot-water washer or a dryer. And, as with any stained surface, it is always wise for parents to check a small area before washing a whole surface; some house paints, for example, may also be removed when washed.

The patented washable crayons were developed in response to requests from parents, who have over the years called or written the manufacturer by the thousands each year, for help in trying to remove crayon stains. Because experience has shown that most "mishaps" with traditional crayons occur with children under age 5, the new washable Crayola crayons were introduced in only 2 sizes: large and So Big (even larger); both are designed to be easier for small hands to hold and harder to break than the smaller crayons meant for older children. The box of 8 large washable crayons contains the same colors as the first box of Crayola crayons which sold for five cents in 1903: red, green, yellow, orange, blue, black, brown, and violet. The So Big washable crayons come in boxes of 6, without the orange and violet. The only thing missing is the familiar waxy aroma of the traditional crayons, which continue to sell in the billions. Washable Crayola crayons are available in retail stores. Washable markers are also available from Crayola. (For more information, contact: Binney & Smith, Inc., 1100 Church Lane, P.O. Box 431, Easton, PA 18044-0431; 800-CRAYOLA [272-9652] or 215-253-6271.)

Arts and Crafts for Fun

For many parents, enhancing their children's artistic skills is a top priority. Several books have recently been published to help them do just that. The "Come Look with Me" series shows parents (or other adults) how to introduce children to art, using examples of paintings by such artists as Holbein, Rousseau, and Picasso. Written by Gladys S. Blizzard and published by Thomasson-Grant, titles include *Enjoying Art with Children* (1991) and *Exploring Landscape Art with Children* (1992). Use them for kids ages 6 and up. Another useful title is *A Parent's Guide to Teaching Art*, by Donna B. Gray (Betterway, 1991), with photographs, illustrations, and a color insert.

Many recent titles focus on hands-on arts and crafts, including these:

For Preschoolers

• *I Can Draw*, by Merry Fleming Thomasson (Thomasson-Grant, 1992). This book, for ages 2 to 7, helps children create their own illustrations. It is part of the "Hey, Look at Me!" series, in which a child's photo is placed in the back cover, making him or her the "star" of the book.

For Kids in Kindergarten and Primary School

• The "Rainy Day" series, published by Gloucester/Watts, with color photos and illustrations, and projects to do, for children in grades K through 4, includes these titles: *Kites and Flying Objects* (1992), *Masks and Funny Faces* (1992), *Grow It for Fun: Hands-on Projects* (1991), and *Cooking: Hands-on Projects* (1991), all by Denny Robson; and *Puppets: Games and Projects* (1991), *Shadow Theater: Games and Projects* (1991), *Magic Tricks: Games and Projects for Children*, and *Card Tricks: Games and Projects for Children* (1990), all by Vanessa Bailey.
• The "Why Throw It Away?" series, by Jen Green, published by Gloucester/Watts, with color photos and projects for children in grades

K through 4, includes *Making Crazy Animals* and *Making Mad Machines* (both 1992).

• The "Art and Activities for Kids" series, by Kim Solga, published by North Light Books, for children ages 6 to 11, includes *Draw!*, *Paint!*, *Make Gifts!*, and *Make Prints!* (all 1991).

• *Woodworking with Your Kids*, rev. ed., by Richard Starr (Taunton, 1990). This is for parents to use with children in grades 1 through 9.

• *String: Tying It Up, Tying It Down*, by Jan Adkins (Scribner's, 1992). For ages 10 and up, this is a beginner's guide to tying things, with projects like rigging a hammock, stretching a clothesline, hoisting a bucket, binding a bundle, and more.

For Kids in Middle School and Up

• The "Hands-On Arts and Crafts" series, by Anthony Hodge, published by Watts, for children in grades 5 through 9, includes *Cartooning* (1992), *Collage* (1992), *Drawing* (1991), and *Painting* (1991).

• *Simple Makeup for Young Actors*, by Richard Cummings (Plays, Inc., 1990). For grades 8 and up, this book shows the whole process, from assembling a basic makeup kit to application and removal. It also covers special concerns such as prosthetics and character makeup, including details on makeup for two dozen character types.

For more information on these and other titles, contact your local library or bookstore. Parents may also want to check out "Free Information for Parents" on page 212.

Kidpix: Drawing Without Tears, Painting Without Mess

Are you nurturing a young Picasso or O'Keeffe? Perhaps. For parents who have a home computer, one easy—and nonmessy—way to find out might be to buy the family a copy of the computer program *Kidpix*. This is a simple "paint program," without adult graphics sophistication, but instead with dozens of kid-delighting tools and special effects, including sounds.

Children as young as 3 or 4 can make simple drawings by moving a device called a mouse, movements that the computer program translates into images on the screen. Older children and young adults find a

Kidpix (BRØDERBUND SOFTWARE)

dazzling array of tools, including a pencil for drawing free-form lines; tools for drawing circles, straight lines, and rectangles; and other tools such as a paint bucket, a tool for adding text, a rubber stamp (for moving computer-stored objects, such as a bird, a heart, or a happy face), a moving van, and an electric mixer, which introduces a host of variations, such as reversing colors, slicing a drawing into strips, or "shattering" it like glass.

Even more fun for kids, each tool and its variations has a distinctive sound, such as spraying, scratching (as of a pencil), dripping, or splashing; also, any numbers and letters added to the picture are spoken aloud (in English or Spanish, as chosen when the program is set up). An eraser is provided, so kids can "erase" the last move they made; by clicking the mouse on a little face called the "Undo Guy," they can restore the previous version of the "painting."

Finished works can be printed out, stored on disks, or simply erased—and even this is made fun, as the child can choose several different ways to go, including blowing up the drawing with a firecracker, having a black hole suck it up, having it fade away, or causing it to drop away in pieces. Luckily for parents, *Kidpix* comes with a special feature that preserves other material on the hard disk from damage; they simply set the program in "Small Kids Mode," so the program will disable any command that might cause problems to the computer, the disk, or its contents; it also prevents kids from getting "stuck."

Kidpix can be used with black-and-white machines but is most fun for kids if the computer has color; similarly, only with color printers can a child see the full effect of the "painting" on paper. The program is available for use on Macintosh or IBM computers. (For more information, contact: Brøderbund Software-Direct, P.O. Box 6125, Novato, CA 94948-6125; 800-521-6263 or 415-492-3500.)

Thinga-ma-bib™

That's the name of some new handcrafted bibs for babies—what one reviewer called "the thinking baby's arty alternative to ordinary spill protectors." Each one-of-a-kind bib is made of see-through vinyl plastic, in which are encased colorful bits of Mylar as well as various "doohickeys" and "found objects," such as vintage postcards and other images, which provide color to stimulate babies and humor to tickle adults. Each individual Thinga-ma-bib is unique, but entrepreneur-designer Wendy Kaplan Backer crafts them around various themes, including A.M. (suburban morning life), Apples and Carrots (where they come from and who eats them), La Bamba (music), La Estrella (water activities), Greetings From (travel), El Mundo (tongue-in-cheek anthropology), and Trouble in Paradise (with unexpected conjunctions,

La Estrella Thinga-ma-bib™
(THINGA-MA-BIB)

La Bamba Thinga-ma-bib™
(THINGA-MA-BIB)

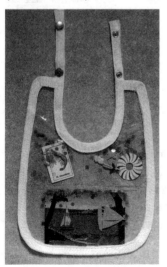

such as dinosaurs wooing a hula girl or an ant in a bouffant hairdo). The wipe-clean bibs are trimmed with stain-resistant, colorfast cotton, and the ties have various snaps to fit babies small or large. (For more information, contact: Thinga-ma-bib, 150 Clipper Street, San Francisco, CA 94114; 415-824-5640.)

A Doll with a Purpose

In the three decades since Barbie® was introduced, many parents and child psychology experts have expressed concern that the unrealistic shape and measurements of Barbie and other "fashion dolls" give young girls a distorted image of what a woman's body should look like, thereby contributing to low self-esteem and eating disorders, including excessive dieting. Cathy Meredig thought she'd do something about helping young girls develop realistic body images and acceptance of themselves as they are—so she developed the Happy To Be Me™ doll. A human-sized Barbie would measure a nearly impossible 39-21-33, with other disproportionate measurements, including a midriff so indented as to be achievable only through surgical removal of ribs. By contrast, a Happy To Be Me doll would in human size measure a more realistic 36-27-38, with other normal proportions, such as hips being broader than the shoulders and rounded tummy and bottom (rather than being impossibly flat or even indented, as in some fashion dolls), and with feet in a flat position, rather than permanently flexed in a high-heel stance. Both types of dolls have bendable arms and legs.

From its introduction in 1991, the Happy To Be Me doll has generated enormous attention, with substantial newspaper, radio, and television coverage not only across North America but also abroad as well. The Happy To Be Me line also includes an Asian-American doll and an African-American doll (both female), as well as a Happy to Be Grandpa doll. Various outfits are available for the Happy dolls for a wide range of activities, from a camping outfit and sweatsuit to old-fashioned caroling outfits and gowns (including bridal wear), to an office-oriented suit-with-skirt or dressy pants suit, to winter coats and everyday wear. In addition, McCall Pattern Company sells patterns for Happy doll clothes—people who sew note that clothes for the Happy doll are much easier to sew than those for fashion dolls. (For more information, contact: High Self-Esteem Toys Corporation, P.O.

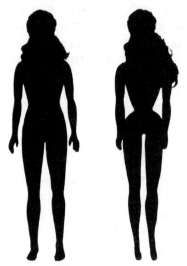

Happy To Be Me™ vs. fashion doll
(HIGH SELF-ESTEEM TOY CORP.)

Happy To Be Me™ doll (HIGH
SELF-ESTEEM TOY CORP.)

Box 25208, Woodbury, MN 55125; 612-731-4767, or to place an order 800-477-9235.)

What Shall We Do Today?

For parents with kids at home on a summer day, winter day, rainy day, too-hot day, Saturday, Sunday, sick day, holiday, or other no-school day, this is a perennial question. A number of authors—generally parents themselves—have come up with activities designed to keep children busy and entertained, and often to enhance their skills and development, and perhaps also the parent-child relationship. Among the recent publications in this area are:

    ♦ *More Prime Time Activities with Kids*, by Donna Erickson (Augsburg, 1992). Offers 80 projects to help build parent-child relationships; it is a sequel to her *Prime Time Together . . . with Kids* (Augsburg, 1989).
    ♦ *Kids and Weekends: Creative Ways to Make Special Days*, by Avery Hart and Paul Mantell (Williamson, 1992). Suggests ideas on

interactive experiences for adults and just one child or the whole neighborhood.

♦ *100 Wonderful Things to Keep Kids Busy and Having Fun*, by Pam Schiller and Joan Rossano (Ten Speed/Celestial Arts, 1992). Describes activities and projects for one or more kids.

♦ *101 Great Ways to Keep Your Child Entertained: While You Get Something Else Done*, by Danelle Hickman and Valerie Teurlay (St. Martin's, 1992). For parents of toddlers and preschoolers.

♦ *Beating the Winter Blues*, by Claudia Arp (Thomas Nelson, 1991). Described as "The Complete Survival Handbook for Moms," it offers creative ways to have fun with children and chase away the winter blues.

♦ *365 TV-Free Activities You Can Do with Your Child*, by Steve Bennett and Ruth Bennett (Bob Adams, 1991). Includes everything from "milk jug catch" and "balancing act" to "scavenger hunt" and "sand paintings," and gives guidance to parents who want to wean their children from TV—or prevent the TV habit from forming in the first place.

♦ *The KIDFUN Activity Book*, by Sharla Feldscher with Susan Lieberman (HarperCollins, 1990). Describes more than 250 activities using ordinary materials.

For more information, contact your local library or bookstore. Parents may also want to take a look at "Is There a Prodigy in Your Future?" on page 39 and "Arts and Crafts for Fun" on page 9.

Countering TV Advertising

If there's a television in the house, one complaint parents are sure to have is about advertising directed at kids. But a new video is intended to educate children ages 6 to 10 about the tricks and deceptions of advertisements, especially the child-oriented ones on Saturday mornings. It's *Buy Me That! A Kid's Survival Guide to TV Advertising* (1989; released 1990), produced by Consumer Reports TV for HBO, for purchase or rental. Reviewers found the video especially effective in its footage of young children talking about their disappointment with heavily advertised products that didn't live up to their advance billing. (For more information, contact: Films, Inc., Video, 5547 North Ravenswood Avenue, Chicago, IL 60640.)

No Zone (LITTLE KIDS, INC.)

For older children, in grades 9 through 12, there is *Caution: This May Be an Advertisement! A Teen Guide to Advertising*, by Kathlyn Gay (Watts, 1992). This explores how the advertising industry works and how its marketing techniques are used to communicate its message about a product and shape the responses of potential buyers. The book also gives teens tips for smart shopping.

For parents themselves, *Consumer Reports* has been a widely used tool for cutting through the fog of advertising to reach the facts needed for intelligent shopping. While that magazine is far from new, parents with home computers may be interested to know that *Consumer Reports* articles are available on the PRODIGY Service®. (See "Is There a Prodigy in Your Future?" on page 39.)

Too Close to the TV?

Parents who are tired of reminding kids not to sit so close to the television now have a new product to do it for them—silently. It's the No Zone™ Television Boundary Mat, from Little Kids, Inc. This colorful, skid-resistant 40- by 24-inch plastic mat, placed in front of the television, is a constant reminder to kids that it's best to watch television from the beach, not from the shark-infested waters—labeled the No Zone—displayed on most of the mat. The mat may help keep the carpet clean as well, by providing a place to put snacks, and can also be used as a coloring mat or a floor protector under a high chair. (For more information, contact Little Kids, Inc., 2757 Pawtucket Avenue, East Providence, RI 02914; 800-LIL-KIDS [545-5437].)

Contests for Kids

The good news for parents is that *All the Best Contests for Kids, 1992–1993*, 3d ed., by Joan M. Bergstrom and Craig Bergstrom (Ten Speed, 1992) is now available. This revised and updated edition lists over 100 contests and competitions, nationwide, that children ages 6 to 12 might want to enter—or that parents, caregivers, or group leaders might want to organize for a local club or organization. General information on how to choose the right contests, enter them, and handle either winning or losing is followed by specific details on contests in areas such as sports, the arts, writing, history, science, entertainment, mathematics, pets, and fairs—everything from a milk-carton derby and a Bill of Rights competition to computer art and a rotten-sneaker championship to pancake eating and limerick writing. Also included is a section on running your own contests and publishing a newspaper.

Getting a Move On: The Gymboree® Way

In the movement movement, the word for the 1980s and 1990s has been Gymboree®. This California-based company now has over 300 locations worldwide, offering a series of age-appropriate developmental play programs for babies through toddlers to preschoolers. For each age, there are weekly parent-child classes with specially trained instructors, generally 45 minutes long, with music, games, sights, sounds, and specially built play equipment unlike that available in the home, including Parachute Time, a variety of rides and other activities involving parachute material, which ends each class. The basic programs are:

• **CradleGym.** For babies from birth through 3 months old, this gives babies sensory stimulation—tactile, auditory, and visual—from special movement to music activities, which include gentle songs, nursery rhymes, and chants. (For more on the importance of such experience, see "Listening for Language Development" on page 128.) Many of the specially designed "Baby Games," often described in handouts to parents, are meant also to be used in the home, since babies (not surprisingly) sometimes fall asleep during sessions. The newest

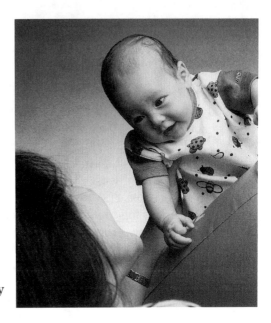

Gymboree® activity
(GYMBOREE CORP.)

Gymboree offering, CradleGym was introduced as a limited pilot program in 1991, and then expanded to most locations during 1992.

• **BabyGym.** For kids 3 to 12 months old, this introduces infants to new colors, textures, sounds, and activities, which include "Baby Boogie" dances, music, games, and bubbles to pop, and provides experience in "socializing."

• **Gymboree I.** For kids 10 to 16 months old, who are "almost/just walkers," this is designed to promote balance, spatial awareness, exploring, and confidence in their newfound mobility, as well as socializing skills and language development.

• **Gymboree II.** For kids 12 to 30 months old, this is designed to refine body movement, practice balance, enhance socializing skills, and build general self-esteem. Weekly classes are built around themes such as "Through" or "Under."

• **Gymboree III.** For kids 24 to 36 months old, this is designed to develop a sense of rhythm through use of instruments, cooperation with others, and imagination, as through new games such as Numberland and Pet Shop.

• **GymGrad.** For kids 2½ to 4 years old, this is designed to prepare children for sports, offering noncompetitive pre-gymnastics activities such as tumbling; games with special props; and Gymbercises for children and parents, which are special exercise routines choreographed to music to develop overall body strength and coordination. Cooperative and socializing skills within the group are also emphasized.

• **GymKids!**®. Another new program, for kids 4 to 5 years old, at the "I can do it!" stage, this is a drop-off program, optional for parents. The 75-minute class offers a wide variety of activities, games, projects, and songs.

In line with Gymboree's commitment to the idea of "positive parenting," these programs, especially CradleGym and BabyGym, are as much for parent as for child. Classes are also resource sessions, providing information and news about parenting and child care, such as sleep patterns, travel tips, finding quality child care, family involvement, and the importance of parents making time for themselves. This is useful for all parents, not just first-timers, because the classes act as discussion and support groups in which parents can share experiences. Gymboree centers also have a lending library of videos and books about parenting and child care, as well as guest speakers, demonstrations, and special projects; in addition, parents are taught at-home activities and songs that creatively use everyday such items as flashlights, scarves, bells, cushions, table leaves, blankets, mirrors, and beach balls.

Gymboree centers sell various program-oriented products, such as a Gymbo and Gymbelle doll, a Gym wacky ball (asymmetrically weighted so it *can't* be thrown straight), and a song book-cassette package. Gymboree stores in 60 locations in the United States offer clothing and accessories for kids up to 7 years old. (For more information, including the location of the nearest Gymboree center, contact Gymboree Corporation, 577 Airport Boulevard, Suite 400, Burlingame, CA 94010-2022; 800-632-2122, ext. GYMBO, from inside CA; 800-227-3900, ext. GYMBO, from outside CA; or 415-579-0600 from outside the U.S. call collect. The latter number should also be used by people interested in opening a Gymboree program franchise in their area, or those seeking information on Gymboree stores.)

Parents who want to help develop their young child's skills, coordination, and bodily strength may also be interested in this recent publication:

• *Hello Toes! Movement Games for Children,* by Anne Lief Barlin and Nurit Kalevwith. A cassette or cassette-paperback package for parents of young children (ages 2 to 5), this provides movement games and activities for parents and children to play together. These include using available objects to promote physical development, large-muscle movement, and creative dance, by means of ethnic stories and rhythmic chants. (For more information, contact: Learning through Movement, 2728 North Country Road 25E, Bellvue, CO 80512.)

Child Athletes: New Guidelines

Younger and younger children are moving into competitive sports, often pushed by social and parental pressures. The result can be physical and emotional damage, if the child moves into the wrong sport, at the wrong time, and at the wrong pace. In the book *The Pediatric Athlete*, the American Academy of Orthopaedic Surgeons (AAOS) attempts to prevent some of this damage by providing guidelines for children and parents.

The AAOS stresses that children are not miniature adults, but rather are still developing physiologically, so their bodies react to athletic activity quite differently than an adult's. For example, children's bodies burn more calories, tire faster, have less power for their size (because they use glycogen less efficiently), adjust less quickly to changes in heat and humidity, produce more heat and lose it more slowly (so are at increased risk for heat-related illnesses), breathe faster (and so may take in more polluted air), and recover faster from strenuous activity. The AAOS cautions that children should not undertake training programs intended for adults, noting that excessive training can lead to early "burnout."

The report also stresses the importance of annual medical evaluations of children, generally before each school year, and the selection of sports and other athletic activities to suit a child's age and stage of development, both to increase the child's chances of success and to minimize the risk of injury. The AAOS suggests that noncontact sports such as baseball, tennis, swimming, and skating may be appropriate for ages 6 to 8, while children ages 8 to 10 might try contact sports such as basketball, soccer, and wrestling, and older children might try collision sports such as football and hockey. They note that boys and girls of similar size have similar strength and sports potential until puberty, and so can compete equally in sports until then, when boys begin to gain more muscle and strength. They also stress keeping in mind a child's particular skills or deficits, suggesting that a child with poor eye-hand coordination might be steered into an individual sport such as swimming or running. (For more information, contact: American Academy of Orthopaedic Surgeons, 222 South Prospect, Park Ridge, IL 60068; 708-823-7186.)

Parents Coaching Kids

More and more parents are becoming involved in their children's sports activities, either as coaches or volunteer assistants. This trend will only increase, as communities across the country feel the pinch of hard times and cut back funding of organized youth sports leagues, while sponsorship from local businesses is also drying up. But while youth leagues in sports such as softball, baseball, soccer, football, basketball, and lacrosse rely increasingly on parents and other volunteers for both funding and coaching, the trend has not been an entirely happy one.

One area of concern is making sure that those people who are working directly with the children have an unimpeachable background. Questions of child abuse, including sexual abuse, are of such concern today that in some communities potential coaches are fingerprinted and undergo a background check with the FBI and local police before they are cleared for coaching or similar work. Conversely, those who work in direct contact with children are now charged with being alert to signs that the child is being abused at home, at school, in sports activities, or elsewhere. One recent work, *For Their Sake: Recognizing, Responding to, and Reporting Child Abuse*, by Rebecca Cowan Johnson, is actually a manual for identifying signs of child abuse, understanding its causes, and working with its victims, and includes a list of reporting laws in various states; it was written for camp counselors, recreational staff, child care workers, leaders of children's organizations, teachers, and others in regular contact with children. (For more information, contact: American Camping Association, 5000 State Road, 647 North, Martinsville, IN 46151; 317-342-8456.)

Another problem associated with youth sports leagues—and an embarrassing one for almost everyone, but especially for the children—is misbehaving parents. Many hard-driving parents, carrying their adult competitive attitudes into their children's lives, distort their children's sports activities with their anger and verbal violence, which sometimes even escalates into physical violence. Because of that, many communities have instituted clinics for coaches, not just in coaching skills but also in sensitivity training and many other related activities, including emergency first aid, safety, nutrition, and antidrug programs. Leading this movement is the National Youth Sports Coaches Association (NYSCA), which through 1991—just ten years after its founding—had trained and certified some 100,000 adults for youth sports coaching. The NYSCA spreads the word through pamphlets, instructional videos, and codes of ethics for coaches and parents, all emphasizing the psychology of coaching children; these also teach how to organize interesting and enjoyable activities and to develop children's athletic skills. The NYSCA materials stress that while a professional coach's goals might be winning games, earning money, and providing entertainment, the youth coach's goals are quite different: teaching effectively, caring about the child's well-being, developing the child's potential, and making the sports experience enjoyable and affirmative, rather than negative and emotionally abusive. The aim is for youth coaches to keep their perspective and to focus on helping children learn how to play the game, while directly and as role models helping spectator-parents draw back from the win-at-all-costs attitude that is so damaging to everyone involved. In some communities, where possible, parents are not allowed to coach their own children, and sometimes not those of their friends and neighbors either, to relieve the pressures on all. (For more information, contact: National Youth Sports Coaches Association, 2611 Old Okeechobee Road, West Palm Beach, FL 33409; 407-684-1141; or one of its 1,700 chapters around the nation.)

Safety is also a prime concern for parents and coaches of young children involved in sports. Through organizations like the NYSCA, adults can become informed of the latest in protective gear for children. An example is the Thoradom Batting Vest®, which encircles the child's chest and midsection, protecting the spinal column and vital organs such as the kidneys, liver, spleen, pancreas, and stomach, without restricting shoulders, arms, and neck. (For more information, contact: Thoradom, Inc., 501 Village Trace, Building 9, Marietta, GA 30067; 800-932-4406.) Though the Thoradom has been sold for some years, its use took on even more urgency with the death of a 10-year-old Tampa boy, Ryan Wojick, after he was hit in the chest by a pitched ball. Another alternative for protection from pitched balls is the Bat-R-Vest™. (For more information, contact: Carroll Industries, P.O. Box 577, Madison, MS 39130; 601-856-2062.)

The NYSCA also publishes numerous books on special coaching

concerns, including: *Youth League Basketball, Youth League Baseball, Power Volleyball, Fast and Slow Pitch Softball, Youth League Football, FUNdamental Soccer Tactics, FUNdamental Soccer Practice, FUNdamental Soccer Goalkeeping, The Teaching of Soccer, The Coach's Pocket Planner, Basketball Manual for Parents and Youth, Basketball Practice Guide,* and a series of baseball books, such as *Baseball Book, Pitching Book, Fielding Book,* and *Developmental Tee Ball.* NYSCA also distributes to parents other works, such as Pat McInally's *Moms & Dads, Kids & Sports;* videos such as *Soccer-Magic* and *A New Reference Video to Improve Baseball Skills;* and audiocassettes of the National Summit for Safety in Youth Baseball and Softball.

A number of other books have been published to help parents and other sports volunteers be more effective in their work; among the most recent are:

On Coaching in General

• *Sports Without Pressure: A Guide for Parents, Coaches and Athletes,* by Eric Margenau (Gardner Press, 1991). This uses case histories to highlight the dangers of pressure on young people in sports; it also provides guidelines for how, at about age 12, talented young people and their parents can most wisely decide whether to maintain a recreational stance or point toward a professional career.

• *Sportswise: An Essential Guide for Young Athletes, Parents, and Coaches* (Houghton Mifflin, 1990), by Lyle J. Micheli, a past president of the American College of Sports Medicine. It reviews common sports injuries, treatments, and prevention, especially through conditioning, nutrition, and coaching; it includes separate chapters on the special needs of girls and of children with chronic illnesses or disabilities.

• *The Quality of Effort: Integrity in Sport and Life for Student-Athletes, Parents, and Coaches,* by Reggie Marra (From the Heart Press, 1991).

On Health Concerns

• *Youth Sports Injuries: A Medical Handbook for Parents and Coaches,* by John Duff (Macmillan, 1992). This is a care guide to 13 of the most common injuries incurred at home or school.

♦ *Keeping Young Athletes Healthy: What Every Parent and Volunteer Coach Should Know*, by Alan R. Figelman (Simon & Schuster, 1991).

On Coaching Specific Sports

♦ *Soccer Coach's Guide to Practices, Drills and Skills Training*, by Butch Lauffer and Sandy Davie (Sterling, 1992). This is a basic guide for parent or community volunteer coaches in developing children's skills in youth league soccer, and includes drawings and photographs of specific skills and drills for each age group.

♦ The "Rookie Coaches Guide" series, by the American Coaching Effectiveness Program (ACEP), published by Leisure Press, offers parent or community volunteer coaches basic coaching techniques, which include communications and first-aid skills, and specific drills to increase children's skills and awareness of team play in the particular sport. Among the titles are *Rookie Coaches Softball Guide* (1992), *Rookie Coaches Wrestling Guide* (1991), *Rookie Coaches Soccer Guide* (1991), *Rookie Coaches Tennis Guide* (1991), and *Rookie Coaches Basketball Guide* (1991).

♦ *The Complete Book of Coaching Youth Soccer*, by Simon Whitehead (Contemporary, 1991).

♦ *Youth Soccer: A Complete Handbook for Coaches and Parents*, edited by Vern Seefeldt (William C. Brown, 1991).

♦ *A Parent's Guide to Coaching Football*, by John P. McCarthy (Betterway, 1991).

♦ *Youth League Football Coaching and Playing*, by Jack Bicknell (Athletic Institute, 1991).

♦ *A Parent's Guide to Coaching Tennis* by Pierce Kelley, the president of the Youth Tennis Foundation of Florida (Betterway, 1991).

♦ *The Junior Tennis Handbook: A Complete Guide to Tennis for Juniors, Parents, and Coaches*, by Skip Skingleton (Betterway, 1991). For children in grades 5 through 12.

♦ *Pass the Biscuit: Spirited Practices for Youth Hockey Coaches and Players*, by Gary Wright (Ashworth Press, 1991).

♦ *A Parent's Guide to Coaching Soccer*, by John P. McCarthy (Betterway, 1990).

♦ *A Parent's Guide to Coaching Baseball*, by John P. McCarthy (Betterway, 1989).

Personal Experiences

* *Little League Confidential: A Father, a Son and a Daughter Playing Ball,* by William Geist (Macmillan, 1992). This presents view of Little League from the inside, with personal experiences, shrewd analyses, and large dollops of humor.
* *My Season on the Brink: A Father's Seven Weeks as a Little League Manager,* by Paul B. Brown (St. Martin's, 1992). This describes a season with 6- to 8-year-olds in the "instructional league," in which everybody gets to play, under special rules.
* *Dreams of Glory: A Mother's Season With Her Son's High School Football Team,* by Judy Oppenheimer (Summit, 1991). This offers a mother's perspective of the experiences of a high school football team—the students, coaches, and parents.

On General Fitness for Kids

* *Kid Fitness—A Complete Shape Up Program from Birth Through High School,* by Kenneth Cooper (Bantam, 1991). The "father of aerobics" describes how families can turn children toward fitness, especially through rewarding children for the *process,* not the results, and through family involvement in general fitness, not sports only. Cooper explores the differing stages of development—mental, skeletal, and physiological—of boys and girls from infancy through their teens, and stresses nutrition with fitness-oriented recipes and diets, useful for parents and coaches.
* *Weight and Strength Training for Kids and Teenagers,* by Ken Sprague and Chris Sprague (Tarcher, 1991).

Parents will also want to check out "Danger: Exercise Equipment" on page 63.

Safe Sledding

Every winter some 33,000 people are injured sledding in the United States. Some are adults, like Barbara Bush in the most famous sledding accident of recent memory, but most are children ages 5 to 9. The *American Journal of Diseases of Children* (October 1990) put forward

the following safety checklist for sledding:
   S: Snow packed, not icy.
   L: Long, flat runoff at bottom.
   E: Examine area for hazards and traffic.
   D: Dress with helmet, boots, and gloves.
   D: Don't ride in prone position (head first).
   I: Incline not too steep or long.
   N: Non-reckless behavior.
   G: Good condition of sled.

On the Go With Young Kids? No Problem!

Parents who live active lives can now share their walking, jogging, running, bicycling, and other outdoor activities more readily with their young children. Instead of parking them with babysitters, parents can take little ones along because of the advent of several attractive alternatives to conventional strollers and wagons:

• The Buddy Buggy® is a lightweight but heavy-duty rickshaw-type seat on wheels, for one or two small children ages 1 to 6, designed to be pulled. Kids don't have to be lifted in and out; they just step in and sit down. They are out in the open, and so can easily interact with each other and their surroundings, but are secured in place by seat belts or optional special harnesses. Other safety features include high-visibility reflectors for after-dark use, protective wheel covers, and an anti-tipping device. Options include an umbrella or canopy for shade or protection, and a basket attachment for shopping or supplies. Because the children's weight is centered over the two 16-inch wheels, the well-balanced buggy is easy for parents to pull, not just at malls, zoos, or fairs, but also over rough terrain, such as beaches or parks. The steel handle readily detaches, so the lightweight molded plastic bucket seat can be tucked into a car trunk. It also cleans up with just mild soap and water, since there's no cloth or canvas to stain. For young children with disabilities, the Buddy Buggy is an attractive, easy-access alternative to a wheelchair. (For more information, contact: Buddy Buggy, 6400 East El Dorado Circle, Tucson, AZ 85715; 800-458-7400.)

• Runabouts™ are one-, two-, or three-seat walking-jogging "karts" for young children up to 50 pounds, designed to be pushed. Children sit in molded plastic seats, which are adjustable to recline from a 10- to 30-

Buddy Buggy® (BUDDY
BUGGY)

degree angle and are covered with washable seat pads. Other features
include a padded headrest and roll bar; three-point safety harness/seat
belt; padded snap-on, quick-release seat grab bar; and vinyl-covered
foot pegs for legs too long for the footrests. Runabouts are unique in
that seats can be added as the family grows; the seats are also designed
to bolt on or off quickly, so the kart can be readily broken down to fit
into even compact cars. In a multiseat version, children sit in a gradu-
ated line, with each behind and slightly higher than the one in front;
that makes the Runabout narrow enough (22 inches wide) to fit through
doorways. Parents benefit from the solid, well-balanced construction;
foam-padded handlebar adjustable to the walker's height; nylon safety
wrist cord; positive parking brake; easy-handling ball-bearing 12-inch
front and 16-inch rear wheels; smooth-running balloon air tires; protective wheel covers; and safety reflectors for after-dark use. Options
include a removable sun/rain bonnet, 16-inch front and 20-inch rear
wheels, a nylon basket, chrome-plated fenders, and attachable beverage bottles.

Runabout/USA also has several other walking/jogging kart designs,
including the more basic Puddle Jumper, a one- or two-seater; the
Runabout/Sport, with larger wheels; and the stylish Runabout/Aero,

which adds padded arm rests, a child's steering wheel and horn, a grocery bag–sized trunk, and options such as a tinted lexan bubble canopy, a retractable sun/rain bonnet, and a baby's "rumble seat." (For more information, contact: Runabout/USA, Inc., 8025 SW 185th, Aloha, OR 97007; 503-649-7922.)

♦ The Baby Jogger® is designed to carry one child, from one month to four years, or up to 50 pounds, and to be pushed by walkers, runners, and joggers. Advertised as "the ultimate all-terrain stroller," the Baby Jogger has a lightweight aluminum frame, stable tripod shape, and easy-rolling design, so it readily goes not just on pavement, sidewalks, or in malls, but also on dirt roads, grass, gravel, and sand. The child is belted in a deep, sling seat made of washable Cordura, in a choice of colors; the Baby Jogger also has a locking hand brake and a

Runabout™ (RUNABOUT/ USA)

Runabout Aero
(RUNABOUT/USA)

Baby Jogger® (RACING STROLLERS, INC.)

safety leash. Options include a higher handle for extra-tall runners; a nylon, water-repellent, all-weather canopy; and a wire basket. The makers note that little babies need head support in the Jogger, as from folded diapers or a blanket. The Baby Jogger can readily be collapsed for transport or storage. Racing Strollers, Inc., also makes a smaller, even more portable version called the Walkabout; a two-seater called the Twinner; and the Super Jogger, a lighter, smoother, faster model, with a larger-capacity seat for older children and easier-to-remove quick-release wheels for easier storing. Racing Strollers also can modify their strollers for children with disabilities; they can, for example, make them larger or stronger for bigger children, or build a stroller with a wheelchair insert. (For more information, contact: Racing Strollers, Inc., P.O. Box 2189, Yakima, WA 98907; 800-548-7230, ext. 3, or 509-457-0925.)

♦ Among bicycling families, Burley is well known for its line of strong, lightweight aluminum trailers. These attach to a bicycle with a strong hitch backed by a safety strap, and have an easy-to-hitch-and-unhitch design; a strong, lightweight aluminum frame; a wide track; and a low center of gravity. Trailer models include the basic Burley Lite; the folding Burley d'Lite; and the even less expensive folding trailer, the Burley-Roo. What's new for parents of small children is the optional Walk 'n Roller™, a seat-on-wheels that hitches onto a bicycle

Walk 'n Roller™ (BURLEY DESIGN COOPERATIVE)

Burley d'Lite (BURLEY DESIGN COOPERATIVE)

like a trailer; it holds one or two children, who ride in a "roll cage," where they can see and be seen, secured by lap and chest belts. More than that, the Walk 'n Roller can be readily unhitched and used as a three-wheeled walking or jogging cart, over smooth or rough terrain. Safety features of the Walk 'n Roller include bright yellow side and top panels for maximum visibility; close-fitting side panels to keep small fingers inside; reflectors and reflector tape; and a 6-foot safety flag. Options include a 2-in-1 all-weather cover, with a vinyl see-through window, convertible to a nylon mesh sunscreen; side windows for a better view (standard with the d'Lite); side pockets for toys, snacks, or extra clothes; and straps to allow the Burley Lite (with wheels removed) to be transported atop a car, doubling as a car-top carrier. Parents who already have earlier versions of Burley trailers can add the Walk 'n Roller as an option. (For more information, contact: Burley Design Cooperative, 4080 Stewart Road, Eugene, OR 97402; 503-687-1644; Dealer Order Line, 800-423-8445.)

These products must meet federal regulations for strollers. However, parents should realize that they must still keep a close eye on their children's safety. In all of these products, after all, the child is strapped into a wheeled vehicle that has the potential to roll away unless it is properly parked and braked—it is for good reason that several of these strollers have a safety strap, which stays around a parent's wrist, even when the parent does not have a hand directly on the push-or-pull handle. And in all cases, parents must walk, run, or ride defensively, attempting to avoid danger from other vehicles to the stroller, cart, or trailer in which the child is sitting.

Stroll'r Hold'r™ (KEL-GAR, INC.)

For stroller-using parents who always have more things to carry than they have hands, there is an answer to the question "Where do you put all your stuff?" It's a specially designed accessory called the Stroll'r Hold'r™. This handy product hangs on a stroller handle (or any tubular surface, such as a bicycle or grocery cart), and provides three hooks on which to hang purses, shopping bags, diaper bags, jackets, and the like, along with a detachable holder for drink containers. (For more information, contact: Kel-Gar, Inc., P.O. Box 796934, Dallas, TX 75379-6934; 214-250-3838.)

Safety 1st® offers a stroller bag, a loose-knit affair similar to a French-style shopping bag, which fits over the handle of the stroller. The firm also has a new product, the Stroll N' Go Drink Holder, a device that attaches to a stroller handle and holds a soft drink can. (For more information, contact: Safety 1st, 210 Boylston Street, Chestnut Hill, MA 02167; 800-962-7233 outside MA, or 617-964-7744.)

Have Kids, Will Travel

Travel offers change more often than the seasons, but parents should be aware that special bargains are often available for children.

• Many countries and regions abroad have discount airfares for foreign visitors, unavailable to local residents. These may include passes for relatively unrestricted travel in a specific time period, heavily discounted single flights or coupon books, or more general discounts. Parents traveling abroad should realize that additional discounts are often available for children ages 2 to 11, with infants often flying at even heavier discounts or free. In one recent period, for example, British Airways' UK Air Pass offered children's passes at 67 percent of the adult discounted fare, with passes for infants set at 10 percent; while the Explore Australia Airpass was discounted for children at 50 percent off the full airfare. Fares for infants under 2 often do not include a separate seat reservation, so an accompanying adult may have to hold the infant if the plane is full. (For more information, contact a travel agent.)

• Similarly, Amtrak has extended its children's discounts—50 percent off the cheapest coach fare—to kids through age 15. Each adult-fare traveler can be accompanied by up to two children at the discount fare. (For more information, contact: Amtrak, 800-872-7245.)

• USAir has introduced a new twist for kids: discounts for grandchildren traveling with their grandparents. Grandparents 62 or over who are traveling on USAir's senior coupons can use those coupons for their grandchildren ages 2 to 11; the offer applies for one grandchild per grandparent, and they must travel on the same itinerary. Otherwise, regular rules for senior coupons apply. (For more information, contact: USAir, 800-428-4322.)

• Club Med also has numerous special programs and rates for families, including occasional free weeks for young kids. (See "Club Med—With Kids" on page 34.)

Remember: The details of travel offers may change in the blink of an eye, so be sure to call the supplier or travel agent for up-to-date information.

Parents may also want to check out some recent books to ease travel with children, such as:

• *Trouble-Free Travel with Children: Helpful Hints for Parents on the Go*, 2d ed., by Vicki Lansky (BookPeddlers, 1991).

• *Traveling with Children and Enjoying It: A Complete Guide to Family Travel by Car, Plane, and Train*, by Arlene K. Butler (Globe Pequot, 1991).

• *Take Your Kids to Europe*, by Cynthia W. Harriman (Mason-Grant, 1991).

Child-oriented books are also available for several specific cities or regions, such as Frommer's Family Travel Guides (published by Prentice Hall), which focus on sight-seeing, hotels, and restaurants particularly congenial to children and families in such cities as New York, San Francisco, Los Angeles, and Washington, D.C.; Colormore's series of Travel Guides for Kids, for such cities as Richmond, Virginia (1991), Honolulu, Hawaii (1992), Dallas, Texas (1992), and San Diego, California (1991); and *Disney World and Beyond: The Ultimate Family Guidebook*, by Stacy Ritz (Ulysses Press, 1991).

In addition, various activity packages have recently been published to help travel time pass more quickly for kids. Among them are:

• *Family Travel Kit* (Focus on the Family, 1992). This includes an activity book, color markers, and a cassette of sing-along songs.

• *Little Visits on the Go*, by Mary Manz Simon (Concordia, 1992). A Christian-oriented book and audiocassette package, it contains activities, devotions, and songs for family outings, and tips for traveling with kids.

If your family is traveling abroad, don't forget about getting the proper vaccinations ahead of time. (See "Protecting Children Against Disease: Immunization" on page 87.)

Club Med—With Kids

The "original all-inclusive vacation," as Club Med bills itself, has looked at the needs and desires of families with young children, and met them in a big way. Various Club Med "villages" provide (at no extra charge) staffed, supervised programs specifically designed for children of different ages, from infants to teens, and centered on special clubhouses with downsized facilities for kids.

As of April 1992, Baby Clubs for infants were available from 8 A.M. to 6 P.M. at two locations: at Sandpiper, Florida, for ages 4 to 23 months; and at Ixtapa, Mexico, for ages 12 to 23 months. Meals for infants are prepared in a special "Baby Restaurant"; sterilizers and bottle warmers are available around the clock; and (at least at Sandpiper) Twilight Care provides baby-sitting for infants from 7 to 11 P.M. After kid-club hours, Club Med offers "free use of nursery monitors"; local baby-sitting services are often available, at an extra charge. Club Med stresses that it has two registered nurses on duty 24 hours a day, and that a doctor (independent of Club Med) is always available nearby.

For older children, these and some other Club Med sites have Petit Clubs (for kids 2 to 3 years old), Mini Clubs (4 to 7), and Kids Clubs (8 to 11), operating from 9 A.M. to 9 P.M. Specific sports and activities vary from village to village; Club Med's brochures outline which sites have programs best suited to which ages and interests. The Sandpiper, for example, has a circus program, a wading pool, intensive tennis from age 8, and scuba diving for ages 4 to 12, with child-sized tanks and fins. The Ixtapa site has similar programs, plus snorkeling boat trips for ages 8 to 11. These are special features in a whole program of sports, activities, excursions, contests, and shows, under the supervision of trained instructors, entertainers, and others—all dubbed *gentil organisateurs* (French for "congenial hosts") or G.O.s. Kids also have

Horseback riding at Club Med Mini Club (CLUB MED)

meals in their own restaurant, where they are offered "child-tested" menus, at early mealtimes, if desired, so they can dine with their peers; or they can eat with their parents in family dining areas. It's no wonder that Club Med Mini Clubs' advertising slogan is "It's 11:45. Do you know where your parents are? Do you care?" Parents are free to pursue their own interests, or just lie on the beach, and all can "come together as a family at any time, day or night."

Club Med sites geared for families with children ages 2 and up are St. Lucia, West Indies; Punta Cana, Dominican Republic; and Eleuthera, Bahamas. For children ages 4 and up, Club Med has Caravelle, Guadeloupe (new for kids in 1992); and Moorea, French Polynesia. For 6 and up, there are Magic Isle, Haiti; Huatulco, Mexico (also new in 1992); Sonora Bay, Mexico; and Bora Bora, French Polynesia. For ages 12 and up, there are Columbus Isle, Bahamas; Buccaneer's Creek, Martinique; Turkoise, Turks & Caicos; Paradise Island, Bahamas; Cancun, Mexico; Playa Blanca, Mexico; and the cruise ship *Club Med 1*.

Some things to know in advance: Children under age 6 sleep in the same room as their parents. The age of the child is as of the time of arrival, not when the reservation is made. Also, children who show signs of having a contagious illness, in the opinion of the doctor or (in his or her absence) the nurse, may be excluded from club activities, and even from the Club Med village, if necessary; parents are advised to have their own and their children's health verified by a doctor before departing on the trip.

Perhaps even more attractive for parents in recession times, Club Med offers free weeks for kids of certain ages during some periods. In 1992, for example, children ages 2 to 5 could stay free at St. Lucia, Eleuthera, and Sandpiper during the weeks of May 2d through June 20th or August 29th through December 12th, as could babies 4 to 23 months at Sandpiper on the same dates; similar offers were available at other sites. At many of these Family Villages, Club Med also had Extra-Value Programs, which in 1992 offered additional savings of up to $100 per adult for land-and-air travel from certain gateway cities. Specifics change all the time, of course, but parents looking for value may well want to explore Club Med's current offerings for families. (For more information, contact a travel agent or Club Med, 40 West 57th Street, New York, NY 19919; 800-CLUB-MED [258-2633] or 212-977-2100.)

Summer Opportunities for Kids and Teens

Parents seeking new and special experiences for their children now have the perfect guidebook: the annual *Peterson's Summer Opportunities for Kids and Teenagers.* The 9th edition, for 1992, lists over 1,300 educational and recreational summer programs in North America and abroad, including sports, academics, arts, and wilderness or outdoors activities over a wide range, from camping in the Adirondacks or living on an Israeli kibbutz to learning Japanese or studying about Zimbabwe. For each program in the main Program Profiles section, the book describes the activity; gives program information, such as age level, dates, costs, and (in some cases) jobs for teens; and provides the program's address and contact person. Those programs that pay a fee to Peterson's have a more detailed profile in an "In-Depth Descriptions" section.

One new feature in the 1992 edition is a section to help parents and their child work together to choose the right program and to prepare for it, exploring some of the personal, academic, and financial questions to be considered. An Activities Directory, an alphabetical list of activities, leads users quickly to the type of program they are seeking, while a Quick-Reference Chart allows them to zero in on programs in a particular state or country. Readers will also find indexes of special types of programs, including those for the academically talented, the developmentally disabled, the hearing impaired, or the emotionally disturbed, as well as those that have religious affiliations, that offer financial aid, and the like.

Parents of kids heading to summer camp may want to consult *The Smart Parent's Guide to Summer Camp*, by Sheldon Silver (Farrar, Straus & Giroux, 1991). A camp director, educator, and parent himself, Silver advises parents on evaluating what their child needs as well as the quality of a camp. He also profiles 150 camps, including comments on each from the camp director and from a parent. The book provides a list of camps for children with special needs, too.

Parents looking for international experiences for their teens should point them toward *The Teenager's Guide to Study, Travel, and Adventure Abroad*, 3d ed., by the Council on International Educational Exchange (St. Martin's, 1991). This work starts with a large section on the basics—assessing readiness, getting ready, making the right choices, making preparations, and guidelines for traveling abroad and returning home. The CIEE guide then describes and provides vital details on over 200 programs from around the world for junior and senior high schoolers, in various topic areas: Study Abroad, Language Institutes, Creative Arts, Organized Tours, Work/Volunteer, Outdoor Activities, and Homestays.

College-age students, or families with teens, may also want to explore the opportunities described in Stephanie Ocko's *Environmental Vacations: Volunteer Projects to Save the Planet* (John Muir, 1990). Here are described numerous volunteer projects in which adults must pay to work on a scientific project, such as "digging for artifacts of the ancient Anasazi in the American Southwest, tracking hamsters in Siberia, listening for volcanoes in Yellowstone, counting monkeys in Liberia, bird-watching in China . . . or diving to a wreck off Belize." Activities change every few months, and involve hard work, but provide unique opportunities for joining scientists in hands-on fieldwork. Some environmentally oriented activities for high school or college students and adults are also described in *The Green Encyclopedia*, by Irene Franck and David Brownstone (Prentice Hall, 1992), especially under the heading "Ecotourism," including such activities as building wilderness trails and helping to restore damaged environments.

Who in the World is Carmen Sandiego?

Only the most notorious criminal mastermind known to the 8-and-up computer set. Since 1985, when Brøderbund published its computer software game *Where in the World Is Carmen Sandiego?*®, budding detectives have been following geographical clues to locate the archcriminal before she can steal again. In this interactive program, the actual routes followed in pursuit of Carmen are determined by choices children make as detectives, based on their memory of clues given about the habits of Carmen and her henchpeople. And—whether they know it or not—the children have been learning a great deal of geography in the process, often consulting the reference book that comes packed with the game.

Many families have purchased the game for use on their home computers. A deluxe edition of the original program is designed to take full advantage of the latest computer technology in high-end IBM or compatible machines. This includes realistic digitized slides provided by the National Geographic Society, over 62 animations, a new musical score, and digitized sound, and has been expanded to have over 2,500 clues and twice as many countries and villains as the original.

Many other people play a version of *Where in the World . . .* as part of a computer service (see "Is There a Prodigy in Your Future?" on page 39). There the mysteries change with the seasons—for example, in

Where in the World Is Carmen Sandiego?® Deluxe Edition (BRØDERBUND SOFTWARE)

April, baseball bats are stolen, and in December, players might solve the theft of the White House Christmas tree. On computer, players refer to on-screen encyclopedias, or their own information sources, and can even compare their scores to those of others.

The original game was followed by *Where in the U.S.A. . . .*®, *Where in Europe . . .*™, *Where in Time . . .*™, and *Where in America's Past . . .*™, the latter two focusing on historical clues. *Where in America's Past . . .* has kids using a 1,300-page reference guide to try to solve the mystery of the missing Liberty Bell, chasing Carmen and her associate villains, such as Homer DeBrave, before they go after Plymouth Rock or even the Statue of Liberty. Reviewers note that the history games are somewhat more sophisticated than the geography-oriented ones, and so—except for those already familiar with other Carmen Sandiego games—may be best for children in grades 6 through 12.

In fall 1991, many new detectives were created when the Public Broadcasting System (PBS) premiered a game show, also called *Where in the World Is Carmen Sandiego?* Interestingly, one reviewer noted that his own children, already familiar with the fully interactive computer game, were less satisfied to simply watch other people on television make the choices that would lead to Sandiego's capture. Also in 1991, Golden Press brought out a series of books based on the software titles, each containing games and collectible cards based on the super-criminal.

Clearly crime does pay, not just for Brøderbund and its colleagues, but for the many children learning geography and history from the games, in what some have dubbed "edu-tainment." Not a few adults have also found themselves drawn into the search for the globe-trotting, time-traveling thieves. (For more information, including which programs are available for which types of computers, contact: Brøderbund Software-Direct, P.O. Box 6125, Novato, CA 94948-6125; 800-521-6263 or 415-492-3500.)

Is There a Prodigy in Your Future?

There just might be, if you have a home computer, even if it's currently gathering dust in a corner. The PRODIGY Service® is an easy-to-use, consumer-oriented system for casual computer users—no one has to be a computer whiz, since the program presents you with a list of options, called a *menu*, and allows you to choose what you want to do, and where you want to go among the service's over 800 activities.

Designed for family needs and interests, Prodigy offers everything from parenting advice to on-screen shopping, from homework help for kids to guidance on researching your family's past, from information on new products to advice on how to fix old ones. Not surprisingly—since it is a joint project of IBM and Sears, Roebuck—Prodigy has dozens of shopping services. You can, for example, read about a book, toy, game, crib, or whatever, and order it then and there. But Prodigy also has much, much more for family members of all ages.

Of particular interest to children or teenagers are such offerings as:

• An encyclopedia, specifically the *Academic American Encyclopedia*, updated quarterly and available on-screen for students (and parents) to refer to at will. (For more on the AAE, see "Children's Encyclopedias: What's New? What's Not?" on page 172.)

• A geographic magazine from the National Geographic Society, including color graphics.

• A science center for kids, entitled *Nova* and created by Boston's PBS station WGBH, which includes a scientific column, a weekly lab experiment that students can perform using everyday household items, and an adventure-oriented on-screen monthly experiment, such as exploring the inside of the space shuttle.

• A craft center for kids, with illustrated instructions (which they can print out) for a new project to make each month, with a glossary and bibliography for further exploration.

• Stories for kids, including weekly installments of action tales and mysteries kids can solve themselves. They can even write their own endings.

• A wide range of games for kids, including the bestselling *Where in the World Is Carmen Sandiego?*® (see "Who in the World Is Carmen Sandiego?" on page 38.); MadMaze, in which kids use math and logic skills to defeat mythical opponents in an imaginary land; and various word games, news quizzes, and two-player board games. For high schoolers (and adults), there are games like CEO, a multiplayer business simulation game created by the Wharton School of Business; and Guts, a popular competitive all-or-nothing question-and-answer game asking 7 questions in 7 weeks, which some have described as an informational scavenger hunt.

• Quizzes for kids under the heading "smartkids," with high scorers getting their names displayed on the service.

• The *Weekly Reader*®, with kid-oriented news, stories, games, and puzzles every week.

• A special "club" for members under 18, which allows children and teens to communicate through the computer with other kids about their special interests—sports, hobbies, music, fashion, or whatever, comparing notes on everything from sneaker styles to views on the breakup of the Soviet Union. Older children may also be interested in various special-interest clubs for adults (see below).

Of more general interest for parents and the whole family are:

• News, information, and commentary, ranging from the day's sports scores and weather forecast to ski reports and stock quotes, often with special information highlighted by season, such as Oscar information in March or baseball tips in April, or triggered by current events, such as the Gulf Update introduced during the Persian Gulf War.

• Parenting advice, including twice-a-week articles from the National Parenting Center on such topics as prenatal care, children's books, and living with teenagers, as well as on-screen access to the publication *Parenting Guide*, with more information and useful articles.

• Political information, including current political news and poll results, with daily coverage during presidential campaigns; political profiles of incumbents and candidates, with information on voting record and campaign funding; columns by such well-known figures as Jack Germond and Robert Novak; and even games based on current political races.

• Reviews of new books, including children's books, with a new column added each day from *Los Angeles Times Book Review* founding editor Digby Diehl, plus current best-seller lists.

• Movie news and information, including reviews of current movies, synopses of over 13,000 movies, columns by movie reviewer Leonard Maltin, box-office leaders, and members' ratings of current movies, as well as Hollywood and celebrity news.

• Television news and information, including television for kids, ratings and charts, and soap opera information.

• Video news and information, including new releases and chart leaders of kids' videos and music videos.

* Music news and information, including reviews of new releases, music charts, rock history and trivia, and columns on classical music and rock music.

* A homelife club, for parents to compare notes on various topics, from parenting and pets to house and garage to hobbies and crafts.

* An arts club, for Prodigy members to carry on written discussions about books, music, television, movies, and the other arts.

* A sports club, for members to communicate about their favorite players, teams, and the fine points of playing.

* Cooking advice, including a basic "cooking class," a cookbook with recipes (which can be selected by type of cuisine, ingredients, and the like, and can then be printed out for home use), and wine information from noted expert Robert Parker.

* An on-screen food-and-wine club, in which members share ideas and recipes with each other.

* Travel information and advice, including columns on family travel, as well as luxury and business travel; the *Mobil Travel Guide* for information on United States sites; *Zagat's Restaurant Survey* with eatery evaluations from consumer patrons nationwide; and a travel club bulletin board for current advice, plus the EAASY SABRE™ system for booking and confirming reservations with major airlines, hotels, and car rental companies, and the QuikTix electronic ticket delivery network.

* Genealogical advice, with information from genealogist Myra Vanderpool on researching your family roots and making a personalized family tree.

* Consumer advice, including recent articles from *Consumer Reports*.

* Personal advice, with articles by columnist Jane Dare on a wide range of topics from sex and reproductive technology to families and death.

* On-line banking and money handling, including electronic check payment, investing, and stock trading.

* Financial counsel, with advice on taxes, investing, and planning, all as part of the Family Financial Guide.

* Electronic mail, or E-mail, allowing members to write to each other through Prodigy.

* Classified advertising, whereby Prodigy members can buy and sell goods and services in 24 categories, and place personal ads.

* Interactive games with members competing with other members, nationwide.

One of the most attractive features of Prodigy is that it is available for a single flat fee per month, no matter how much the service is used. (By contrast, most other computer databases charge per minute of use, with fees that range from modest to enormous.) Families who make heavy use of Prodigy, therefore, get a very good deal. After startup, the only additional costs are for the telephone call to the nearest Prodigy installation and, for the comparatively few heavy users of electronic mail, a charge of twenty-five cents (as of spring 1992), for each message over 30 per month. Some other products and services are available to Prodigy members for a special fee.

Among the most popular features of Prodigy are electronic mail or E-mail, whereby members pass written messages back and forth to each other on computer over the phone lines; and bulletin boards, on which members post messages for anyone to read, often as part of special-interest clubs, such as arts or homelife, as noted above. Use of these is unrestricted, however, being a family service, Prodigy does screen bulletin board messages, and will pull a message that is found objectionable, or that does not pertain to the topic of that particular bulletin board, informing the member as to why it was not posted.

Each member of a family receives his or her own Prodigy identification number (up to six per subscribing household). These IDs are used in communicating with other members through electronic mail, or in the various clubs. In addition, each family member creates his or her own unique and secret password, so that their private interactions and messages are protected. Without knowing these private passwords, parents cannot read their children's electronic mail, for example, and kids cannot use their parents' credit cards. Some services, such as banking, brokerage, and airline ticketing, require additional secret Personal Identification Numbers, as an added level of security.

Prodigy's basic requirements are a computer, a startup kit (purchased from Prodigy, though sometimes available free as part of special offers), and a modem (a device that allows the computer to communicate over a telephone line); if you don't have a modem (or the right kind of modem), Prodigy often has a special discount for buying one. A printer is not necessary, but most families will want to have one to be able to print out information and articles from the service. Because of the way Prodigy is organized, material can be read on screen or printed out on paper, but not transferred onto computer disks. Prodigy works perfectly well with a black-and-white monitor, though a color monitor makes better use of the service's graphics. The computer can be of either of the main types—IBM (or IBM-compatible) or Macintosh

(Apple)—and need not have a very large memory, since relatively little needs to be stored permanently on it. Instead, Prodigy works by connecting the home computer to massive computers in the region or locality; when accessed by members, these supply the data needed to allow users to reach all the kinds of services listed above. Members can also set up a "personal path," going quickly to those features of greatest interest to them.

For people used to professional or more sophisticated computer services, Prodigy might seem slow; however, it is far more sophisticated than others in its use of color and graphics. Some users dislike the fact that the bottom of the screen is generally given over to ads, though many seem to enjoy it, and a special feature allows users to review the last group of ads displayed, if something catches their eye. Prodigy seems to provide an attractive service to many families: By January 1992, Prodigy claimed 1,400,000 subscribers. Over 90 percent of the members have gone to college, and 28 percent have a master's or doctoral degree; interestingly, 10 percent of the members are children. (For more information, contact: Prodigy Services Company, 45 Hamilton Avenue, White Plains, NY 10601; 800-PRODIGY [776-3449].)

Where in the World Is Carmen Sandiego?® on Prodigy®
(PRODIGY SERVICES COMPANY)

Headline News on Prodigy®
(PRODIGY SERVICES COMPANY)

People can learn all about what's available right on the screen, and through the *Prodigy Star* newsletter, once they've joined the Prodigy service. But for people who want to know even more, there's *The Official Guide to the PRODIGY Service*, by computer author John Viescas (Microsoft, 1991). It includes nine chapters: Getting Started, Getting Around, Having Fun, Information, Shopping, Communications, Travel, Money, and Customizing Your Account, as well as coverage of special features added only in 1991. The book is available from a bookstore, or can be purchased on-line through Prodigy's shopping service.

Another consumer-oriented computer database service is America Online®, which takes a different approach. It has a lower monthly fee, which includes one free evening or weekend hour; above that, subscribers pay a low time-based fee, somewhat higher during business hours; free online help is also provided on evenings and weekends. America Online's software and *Getting Started* guide are free, and new subscribers receive the first month's membership free, including an evening or weekend hour. Like Prodigy, America Online has a wide variety of games (including an advanced version of the popular *Dungeons & Dragons*), computer forums, electronic mail, interactive message boards, travel services, news from around the world, including business and sports, and an online encyclopedia (*Compton's Electronic Encyclopedia*). But it offers some services not (as of mid-1992) available on Prodigy, including online classes, taught by professional teachers, and nightly online homework help for kids. Where information on Prodigy can only be printed out, programs, articles, and other information from America Online can be "downloaded" or read right into the user's computer; this includes many free or shareware programs (for which users pay on the honor system). America Online also has special relationships with such organizations as the National Geographic Society (which offers a Kids Network), Senior Net, and the National Education Association; and also regional editions, such as Chicago Online and Florida Online. America Online's wide-ranging offerings are organized into eight departments: Computing and Software; News and Finance; Learning and Reference; Travel and Shopping; What's New and Online Support; People Connection; Lifestyles and Interests; and Games and Entertainment. The service is available for use with Macintosh, Apple II, IBM or IBM-compatible computers. (For more information, contact: America Online, 8619 Westwood Center Drive, Vienna, VA 22182; 703-893-6288 or 800-827-6364.)

What's *New* in Family Health and Safety

Babyproofing

That's the watchword among parents of young children, especially the parents of those who have just started to crawl or walk. Ordinary objects ranging from electrical outlets and toilets to hot-water faucets and cat boxes suddenly become fraught with danger. What about that tall lamp, which might be pulled down? Or the potentially toxic detergents under the sink? Or the key to the fireplace gas jet? Or the poisonous plant on the coffee table. Or the crib attachments that a child can use to climb out of the crib and fall? From hazards seen and unseen, more children die in avoidable accidents each year than from the life-threatening diseases of children, according to the National Safety Council.

No parent can watch a child every minute of every day. Anticipation is the key to preventing injury, but too few parents—especially first-time parents—have the ability to identify the many potential hazards to their young child, much less know how to remove or modify them so as to reduce or eliminate the danger. For every hazard they might spy, another might go unnoticed. Hence the emergence of a new service for parents: babyproofing.

Babyproofing services are hired to come into the home, evaluate its dangers from a *child's* point of view, and remove, replace, or install what is necessary to make the home safe. They offer the advantages of experience in spotting potential dangers and ready access to the devices and skills for the necessary changes, modifications, or installations. These include not just the familiar gates for stairways, shields for electrical outlets, or coverings for balcony railings (now often of plexiglass), but also less-familiar items such as latches on drawers, locks on refrigerators, corner guards on glass or stone coffee tables, latches on toilets, and metal attachments to keep windows from opening so far that a child might fall out. Though many such devices are available to everyone and could be installed by do-it-yourselfers, the sheer inconvenience of trying to get devices from a couple of dozen different suppliers makes many people turn instead to babyproofing services—especially because charges for services at a modest-sized apartment or home may be little more than the cost of a visit or two to the emergency room, in case of an accident—to say nothing of the anguish saved.

The acknowledged granddaddy of babyproofing is Danny McNeill, who became "Mr. Baby Proofer" when he opened a store of that name in Los Angeles in 1985. Since that time, McNeill and a partner have founded Baby Proofers International, a network of babyproofing services around the United States. These are independently owned and operated, under various names; the Chicago dealership, for example, is called Safe 'n' Sound Childproofers, Inc. (see below). Parents can generally locate a Baby Proofers International dealership or other childproofing service in their area by looking in the yellow pages under child or baby services. Indeed, some parents have become home-based dealers themselves, with products and training supplied to affiliates by Baby Proofers International. (For more information, contact: Baby Proofers International, 1610 South La Cienega Boulevard, Suite 205, Los Angeles, CA 90035; 800-783-8793 or 310-550-7741. Safe 'n' Sound Childproofers, who kindly supplied the accompanying photos, can be reached at 345 Fullerton Parkway, Suite 1502, Chicago, IL 60614; 312-281-BABY[2229].)

Parents who choose to do their own babyproofing will have to shop around for the right devices to install in their homes. One firm that makes something of a specialty of such products is Safety 1st®. Among the many child-resistant or childproof products the firm offers are outlet plugs or covers, locks for switches (as for a garbage disposal unit), cabinet and drawer latches, oven and cabinet locks, stove knob

A simple latch on a
cabinet door . . .
(SAFE 'N SOUND
CHILDPROOFERS, INC.)

can prevent this.
(SAFE 'N SOUND
CHILDPROOFERS, INC.)

covers, stove guards, Velcro-type appliance latches, VCR locks, edge-and-corner bumpers, balcony guards, door stoppers (to protect children's fingers), cord shorteners, window locks, and even a small-object tester, to see if an object is small enough to fit into a child's mouth. (For more information, contact: Safety 1st, 210 Boylston Street, Chestnut Hill, MA 02167; 800-962-7233 outside MA, or 617-964-7744.)

Parents can also get help from some of the useful books that have recently been published in the area of child safety, among them:

• *Parents Book of Child Safety*, by David Laskin (Ballantine, 1991). Guides parents in childproofing their home, choosing safe products, and staying ahead of their child's developing capabilities, focusing on children from birth through the early school years. Published under the auspices of *Parents* magazine, the book also includes information on safety issues outside the home—as in outdoor play and day care—and instructions on performing emergency procedures, such as cardiopulmonary resuscitation (CPR) for children. Laskin is also the author of the *Parents Book for New Fathers* (Ballantine, 1988), and coauthor, with Kathleen O. Laskin, of *The Little Girl Book* (Ballantine, 1992).

• *Baby Proofing Basics: How to Keep Your Child Safe*, by Vicki Lansky (Book Peddlers, 1991). A parent's guide to babyproofing not only in the house, but also outdoors, while traveling, playing, and so on. The book includes helpful descriptions of safe baby equipment and information on poisoning prevention.

• *The Perfectly Safe Home*, by Jeanne E. Miller (Simon & Schuster/Fireside, 1991). Focuses on child safety from infancy to age 7, with special emphasis on sites of greatest danger, indoors and out, including play, sports, and travel. It provides counsel on general fire safety, first aid, and poisoning prevention; critiques furniture, equipment, and toys; and notes many common dangerous household objects and products.

To look at or buy these books, contact your local bookstore or library; the Laskin book can be purchased directly by calling 800-733-3000.

Singly or in groups, parents may also want to buy or rent the 18-minute video called *One Step Ahead*, produced by Kristine Samuelson, which teaches parents safety awareness, by presenting a "child's eye" view of household hazards, and also stresses the importance of being prepared with emergency phone numbers and procedures in case of crisis. (Contact: Carle Media, 611 West Park, Urbana, IL 61801; 217-384-8280.)

When Do Kids Need Protection from the Sun?

The answer is: *Much* more often than they get it. Though sunlight is essential for all life, doctors are learning more and more about the dangers for humans of long-term daily exposure to the sun, including sunburn, damage to the retina in the eye, cataracts, and skin cancer. With the continuing passion for tanning and outdoor activities, and probably also because of the progressive thinning of the ozone layer in the earth's upper atmosphere, skin cancer rates are rising. In 1991, some 600,000 people in the United States alone were diagnosed with some form of skin cancer, with numbers recently increasing 3 to 5 percent a year. Of these, about 32,000 have melanoma, and about 8,000 die annually, a figure doubled from the previous decade. Skin cancers are triggered by accumulated skin damage from the sun's rays. Much of that damage takes place during childhood; experts estimate that half of a person's total exposure to the sun occurs before age 18. Strikingly, doctors are now routinely seeing melanoma patients in their 20s, when in the past the disease was rare in persons under age 40.

Among the sun's rays, the particular culprit—as researchers confirmed definitively for the first time in 1991—is ultraviolet radiation, light from the purple end of the rainbow. Studies focused on a gene called p53, which normally keeps cell growth in check; it was found that ultraviolet radiation can cripple the p53 gene and allow the unchecked cell division that, with other kinds of damage and mutations, leads to what we know as cancer.

There are three kinds of ultraviolet light, all of which can damage the skin:

* Type C (UVC), the most penetrating and most damaging. During the period of human life on earth, this type of radiation has been largely absorbed by the ozone layer in the earth's upper atmosphere before reaching the ground. However, progressive thinning of the ozone layer may be weakening this blocking action, and so is causing concerns about increasing UVC danger to humans and other life.

* Type B (UVB), a high-energy form that passes right through the earth's atmosphere. This is the type of radiation that produces sunburn and most tanning, as well as aging the skin and causing skin cancer, especially the potentially deadly melanoma.

• Type A (UVA), a lower-energy form that also penetrates the earth's atmosphere, unblocked by the ozone layer. This type of radiation produces some tanning and causes two types of skin cancer, though apparently not melanoma.

Tanning is actually the body's attempt to prevent further skin damage; skin cells produce a pigment called *melanin*, which blocks some of the ultraviolet light. As the experts bluntly put it: Tanned skin is damaged skin, and the deeper the color of the tan, the more extensive the damage. People who are very fair-skinned do not have many of the type of cells that produce melanin, and so will not get tanned, no matter how much damage they cause to their skin. People who have very dark skin have more melanin, but are still subject to damage from sun exposure. Sunburn results when the skin has been damaged so much that it is painful to remain in the sun. Tanning devices produce the same kinds of UVA and UVB rays, deliberately causing skin damage.

Sunscreens are designed to offer some protection from ultraviolet rays. Most block out only UVB radiation and are rated by their ability to do just that. They are given a *sun protection factor* (SPF), indicating how long a person can remain in the sun without burning; if a person would normally get a sunburn after 10 minutes unprotected, application of a sunscreen with an SPF of 15 would mean the person could stay in the sun for 150 minutes before burning. As of early 1992, the FDA endorsed sunscreens only up to 15. Sunscreens as high as 50 are on the market, and federal experts think that they may be valuable, especially for people who have very fair skin—and for children—though the FDA has not been able to develop procedures for determining the effectiveness of SPF's above 15.

Most sunscreens do not block out UVAs, however. Even for the relatively few sunscreens that do, none blocks *all* UVAs, and no rating system yet exists for evaluating UVA protection, though some experts estimate that their SPF is equivalent to 3 or 4. Despite advertising claims to the contrary, no sunscreens are sunblocks. Only totally opaque substances, such as zinc oxide or titanium dioxide, block all rays. These are usually practical to use only on areas most exposed and vulnerable, such as nose or lips.

Ironically, the advent of UVB sunscreens may be causing more UVA damage, for when people are protected from burning, they have the illusion of safety and stay in the sun longer, unprotected from UVA radiation. The same is true on cool, breezy, or overcast days, when—

because ultraviolet rays carry no warmth—people are unaware that they are still at risk from ultraviolet radiation. (Clouds block out the heat-producing infrared rays, but ultraviolet rays pass right through them.) Shade often offers little protection, for ultraviolet rays bounce off bright surfaces, such as sand, water, snow, and white concrete. The rays even penetrate several feet under water, and through glass.

How are parents to best protect their children? Federal agencies and medical organizations make the following recommendations:

• Infants under six months old (some say up to a year) should be kept out of the sun altogether, or as much as possible. Their eyes are particularly vulnerable to sunlight, and sunscreens are not recommended, because they irritate sensitive baby skin.

• Children and parents going out in the sun should wear a hat and tightly woven clothing, fully covering arms and legs. Loosely woven, gauzy, or wet clothes offer little protection.

• Children and their families should avoid being out in the midday sun for any prolonged period of time, in all areas (though especially near the equator and in higher altitudes, where the atmosphere is thinner) and all times of the year (though especially in the warmer months, when the rays are more direct). Some experts have suggested that schools, child-care centers, and camps reschedule their outdoor play times for early morning and late afternoon, rather than between 10 A.M. and 2 to 3 P.M.

• Parents should see that their children routinely wear sunscreen with an SPF of 15 or more. A waterproof sunscreen is recommended for children, who sweat more heavily and dash in and out of water more frequently than most adults. (Active adults, especially swimmers, should also use a waterproof sunscreen.) For adults and children, sunscreen is recommended even for casual exposure, such as driving a car, walking to the store, or taking an outdoor lunch break, since all exposure contributes to cumulative damage.

• Before using a new sunscreen, test it on a small area of skin (such as the underpart of the forearm). Apply some, cover it with a bandage for 24 hours, then expose it to sunlight for 15 minutes; if the skin is sensitive to the ingredients in the sunscreen, the patch will be red and swollen the next day. Many people are sensitive to the widely used substance PABA (para-aminobenzoic acid), which can also stain clothing. Many newer sunscreens are labeled as greaseless, hypoallergenic, or PABA-free; allergies to non-PABA sunscreens have been less common. Higher SPF strengths, however, cause increased irritation, where sensitivity exists. Parents should also check with their doctor or pharmacist about any medications that can increase sensitivity to sunscreen ingredients, such as certain antibiotics (notably tetracycline, given for acne), antihistamines, birth control pills, diuretics, sulfa drugs, and antidepressants.

• Apply sunscreen liberally. Recent studies have found that most people use only half as much as they should, the result being that they may get only an SPF 7 protection from an SPF 15 sunscreen. Actual amounts vary with the brand and the form, but for one application at the beach, an adult should use an ounce or two per application, with proportionately less for children.

• Put sunscreen on every exposed area, including ears, feet, and the part in the hair. For protection in places with snow, water, sand, white concrete, or other light, bright surfaces that reflect ultraviolet rays, do not neglect areas susceptible to light reflecting upward, such as the underchin, the area under the nose, and the upper lip.

• Put the sunscreen on 30 minutes before going outdoors, to give the skin time to soak it up.

• Put on more sunscreen every two hours, and immediately after being in the water (unless the sunscreen is waterproof).

(For more information, contact: Food and Drug Administration, 301-443-3170 or 301-443-2410.)

Eyes also need protection from ultraviolet radiation. For extended outdoor activity, especially in snow, on water, or at the beach, sunglasses that filter out all UVA and UVB light are recommended for everyone. Large lenses or wraparound styles are preferred, since they lessen the amount of light entering from around the frames. Some experts recommend that regular glasses for indoor or short-term outdoor wear also have an ultraviolet coating; however, others say that such coatings will not hurt, but are unnecessary, since people who wear glasses with plastic lenses—which is most eyeglass wearers today—already have 95 percent of the UV rays blocked, and so do not need any extra protective coating.

As far as it is known, there are no significant indoor sources of ultraviolet radiation. Though many people are sold coatings to block out UV from computers, impartial experts note that computers and television screens emit less UV radiation than do fluorescent lights, at $\frac{1}{10,000}$th of the level believed to cause problems. Scientists have, however, found that tungsten-halogen lamps emit possibly harmful UV rays, and so should not be used near people, as at a desk, unless a UV filter is installed. The FDA has found that some filters are inadequate, and that people sometimes fail to replace the filter after changing a bulb.

Mercury vapor lamps can also emit intense ultraviolet radiation, which has caused various injuries and burns, including burns to the cornea of the eye; such lamps are normally protected by filters, and most injuries occur when this outer envelope is broken, generally through activities in school gymnasiums. Since 1980, the FDA has recommended that mercury vapor lamps used in proximity to people be of a self-extinguishing type, which shuts off within 15 minutes. But non–self-extinguishing lamps are still widely found. The FDA recommends that such lamps be checked regularly (with the lamp off) for missing, broken, or punctured outer envelopes; that broken lamps be turned off immediately, and parts replaced only while the lamps are off; that people near broken lamps should leave or protect their eyes and skin from UV exposure by putting on coats or sweaters and sunglasses; and that people exposed to UV rays from broken lamps see a doctor if they have any symptoms of skin burns or eye irritation.

Families who are installing sun rooms, greenhouses, skylights, or extra-large windows and doors are also advised to get *low-emissivity glass*, or *low-e*, to cut down on ultraviolet radiation. Ordinary clear glass allows most of the sun's rays, including UV and heat, to pass through into the house; they can be made tinted or reflective to block UV and many other rays, but that produces darker rooms and hinders growth of houseplants. By contrast, low-e glass is coated with metal oxides to block ultraviolet rays and heat from outdoors, while still allowing visible light to pass through; low-e also retains indoor heat, for energy efficiency. Even more effective in blocking UV radiation are low-e films; one type, called Heat Mirror, is placed between double-paned glass for nearly complete ultraviolet blockage. Many hardware stores now sell low-e film, such as Gila/Sunshine (manufactured by Courtaulds Performance Films, of Chandler, Arizona), which homeowners can apply to ordinary windows.

No More Lost or Missing Kids

That's the aim of Phone Home™, a new automatic dialing device that allows children to phone home, even if they have no money, don't know the number, and don't even know how to use a telephone. The small electronic device—no larger than a child's hand—can simply be clipped to a child's clothing, such as the inside of a pocket, or to a key chain. It allows a child to make a collect call to a preprogrammed telephone number, normally the home number.

To use the Phone Home device, the child simply holds it up to the mouthpiece of a telephone and presses the large button (marked "Home"). Phone Home then automatically dials 16 digits: "0" for operator, the three-digit area code, and the seven-digit number. When the parents receive the collect call, they should immediately say to the operator that this is an emergency call, that the child is lost and the call must be traced, and ask for time and charges on the call; the operator will then hook up with appropriate emergency systems in that area to find and rescue the child. The child does not even have to be able to talk

Phone Home™ (NIMROD INTERNATIONAL)

into the telephone, though parents will want to teach their child to do so. The battery-operated device cannot be tampered with, since it can be programmed only with the special device supplied with the product.

When Phone Home was tested with children ages 3 to 12, all were able to use the device successfully and could understand that Phone Home was for emergency use only, once it was explained to them by a parent or other adult. Even small children who are unable to reach or operate a pay telephone can be taught to knock a phone off the hook, in order to use Phone Home. Parents will want to teach their child to use the device *regardless of what anyone else tells them*; doing so will counteract some of the standard lies told by abductors, including non-custodial parents, such as that their other parent is dead or that their family doesn't want them anymore. As a more general safety precaution, experts in the field suggest that parents establish a family password, and teach their children never to go anywhere with anyone who does not know the password. Phone Home has been endorsed by the Vanished Children's Alliance.

Phone Home can also be used by older children or adults, such as those with mental retardation, some physical disabilities, or Alzheimer's disease. On a lighter note, it may also act as a reminder for children away at college or camp to . . . phone home. Phone Home is available in discount and variety stores. (For more information, contact: Nimrod International, P.O. Box 565, Clarksburg, NJ 08510; to order, call Capitol Sales, 800-477-5196.)

New Twists in Car Safety Seats

As years of experience have now shown, car safety seats save children's lives. The U.S. Department of Transportation estimates that car safety restraints are used for 80 percent of all children ages 1 to 4, and many states require them for children under a certain age. Parents today have a variety of seats to choose from, including seats designed specifically for infants, toddlers, and older children, as well as convertible seats that, with appropriate shifts or modifications, can be used for young children up to about age 4 or 40 pounds. Children under 28 inches tall and under one year old should always be placed in a rear-facing infant seat (either a special infant seat or a convertible one), since an infant's neck and spine are not developed enough to support the weight of the head, in case of a collision.

To the wide array of car safety seats for children over one year and 20 pounds, several recent entries have been added:

• Chrysler has built-in child seats available on certain car models, eliminating the need for parents to purchase separate child safety seats and booster seats, and preventing problems that can result from improper installation of an add-on child safety seat. When closed, the Integrated Child Seat is just like a normal car seat, but it opens up to form a toddler seat for children, with a flip-up headrest, a flip-down child's seat cushion, and a built-in 5-point harness. The seat includes a vinyl pad that is attached to the seat frame with Velcro® fasteners, but can be easily removed for washing. For children over 40 pounds, the seat works as a booster seat, using the vehicle's lap and shoulder belt. Chrysler stresses that the lap-and-shoulder-belt protection should also be used for children whose shoulders are above the shoulder belt anchorages of the 5-point harness, since otherwise they risk spine injury during a collision. The toddler seat is recommended for children who weigh 20 to 40 pounds, are 28 to 40 inches tall, and can sit upright alone; parents may want to get a ring-type neck pillow for children who may

Integrated Child Seat
(CHRYSLER CORP.)

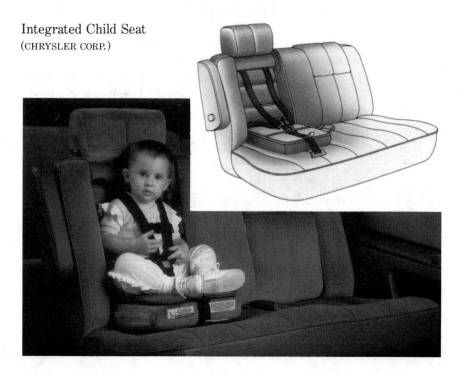

sleep in the car seat. The Integrated Child Seat is available on various models, including the Dodge Caravan and the Plymouth Voyager mini-vans (on the right and left sides of the middle passenger bench) and the LH series of midsized sedans (in the middle of the back seat). Another safety feature, offered on these and other models, is a child-protection lock, which allows parents to flip a small lever on the latch, so the door cannot be opened from the outside. (For more information, contact your local Dodge or Plymouth dealer.)

• Fisher-Price™ has a new T-Shield Booster Car Seat (patent pending), designed for children who are too big for regular car seats. It has the great advantage of opening from the right or from the left. The child simply sits (or is placed in) the base seat; a T-shaped piece fits into the base, holding the child in place and also functioning as an armrest; then the automobile's lap seat belt fits into the groove of the T-shaped armrest, to secure the whole seat—and therefore the child. To remove the child, the parent simply releases the seat belt and pulls out the T-shaped insert; this can be done from either the right or left side, making it easy for parents to seat children on either side of the car. The seat is padded for the child's comfort, and comes with a seat guard that fits under it, to keep the car's upholstery unmarked. The T-Shield Booster Car Seat is designed to be used in this way with children 40 to 60 pounds, or if both lap and shoulder belt are used, 30 to 60 pounds. Without the T-shaped piece, the base alone can be used as a booster seat, with lap-and-shoulder-belt safety systems.

Fisher-Price has also recently introduced a new deluxe convertible car seat for infants and toddlers, which has a built-in pillow and adjustable side "cuddle cushions." The seat reclines and adjusts for a more comfortable fit, seat belts adjust automatically, and the deluxe pad can be removed for washing. Most convenient for parents, the armrest-and-restraint system has a retractor that can be operated with one hand, making it easy to get the child in and out of the seat. In addition, Fisher-Price's standard infant car seat, which received a gold award in the 1990 Industrial Design Excellent Awards, now comes in a variety of bright, new colors. (For more information, contact a store selling Fisher-Price products, or Fisher-Price, Inc., East Aurora, NY 14052; 800-433-5437 or 716-687-3000.)

• From Downunder Design, Inc., modeled on an Australian prototype, comes the Kangaroo Booster® (patent pending), for children who have outgrown their car seats and weigh between 50 to 80 pounds (in Canada, 40 to 80 pounds and over 33 inches, or 85 cm, tall). The Kangaroo Booster's prime advantages are that it gives the child full

T-Shield Booster Car Seat
(FISHER-PRICE, INC.)

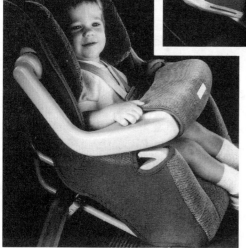

Deluxe Infant Car Seat
(FISHER-PRICE, INC.)

view from the car windows; positions the lap and shoulder belt properly for protection (that is, across the shoulder and the pelvis, not the neck and the abdomen, where the belts can cause injury in case of accidents); is easy to use, involving no complicated mechanisms or straps; is light and portable, and so can be readily moved from car to car; can be easily cleaned, since the fabric cover removes for washing and is treated with Scotchguard™; and is comfortable, offering the child a velour-covered foam seat (in contrast to some barely cushioned plastic boosters), with side cushions that provide support, so a child can rest or sleep on long trips. Citing the National Transportation Safety Board, Downunder

Kangaroo Booster™
(DOWNUNDER DESIGN, INC.)

Design notes that every year 3 million children ages 5 to 9 outgrow their car seats, but only 37 percent go on to use any form of safety restraint, including seat belts and booster seats—one reason that the leading cause of death among children continues to be automobile accidents. One problem is that, with seat belts alone, children can't see when buckled in; also, many booster seats are hard and uncomfortable, and offer no shoulder support. The Kangaroo Booster is designed to meet the needs of these children, making them feel more "grown up" and helping parents avoid hassles about buckling up. Downunder Design stresses that (as with all belt-positioning boosters) the Kangaroo Booster should be used only with lap-and-shoulder systems, noting that "lap belts alone can produce severe or fatal injuries in even minor accidents." For cars with only lap belts, Downunder recommends getting a retrofit kit, either from the car dealer or from a specialty supplier, such as Cassidy's Safety Belts, 1012 King Street, Olean, NY 14760; 716-372-8602. (For more information, contact: Downunder Design, Inc., P.O. Box 709, Concord, MA 01742; 800-677-1718 or 508-371-0100.)

Downunder Design offers a useful guide to choosing car restraints for children of different ages, based on information from the American Academy of Pediatrics Safe Ride Program:

It is important that parents know and follow the specifications for any car safety seats they purchase, and use them only in the prescribed

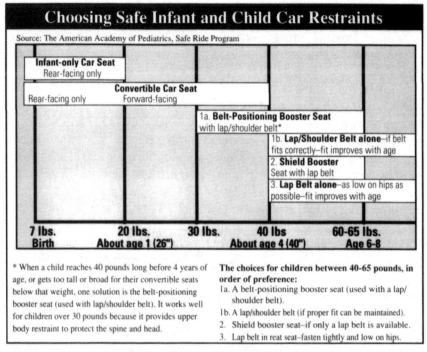

Choosing Safe Infant and Child Car Restraints (DOWNUNDER DESIGN, INC.)

ways and for children of the right ages and sizes for the particular seat. Otherwise, they may cause severe internal or spinal injuries during accidents, instead of protecting their children from danger.

Additionally, parents should be sure to return the registration card now included with all car seats, so that they may be notified in the event of a recall.

Shopping Carts—A Child Safety Hazard

The familiar grocery-store shopping cart has proven to be a surprising safety hazard, especially to children. In 1991, federal safety figures showed that over 32,000 people required hospital emergency care for injuries involving such carts; of these, 19,000 were children 4 years old or under. Young children are particularly vulnerable because many of the accidents involve falls from the cart, when the child climbs out of the seat provided; among the serious results are concussions and other head injuries, fractures, and internal injuries. In a 1991 report, the Consumer Product Safety Commission warned parents and caregivers to watch young children carefully, and to use seat belts when they are provided.

Many parents have taken the offensive by buying a seat belt of their own to take with them to stores. Several companies, including Fisher-Price and Safety 1st, offer portable seat belts for use in shopping carts and other such situations—generally simple straps that fit and buckle around the child and part of the shopping cart. In some cases, the child can, however, wiggle out of the seat belt. The new Sit-Tite™ child restraint system goes these seat belts one better by using a Y-front harness design that actually keeps the child seated and secure.

The Sit-Tite was born out of experience. In 1990, when Elizabeth Duval was distracted by one daughter, her other 2 year old daughter fell from a shopping cart onto the hard floor. Luckily the facial injuries were not serious, but when she was unable to find a child restraint that satisfied her needs, Duval decided to take action to protect other parents and children from similar experiences. The Sit-Tite uses 1-inch-wide straps of heavy-duty, non-stretching, polypropylene webbing, with buckles and one-way Pull-The-Dot snaps to hold the straps securely. The Sit-Tite has adjustable straps to fit children of various ages, will hold children up to age 3 comfortably, and is easy to use: The bottom of the "Y" is attached to a cart between the child's legs, then the straps are brought up over the child's chest and shoulders, and are attached to the back of the seat. In addition to grocery carts, the Sit-Tite can also be easily used in strollers, high chairs, and table seats. When not in use, it is compact enough to fit into a purse, small bag, or pocket, and can be washed in warm water with mild detergent. Rood/Duval Enterprises cautions, however, that the Sit-Tite is not for use in any motorized vehicle, bicycle seat, or aircraft, and that children should not be left unattended, noting: "The Sit-Tite Child Restraint System requires adult supervision at all times." The child is, after all, harnessed into a wheeled device that can roll away if unattended. (For more information, contact: Rood/Duval Enterprises, P.O. Box 8218, Grand Rapids, MI 49518; 616-281-9400.)

Safety 1st also has a "Parent's Helper" Safety Harness, to use in a shopping cart, stroller, or high chair, to prevent sliding out of seats. The adjustable straps loop around the shoulders, and buckle to a waistband, which is then fixed to the cart or seat. Outside a cart or chair, the parent or caregiver can simply loop a hand through the back to keep

Sit-Tite™ (ROOD/DUVAL ENTERPRISES)

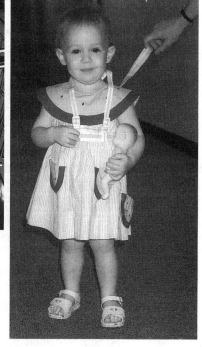

Parent's Helper Safety Harness
(SAFETY 1ST)

the child from roaming too far. More convenient if a child is going to be walking far, whether in a store or elsewhere, is the Totalong, also from Safety 1st. This is simply an adjustable waistband attached to a long strap that ends in a wrist strap for the adult accompanying the child. Both of these items are made of soft, expandable material and are washable. (For more information, contact: Safety 1st, 210 Boylston Street, Chestnut Hill, MA 02167; 800-962-7233 outside MA, or 617-964-7744.)

Danger: Exercise Equipment

Pediatrician John H. Gould was alerted to the problem when he saw, in his own office alone, two cases in which a child's finger had been torn off by a home exercise bike. Gould and fellow pediatrician Allan R. Dejong, both affiliated with Philadelphia's Thomas Jefferson University, found no medical articles dealing with the problem of injuries related to home exercise equipment. But when they examined case reports collected by the Consumer Product Safety Commission (CPSC), they found that in 1990, over 25,250 people received treatment in hospital emergency rooms for injuries caused by exercise equipment—four times as many as in 1982. Of most concern to parents, over half of these injuries involved children under age 15.

In their 1992 report to pediatric research societies, Gould and Dejong found that the most dangerous types of equipment were exercise bikes, involved in 55 percent of the accidents, generally amputating a finger or toe. Even more serious, jump ropes were involved in 25 percent of the accidents, in a majority of which the rope user was strangled to death. In the accidents involving children, over 80 percent of the injuries occurred when the children were playing or exercising alone or unsupervised.

The obvious conclusions for parents are:

• Be careful of yourselves and your children when using exercise equipment.
• Do not let children use exercise equipment alone or unsupervised by an adult.
• Do not store exercise equipment in ways and places that might "attract" use by children.
• If it is possible to lock up or lock away exercise equipment, to prevent potentially dangerous use by children, do so.

(For more information, contact: Consumer Product Safety Commission, Product Safety Hotline, 800-638-CPSC [2772].)

Get the Lead Out

Lead has long been recognized as an environmental hazard that accumulates in the body. But lead poisoning is far from a thing of the past. One homeless Wisconsin child died in 1990, after living for four months with his family in an abandoned office building littered with lead-containing paint chips and piles of dust. Nor does lead poisoning respect class, affecting children from both rich and poor families. A 1990 survey showed that, in the United States alone, 57 million private homes built before 1980 have lead-based paint in them, and nearly 10 million of them house children under age 7. Of those 57 million homes, 10.7 million had dangerously high lead levels in surface dust. A 1991 Department of Health and Human Services (HHS) report, *Strategic Plan for the Elimination of Childhood Lead Poisoning,* called lead poisoning "the most common and societally devastating environmental disease of young children."

Infants and children, as well as developing fetuses, are especially vulnerable to lead poisoning. At low levels of exposure, lead poisoning affects children's intellectual and physical development; at high levels, it can cause degenerative brain disease, which if untreated can lead to death. Lead consumption can impair a whole range of reading, writing, math, visual, motor, and language skills, as well as abstract thinking and concentration. Symptoms of high levels of lead in the blood include irritability, insomnia, colic, and anemia. Young children are especially at risk because so many nonfood objects end up in their mouths. Many researchers now think that swallowing lead-contaminated dust is even more dangerous than eating chips of leaded paint; near roadways, a major danger is soil impregnated with lead from years of leaded gasoline.

Health officials have been rapidly revising their assessments of what amounts of lead in children's blood constitute a danger. As recently as 1985, the federal government's "threshold of concern" was set at 25 micrograms per deciliter of blood. But in its revised recommendations on lead levels and children, the threshold of concern is less than half that figure. The problem is that symptoms generally do not appear until lead has reached dangerous and possibly even deadly levels, leaving the vast majority of cases undiagnosed and untreated. The new recommendations are part of a program urging wider testing of lead levels in children's blood, and issuing new guidelines for action to be taken. These new recommendations for areas where children are at risk from lead poisoning are:

Blood Level*	Children Affected	Action
10 or more	4 to 6 million	Consider checking levels in high-risk areas
15 or more	1.2 million	Test children and advise on cleanup or diet changes
20 or more	545,000	Monitor children closely and visit homes to help
25 or more	188,000	Start medical treatment

* measured in micrograms of lead per deciliter of blood

The Wisconsin child who died had a level of 144, so high that the lead had begun to replace calcium in his bones. The HHS estimates that 3 to 4 million children age 6 or under have lead levels of over 14, noting that this is far greater than the number of children affected by other childhood illnesses. The Centers for Disease Control see these recommendations as part of a program to phase in universal screening for young children. Because the problem is so widespread and its full dimensions still unknown, some health experts have called for yearly testing.

The main treatment for lead poisoning is a process called *chelation*, in which the patient is given drugs that chemically bind with the lead and remove it from the bloodstream. Traditionally such drugs have been given by injections. But the FDA recently approved a new chelation drug, called Chemet (succimer), that can be given orally, though its early use has been limited.

In 1991 the Department of Health and Human Services, working with the Centers for Disease Control, launched a plan to eliminate lead paint in America's houses, calling for testing of houses and apartments, and cleaning up those that require it. The least expensive approach involves putting a protective layer of plastic over the lead-based paint, though it is uncertain how long the layer would last under everyday conditions. The most expensive approach involves stripping all the lead-based paint; this has its own hazards, since doing so releases much *more* lead into the air. The Environmental Protection Agency has also proposed various rules to lessen lead in the environment, and especially in the water supply.

Federal agencies have also warned against several other previously little-recognized sources of lead poisoning. In 1991, the Food and Drug Administration (FDA) issued a warning against lead from leaded crystal. Researchers found that crystal decanters and other containers release (leach) lead into liquids stored in them, especially alcoholic or acidic liquids, including fruit juices, and even infant formula. Meanwhile, lead continues to be found in many other areas—at home, in imported ceramicware, houseware decorations, house paint, water pipes, soldered cans, some calcium supplements, and lead-containing wine bottle seals; and in the wider world, in such sources as artist's materials, some older commercial coffee urns, lead-acid batteries, power plant scrubbers, and gasoline. Though many such uses have ended, lead concentrations remain. Some newly recognized sources can be seemingly innocuous, such as the lead-pigmented inks used on plastic wrappers; if these are turned inside out and used to store foods, the contents may become contaminated with lead.

In line with recent understandings about lead hazards, the FDA advises the following:

* Make sure children's hands are clean before they eat.
* If you use leaded crystalware for drinking, do not use it on a daily basis; do not store beverages or foods in it, especially alcoholic beverages and other products with a high acid content (fruit juice, tomato sauce, vinegar, wine, etc.); do not use it while pregnant or of childbearing age; and do not let infants and children drink from leaded crystal baby bottles or glasses.
* Since some imported foods are still packed in lead-soldered cans, limit consumption of imported canned foods, unless your grocer can assure you that a particular product is not packed in a lead-soldered can. The U.S. food processing industry reported to the FDA that, from mid-1991, lead soldering was not being used for domestically produced foods; it has for some time not been used for baby foods (which are usually packed in glass containers) and juices.
* Keep painted surfaces in good shape, so older layers of paint are not exposed, chipping, or peeling. **Be sure children do not eat paint chips.**
* Hire a professional contractor to remove lead-based paints from any surface. **People can poison themselves by burning or scraping off layers of paint. Also, lead dust is generated and, if not properly contained, becomes dispersed in the air and sticks to household surfaces, affecting all of the house's occupants.**
* Get a water analysis to test for lead. For best results, do not run the water for 6 to 8 hours before the test, allowing lead to leach into the still water; first thing in the morning would, therefore, be a good time to test.
* If you know, or suspect, that your household water contains elevated lead levels, let water run for at least 30 seconds or until it runs cool, before the morning's first use, to flush the lines. Use cold water for drinking or cooking, since lead leaches more readily into hot water.
* Contact your local water supplier to find out if your home or apartment has lead water-service connections. If so, and you own the lines, ask for a contractor who can change them; if the supplier owns lead connections, pressure for them to be changed.
* Never use lead solder to repair plumbing.
* If you use older or imported ceramic products, avoid storing acidic foods in them. Better yet, the FDA recommends testing them and, if high lead content is found, disposing of them or using them for decorative purposes only.

(For more information, contact: Food and Drug Administration, 301-443-3170 or 301-443-2410.)

What Causes Sudden Infant Death Syndrome?

The answer is: no one really knows. Sudden infant death syndrome (SIDS), also called crib death or cot death, is the leading cause of death in children under one year old, killing about 7,000 infants a year in the United States alone. But its causes are—by definition—obscure, since the term is applied to the abrupt and unexpected death of an infant, for which no adequate explanation can be found, even after an autopsy, an examination of the scene of death, and a review of the child's medical history.

However, some light has recently been shed in this dark corner. It now seems that some—perhaps many—cases of infant death originally labeled as SIDS may have resulted from infants suffocating in bedding. The problem was recognized just in the last few years, when at least 35 infants died after being put to bed lying face down on beanbag cushions; these molded around their bodies, trapping them to breathe in their own exhaled carbon dioxide, and so to suffocate. All or most of the infants were under 3 months old, and so were too young to raise their heads, or to roll over or away from the cushions. The 12- by 24-inch pillows, filled with plastic foam beads or polystyrene pellets, had been marketed under several names. In April 1990, the U.S. Consumer Product Safety Commission (CPSC) called for a voluntary recall of the 950,000 cushions sold since their introduction in 1985, and reported that all 10 manufacturers of the pillows cooperated, though some such cushions may remain in homes, in closets and attics, and still pose a future hazard.

But the problem appears to be wider than that. Between 1985 and 1990, over 250 infants died lying on adult and youth beds. Many smothered in bedclothes, were trapped between the mattress and part of the bed or a wall, or sank into the mattress or water bed while lying face down. Some have also died sleeping in their parents' bed, when an adult rolled over and smothered them. The CPSC has issued a warning to parents and caregivers about the danger to infants in all these situations. (For more information, contact: Consumer Product Safety Commission, Product Safety Hotline, 800-638-CPSC [2772].)

Two recent studies by Drs. James S. Kemp and Bradley T. Thach of the Washington University School of Medicine in St. Louis have used rabbits to show how infants could suffocate in bedding. One of their reports, published in the July 1991 *New England Journal of Medicine*, described how suffocation could occur using beanbag cushions; and the other, given at the Federation of American Societies for Experimental Biology meeting in April 1992, showed how similar suffocation could occur with a synthetic-filled adult pillow, a thick foam couch cushion, a thick foam pad covered with a comforter, a sheepskin sold as an infant bed, and a soft infant's bassinet cushion covered by a blanket. Kemp and Thach have called for reassessment of the cause of death in many SIDS victims, at least a quarter of whom are found with their faces down.

Parents are warned to keep babies on a firm surface, for anything that conforms to the child's body or that can trap a child lying face down—including adult beds, pillows, cushions, or rugs—is potentially deadly. Newborns are especially vulnerable, since for the first few weeks they breathe only through their nostrils, and the nose with its soft, compressible cartilage is readily obstructed.

Some pediatricians, have come to question the traditional Western pattern of placing babies to sleep on their stomachs (the idea being that babies might otherwise spit up and breathe the fluid into their lungs). For example, Enid Gilbert-Barness of the University of Wisconsin Medical School at Madison, suggests that babies who sleep on their backs may be less prone to SIDS. Dr. Kemp agrees, suggesting that parents should put infants to bed "on their side or back unless there is some medical reason not to." This suggested change in approach will no doubt receive close attention in coming years.

Some additional light on SIDS was shed by a January 1991 report from the Centers for Disease Control. It found that SIDS is more common in the winter, when children are most exposed to viruses and other infections, with the risk twice as high in January as in July. Infants are most vulnerable between the ages of 1 to 4 months, and black infants are at somewhat higher risk than white infants, though SIDS crosses racial and socioeconomic barriers. An infant is at greater risk of SIDS if there were medical complications during pregnancy or delivery, especially if there were multiple births, or if the infant has had to be resuscitated at any time for any reason.

Researchers are continuing to explore links between SIDS and other factors, such as premature birth, sleep apnea (temporary cessation of breathing during sleep), smoking by the parents, low birth weight, bottle-feeding (as opposed to breast-feeding, which provides the infant with some immunity in the early months), adolescent pregnancy, drug or alcohol abuse by the mother, anemia in the mother, socioeconomic disadvantage, and previous loss of a sibling to SIDS. Some cases of SIDS undoubtedly result from undetected birth defects. Whatever the underlying causes, the immediate problem is apparently some interruption of normal heart and breathing rhythms, or a lack of *surfactant*, a substance that normally keeps the air sacs of the lungs from collapsing. Many health professionals recommend that parents learn infant CPR (cardiopulmonary resuscitation), so they can attempt to revive their infant in case of emergency. (For more information, contact: National Sudden Infant Death Syndrome Clearinghouse [NSIDSC], 8102 Greensboro Drive, Suite 600, McLean, VA 22102; 703-821-8955; or the National Sudden Infant Death Syndrome Foundation [NSIDSF], 10500 Little Patuxent Parkway, Suite 420, Columbia, MD 21044; 800-221-SIDS [7437] or 301-964-8000; or National Center for the Prevention of Sudden Infant Death Syndrome [NCPSIDS], 330 North Charles Street, Baltimore, MD 21201; 800-638-SIDS [7437] or 301-547-0300.)

The Diaper Pendulum

The first of the single-use diapers appeared on the market in the 1960s, and by the 1990s they had largely replaced old-fashioned cloth diapers, being used for over 80 percent of all American babies. Unfortunately, these plastic-coated, chemically treated paper diapers were anything but "disposable" as far as the environment was concerned, and soon began to make up a significant percentage of the garbage in already overcrowded landfills. There were also concerns about more—and more serious—diaper rashes on babies in disposable diapers, though precisely why was unclear. For many people, the convenience of disposable diapers outweighs environmental considerations; that is certainly true for many parents who leave their child in day-care centers, where disposables are often required. But as environmental consciousness has grown, from the late 1980s and into the 1990s, increasing numbers of parents have been turning back to cloth diapers.

But, ah, the difference. Cloth diapers no longer mean the all-thumbs-and-pins routine, for ingenuity and modern technology have combined to make cloth diapering not only environmentally sound but also immeasurably more convenient than pre-1960s parents could have dreamed.

The founders of Biobottoms—two environmentally oriented mothers, Anita Dimondstein and Joan Cooper—were among those who sparked the move toward convenient cloth diapering back in 1981, when they introduced cloth diaper covers made of 100 percent wool felt. In addition to using natural, breathable fibers, they employed a major innovation: easy-to-adjust Velcro tabs. Standard cloth diapers are folded into thirds and placed inside the diaper covers; these are then wrapped around the baby's bottom and fixed together with the Velcro. Biobottoms' guide "All About Diapering" recommends that, if the diaper is too long, parents create an extra fold, placing it in front for boys and in back for girls, for maximum coverage. Biobottoms come in three styles: Classic, cream-colored wool, full-cut for maximum coverage; Rainbow Classic, full-cut with rainbow-colored edging; and Rainbow Bikini, rainbow-edged diaper covers cut higher on the legs for extra freedom and better fit, with leg gussets to provide a seal. Rainbow Bikinis come in the full range of sizes: NB (newborn), 4 to 10 pounds; A, 8 to 14 pounds; B, 14 to 18 pounds; C, 18 to 22 pounds; D, 22 to 27 pounds; E, 27 to 32 pounds; and F, 32 to 40 pounds. Sizes C through F have security snaps so older babies won't be able to undo the diapers. The Classic Biobottom and Rainbow Classic come in sizes A through E. To the original Biobottoms diaper covers, sometimes referred to as the

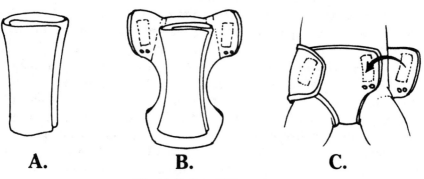

A.   **B.**   **C.**

The A-B-Cs of Diapering

A. Fold standard cloth diaper in thirds.
B. Place diaper on cover, keeping all edges inside to prevent leakage.
C. Adjust Velcro™ to fit.

(FROM "ALL ABOUT DIAPERING," BIOBOTTOMS)

"Cadillac of covers," the firm has since added Tenderbottoms, of 100 percent cotton, in sizes NB through E with rainbow edging; and completely waterproof Cottonbottoms, made of polyester-lined cotton, available in various colors in sizes NB through F. Biobottoms also sells 100 percent cotton cloth diapers; super-absorbent Double-Duty Diapers; contoured Soak-It-Ups™! Diapers, of flannel between cotton terry layers, which concentrate absorbency in the center; Flip Side Diapers, of 100 percent cotton, with terry on one side and bird's-eye on the other, with a center pad; and Soak-It-Ups™! Liners, with cotton terry between flannel layers for extra absorbency without double-diaper bulk, for heavy wetters. "Try Hard" Training Pants are available for the transitional period, in attractive patterns, including dinosaurs, firepeople, calico cats, and violets. For larger children, especially for overnight, Biobottoms has Stay Dry Pants, of cotton with cotton/poly/acrylic padding and a waterproof knit outside, which feel like underpants but absorb up to a cup of urine; these are available in sizes C through F, but also in larger sizes G, 40 to 50 pounds, and H, 51 to 60 pounds. Through its catalog, Biobottoms also sells other related products, including Velcro-fastening diapers from Gerber™ for use with waterproof nylon diaper covers called Rubber Duckies™ (see below), and also the Diaper Duck™, a plastic tool used to squeeze out soiled diapers, while keeping parents' hands dry. (For more information, contact: Biobottoms, 617-C 2nd Street, P.O. Box 6009, Petaluma, CA 94953; 707-778-7168.)

The Rubber Duckies™ mentioned above are nylon pull-on diaper covers used as "outerwear" over cloth or paper diapers. They come in various sizes, ranging from XXS for premature babies (in white only) to XXL for babies 35 pounds and up (in blue, red, pink, and white only); sizes in between also come in turquoise, purple, green, and yellow. A newer alternative is the Pinless WrapUp™, a waterproof nylon diaper cover that uses Velcro closure tabs and a contour design, with a mesh liner designed to hug the baby's legs and reduce leakage, while still letting air circulate. For "dress-up," the R. Duck Company also sells Geoducks, nylon diaper covers in a variety of black-and-white geometric prints, in a pull-on style in sizes XS (newborn to 10 pounds) to XL (30 to 35 pounds), and a wrap-up style in sizes A (4 to 10 pounds) to E (35 pounds and up). Brilliantly colored tropical-print versions are also available: Wild Ducks (pull-ons) and Jungle Wraps (wrap-up style). R. Duck also sells rectangular-shaped 100 percent cotton diapers, which can be used with any type of diaper covers; Di Dee Klips, which hold cloth diapers in place, without sticking into the baby (or diaper changer), for parents who use plain cloth diapers but don't want to use pins; and a non-rustling nylon dropcloth to be used on a child's bed, under a highchair, or even under art projects. R. Duck also has an adult-size division called Top Drawers. (For more information, contact: The R. Duck Company, Inc., 650 Ward Drive, Suite H, Santa Barbara, CA 93111; 800-422-DUCK [3825] or 805-964-4343.)

Wrap Up™ (R. DUCK COMPANY, INC.)

Geoduck (R. DUCK COMPANY, INC.)

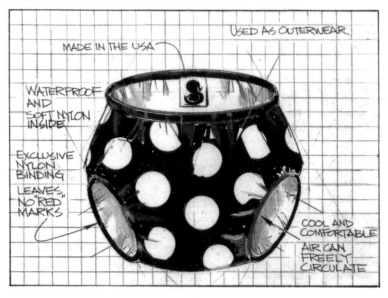

At Natural Comfort Co., Laurel and Jim Adamson have been on a quest for the "perfect diaper," seeking "the convenience of a disposable, without the guilt." They think they have found it in the Buoy™ diapering system. For parents who wish to use standard cloth diapers, they offer the Buoy™ Shell, diaper covers made with two colorful nylon layers housing a waterproof liner, with Lycra™ spandex trim around the legs for better fit; standard diapers are held in place with special elastic holders. The Buoy Shells can be washed along with the diapers, and even bleached. For even more convenience, they offer the Buoy™ All-in-One, which comes with a 100 percent cotton diaper attached at one end to the inside of the shell, and an absorbent inner liner. The semidetached diaper swings out for easy emptying and laundering, and quick drying. Both Buoy models use wide, easy-to-use Velcro strips, with special tabs to cover the Velcro "hooks" in the wash, so they won't damage the fabric. Both the Shells and the All-in-Ones come in three sizes—small, for 7 to 12 pounds; medium, for 12 to 24 pounds, and large, for 25 to 35 pounds—and a choice of colors: pastel pink, bubble gum, powder blue, mint, and of course, white. The two larger sizes come equipped with special "Tike-proof" safety buckles, so older babies can not remove the diapers on their own. All fasteners are designed without sharp edges to poke the baby. In addition, Natural Comfort offers L'il Bumpers, which are more economical versions of the Buoy Shells, available only in white, with a single outside nylon layer and the waterproof lining inside, designed for use with newborns, 5 to 9 pounds, or small babies. The Adamsons feel so strongly about reducing landfill waste that, when babies have outgrown one size of diapers, they will buy them back for a 20 percent credit toward purchase of diapers the next size up; the used diapers are donated to pediatric hospitals. Natural Comfort also offers heavyweight prefolded cloth diapers for use in shells, in newborn or regular sizes, as well as naptime pads, which are even more absorbent. (For more information, contact: Natural Comfort Co., P.O. Box 29990, Greenfield, CA 93927; 800-442-BABY [2229] or 408-674-2222.)

Bumkins® offers three cloth-diapering systems. The All-in-One cloth diaper offers disposable diaper convenience, with a waterproof outer shell, thick cotton flannel inside, an inner absorbent panel for greater absorbency and quick drying, elastic at the legs and waist, an air vent to minimize risk of diaper rash, and Easy-Grip tabs. For long outings, nighttime, older children, or heavy wetters, extra-absorbency cotton flannel inserts can be added. Bumkins' Two-Piece System uses the

Anatomy of the

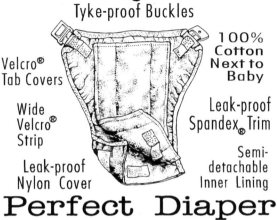

Tyke-proof Buckles

Velcro® Tab Covers

100% Cotton Next to Baby

Wide Velcro® Strip

Leak-proof Spandex® Trim

Leak-proof Nylon Cover

Semi-detachable Inner Lining

Perfect Diaper

Buoy™ All-in-One (NATURAL COMFORT CO.)

same materials, but separately; since the diaper covers do not need to be changed as often as the diapers themselves, not so many need to be bought or washed. Bumkins All-in-Ones and diaper covers come in five sizes: newborn, 6 to 12 pounds; small, 11 to 15 pounds; medium, 15 to 22 pounds; large, 22 to 28 pounds; and extra-large, 28 to 35 pounds, available in an assortment of colors (pink, blue, and white) and prints (zebra, leopard, baby-baby, watercolors, denim, and dinosaur). For older children, a junior size (in white only) is also available. The diapers themselves are specially shaped to fit into the Bumkins diaper cover, and have size adjustability built in, so they grow with the baby. For parents using cloth diaper services or Velcro-closing cloth diapers for which they want a waterproof cover, Bumkins also offers Diaper Covers and Pull-Ons to provide waterproof protection. They also offer disposable diaper liners made of cotton, without chemicals, which also double as wipes, and come by the roll. (For more information, contact: Bumkins, 1945 East Watkins, Phoenix, AZ 85034; 800-553-9302.)

The Nikky® diaper covers also use Velcro and come in wool, all cotton, or cotton with waterproof layers. These have a soft mesh inner lining to keep the baby drier, and soft cloth bindings around the legs to stop leakage. The Natural Baby Co., one of the Nikky distributors, notes that the cotton covers are slightly more waterproof, though somewhat warmer, than the wool; are somewhat more durable; and can also be machine dried. They find the diaper cover with a waterproof layer the most durable, and note that some can be used for a second or even third child. Nikkys are meant to be used with standard cloth diapers. They come in a selection of colors and designs (pink, blue, bear, rainbow edge, or shooting star) and various sizes: newborn, up to 9 pounds; A, 3 months or 9 to 14 pounds; B, 6 months or 14 to 18 pounds; C, 12 months or 18 to 22 pounds; D, 18 months or 22 to 27 pounds; E, 24 months or 27 to 32 pounds; and F, 3 years or over 32 pounds. There is also a Nikky with a built-in diaper; this provides maximum convenience, though ordinarily diaper covers do not need to be changed each time the diaper is changed. (Nikkys are available from various distributors. For more information, contact: The Natural Baby Co., Inc., 114 West Franklin Avenue, Pennington, NJ 08534; 609-737-2895; or Baby Bunz & Co., 800-67-NIKKY [676-4559].)

Natural Baby's top-of-the-line Rainbow diaper is made of thick terrycloth for maximum absorbency with a flannel outside layer for softness against the baby's skin. Unlike standard square diapers made for use with pins, the Rainbow Diaper is contoured to fit into Nikkys, or other diaper covers, without pins. The firm also offers less expensive all-cotton contoured Natural Baby Diapers; extra-absorbent Diaper Doublers, for overnight car trips, or heavy wetters; prefolded diapers as extras or burp cloths; and cloth diapers with Velcro tabs. The latter are supplied by popular demand, even though Natural Baby suggests they are impractical, because they need to be used inside a waterproof

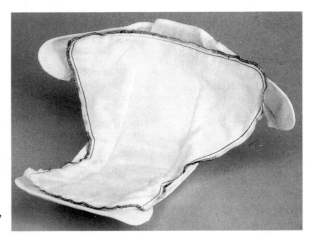

Rainbow Diaper
(NATURAL BABY CO., INC.)

diaper cover. The firm recommends, instead, using shaped diapers with Velcro covers, such as their inexpensive Velcro diaper covers of waterproof nylon taffeta. For older children or adults with bedwetting problems, Natural Baby also offers bathing suit-style Bedwetter Pants, with a thick inside pad that holds a cup of urine, but has an inner mesh that keeps wetness away from the skin. The Natural Baby catalog, formerly called the Natural Diapering Handbook, also offers tips on washing cloth diapers, including advice *not* to use "air freshener" cakes in diaper pails, since they are poisonous, and babies may eat them.

Parents of young babies have other cloth diapering alternatives as well; many of these companies advertise in parents' magazines, or send catalogs to mailing lists of new parents. One general caution: When using any diaper or diaper cover with Velcro, be sure the Velcro tabs are closed on themselves or covered before washing, so other fabrics will not be damaged.

Once Upon a Potty

Once upon a time, a new toilet-training book was published that caught the fancy of parents and toddlers alike. The original *Once Upon a Potty* (Barron's, 1980) featured a young boy named Joshua, his mother, his new potty—and a sense of humor. The book's phenomenal success—in what was and continues to be a very heavily published field—spawned a "Hers" version in 1985, featuring a young girl named Prudence. With over 1 million copies sold, Alona Frankel's books have become "required reading" for over a decade's worth of new parents, and have helped many youngsters on the road from "diapers to dryness." A Spanish version, called *Mi Bacinica y Yo*, appeared in 1987, also in "Hers" and "His" versions.

In 1990, Barron's took the work in a new direction, publishing *Once Upon a Potty* videos, again in "His" and "Hers" versions. The book and its stars, Prudence and Joshua, are brought to life in animated form in the 30-minute videos, introducing the various stages of toilet training and sharing "humorous potty-time experiences." These are prefaced by "The Potty Song," showing real toddlers showing off their potties and bouncing to the musical beat, and followed by a parent's section, with a brief discussion of toilet training from child psychologist Leo Kron, answering commonly asked questions and providing reassuring tips for

Once Upon a Potty—Hers video (BARRON'S
EDUCATIONAL SERIES, INC.)

parents. The videos won a 1991 "Best Kids' Video" award from *Parents* magazine. Barron's also sells a plastic doll on a potty (also his and hers versions), either separately or as part of a gift package including the storybook and videocassette. (For more information, contact: Barron's Educational Series, Inc., 250 Wireless Boulevard, Hauppauge, NY 11788; 800-257-5729 in NY, or 800-645-3476.)

Biobottoms, innovators of Velcro-closed cloth diapering (see "The Diaper Pendulum" on page 70), sells an inexpensive Portable Potty (in blue, pink, or white) that looks much like the one in *Once Upon a Potty*. The firm also sells the doll and book set, in "his" and "her" versions.

Splish Splash, I Was Giving a Bath . . .

For many parents, giving their baby a bath is tantamount to taking a bath themselves, with all the splashing, reaching, and leaning. But several new products are making the whole process just a little easier, and perhaps even a little drier.

Safety 1st® has developed a Swivel Bath Seat that allows the child to sit in the tub, keeping the baby upright without being held every minute by an adult. The Swivel Bath Seat is secured to the bottom by

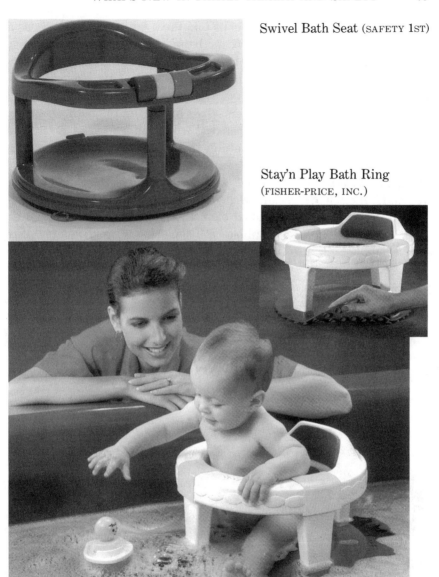

Swivel Bath Seat (SAFETY 1ST)

Stay'n Play Bath Ring
(FISHER-PRICE, INC.)

large suction cups, but swivels around with the touch of a hand, to make the job of washing the baby much easier. Colored cylinders on the arm rest even give the baby something to look at and play with.

From Fisher-Price comes the Stay'n Play Bath Ring. This is also a seat for babies to sit in while in the bath. It is secured to the bottom of the tub by many small suction cups (akin to a bathtub mat) and has a mildew-resistant cushioned back for baby's comfort. The Bath Ring, however, is stationary, rather than a swivel-type. In neither of these products, or any other water-filled area, should parents ever leave a child unattended, of course.

Children can easily injure themselves by hitting the bathtub spout, drain release valve, or faucets, or by turning on water hot enough to burn them. Several firms make products designed to protect them from such injuries. Safety 1st, for example, has an inflatable Sof'Spout, which fits over the bathtub spout, as well as inflatable Tub Knob Covers. Kel-Gar, Inc., has special twist-on faucet protectors. Its Tubbly-Bubbly™ is a three-dimensional elephant-shaped cover that fits over the faucet and doubles as a bubble bath dispenser. Parents simply pour liquid bubble bath into the elephant's trunk and turn on the water to provide bubbles.

Also from Kel-Gar are Tub Team™ valve covers, which fit over the drain release valve with suction cups, to prevent not only injury but accidental release of the tub water. The Tub Team valve covers are made in four designs, one a circus motif, the other three a basketball,

Tubbly-Bubbly™ (KEL-GAR, INC.)

Tub Team™ valve covers (KEL-GAR, INC.)

baseball, or soccer ball. They have finger slots on the sides, so adults can open and close the drain valve without removing the cover itself. These handy devices can also be used elsewhere in the house where protrusions pose a hazard.

For parents themselves, there's the Bathe'r Save'r™, also from Kel-Gar. This ingenious new product offers a knee pad for parents leaning on a hard floor, and another pad that fits over the rim of the bathtub to cushion parents' elbows. The two pads are attached to a wide strip of vinyl that, when in use, fixes to the tub with a suction cup and has an attached pocket that hangs into the tub, to hold washcloths, shampoo, bath toys, or soap. After the bath, the Bathe'r Save'r can simply be hung from the shower head to dry.

Bathe'r Save'r™ (KEL-GAR, INC.)

These products can be found in various stores selling child-related products. (For more information, contact: Safety 1st, 210 Boylston Street, Chestnut Hill, MA 02167; 800-962-7233 outside MA, or 617-964-7744; Fisher-Price, 620 Girard Avenue, East Aurora, NY 14052; 800-433-5347 or 716-687-3000; or Kel-Gar, Inc., P.O. Box 796934, Dallas, TX 75379-6934; 214-250-3838.)

No Spills—A Parent's Dream

Parents who think that juice drinks and messes inevitably go together—think again. Several innovative products can make splattered juice largely a thing of the past.

Little Kids, Inc., has introduced The Tumbler™, the "No Spill Cup" that "eliminates all but the most 'intentional' spills." The 8½-ounce cup (patent pending) has a flexible straw that extends down into the middle of the cup, passing through a screw-on top that is specially designed so that the cup can be turned upside down, dropped, or tipped on its side without spilling the drink, to the amazement of kids—and parents. The Tumbler is sized for use by kids 2 and up, and comes in primary colors. It is advertised as dishwasher safe, and includes a reusable plastic straw, though it can be used with standard straws as well.

Smile Tote, Inc., offers juice cups that attack spills in a different way. The tops of the juice cups have a specially designed mouthpiece-like insert that flips up for drinking and then snaps closed, to create a no-leak, no-spill cup. The Infant Traveling Juice Cup is sized for small hands and can be used by children ages 6 months to 6 years. The Toddler Traveling Juice Cup in a larger 9-ounce size is designed for kids ages 3 and up. Both come in bright, attractive colors. The same design principle has been used in an Insulated Traveling Juice Mug for the whole family, which is handy for carrying coffee or other liquids. Though tagged as "traveling" containers, these cups and mugs may be

(*right*) Toddler Traveling Juice Cup
(SMILE TOTE, INC.)

(*below*) Tumbler™ No Spill Cup
(LITTLE KIDS, INC.)

as useful in the house as in the car, at the beach, at sports events, and elsewhere.

Safety 1st® has developed its own entry into the no-spill sweepstakes. This is the Spill'Proof Cup, a 6-ounce container that contains a flip-top spout with a built-in straw. Children can simply flip up the spout and drink, then flip it down again, to lock it in place, without drips or spills. The cup is shaped for use by small hands, and is described as "top rack dishwasher safe."

Little Kids has also developed some no-spill juice box holders. Standard-sized juice boxes fit into these specially designed plastic holders, with "No Mess" sipper spouts that eliminate the need for messy straws, and also snap shut to reseal the juice box, to save leftover juice and keep it from spilling. The Super Sipper® Juice Box Holder comes in bright colors with bold designs. Super Sippers also come with the colors and logos of all National Football League and Major League Baseball teams, as well as the four Teenage Mutant Ninja Turtles. For infants and toddlers, ages 1 and up, there is the Sipper Gripper® Multi-Stage Juice Box Holder. As with the Super Sipper, the juice box fits into the plastic holder and is held by special "grip ribs." The Sipper Gripper has two easy-to-grip handles, making it easy to use as a training cup for infants. The holder can be used with

Spill'Proof Cup (SAFETY 1ST)

Super Sipper® (LITTLE KIDS, INC.)

standard nipples at the start; it comes with a trainer spout, travel cap, and collar. All of these juice box holders are described as dishwasher safe.

Safety 1st has juice box holders as well. The Sip'n Go has a multistage lid, including a sipper top, a straw top plug, and a hooded nipple cover, so it can be used with a baby's preferred nipples; this variety of lids makes the Sip'n Go suitable for young children from babyhood through first grade. The new Junior Sip'n Go is designed for the recently introduced 4.2 ounce junior juice containers. Both Sip'n Gos have two side handles for easy gripping by young children, come in a variety of colors, and are advertised as top-rack dishwasher safe.

Safety 1st has a new Sipper Top to fit onto soft drink cans. The top flips up for sipping, then closes to prevent spills. Another new two-part product in the kids' drink line is the Soda Pop Holder and Sipper Top. Soft drink cans fit into the two-handled holder, designed for comfortable holding by small hands, and the sipper top fits atop the can, with a flip-top that opens for drinking and closes when not in use. For young children just making the transition from bottle to cup, Safety 1st also has the Sip'n Straw, a flip-top cap for a child's bottle, which contains a built-in straw.

Little Kids produces a Go-Go™ Junior Sports Bottle, modeled after

Sipper Gripper® (LITTLE KIDS, INC.)

(*above left*) Junior Sip'n Go (SAFETY 1ST)

(*above right*) Soda Pop Holder and Sipper Top
(SAFETY 1ST)

(*left*) Go-Go Junior Sports Bottle (LITTLE KIDS,
INC.)

adult bottles, but sized for young hands. The 10-ounce bottle has a pull-up "No-Mess" sipper spout, which can be snapped shut when not in use to seal the bottle against leaks or spills. These refillable bottles are also described as dishwasher safe and come in bright colors with bold designs.

These products are sold in many department stores, toy and specialty stores, supermarkets, and drugstores. (For more information, contact: Little Kids, Inc., 2757 Pawtucket Avenue, East Providence, RI 02914; 800-LIL-KIDS [545-5437]; or Smile Tote, Inc., 12979 Culver Boulevard, Los Angeles, CA 90066; 800-826-6130 or, in CA, 310-827-0156; or Safety 1st, 210 Boylston Street, Chestnut Hill, MA 02167; 800-962-7233 outside MA or 617-964-7744.)

Protecting Children Against Disease: Immunization

As new vaccines are developed and old ones improved, and as studies update knowledge on safety or danger, immunization schedules for children are revised for maximum protection. Among the recent changes for young children are:

   • Improvements in the Hib vaccine, so that it is now recommended for infants from 2 months old, rather than starting at 18 months. New to many parents, for it was originally introduced only in 1985, the Hib vaccine is designed to protect young children against the *Hemophilus influenzae type B*, not actually a "flu" but a bacteria that causes meningitis—inflammation of the membranes covering the brain and spinal cord. The bacterium is especially dangerous to young children, sometimes resulting in brain damage or death; before the advent of antibiotics, it was almost always fatal, and even now it can develop to life-threatening stages within hours of the first symptoms if the child is unimmunized and untreated. The Hib vaccine is produced in different forms, so recommended schedules (see page 88) depend on the type being given. Children under age 5 are recommended to receive the Hib vaccine, if they have not already done so. Those over 5 have generally been exposed to the "H flu" bug, and have developed immunity to it, so immunization is usually considered unnecessary.
   • Approval of a new whooping cough vaccine to fight against the *pertussis* bacteria. The traditional pertussis vaccine is normally given in a combined shot, as diphtheria-tetanus-pertussis (DTP for short), about which many parents have had concerns (see "Are Whooping Cough and Rubella Vaccines Safe?" on page 92). The traditional vaccine is made from whole cells of pertussis bacteria; the new vaccine is not, so it produces fewer and milder reactions. However, the new whooping cough vaccine has (as of spring 1992) been approved for use only for the

fourth and fifth shots, while most adverse reactions occur in the earlier shots of the DTP series.

♦ Use of the injectable inactivated polio vaccine (IPV) in certain situations, rather than the more common oral polio vaccine (OPV). The injectable Salk vaccine is made from inactivated polio viruses, and so cannot cause the disease itself, but it requires clean needles and trained health-care workers for safe administration. By contrast, the oral Sabine vaccine, long favored because it is so easy to administer by mouth, is made from live viruses; some of these are excreted in a child's stool, so there is the rare but real possibility that other people could contract polio from contact with those viruses. The injectable vaccine is therefore favored when the child will be in contact with anyone whose immune system is impaired, such as people receiving chemotherapy or radiation therapy, people on cortisone or other immunosuppressant drugs (including those who have received organ transplants), and people with AIDS. The American Academy of Pediatrics (AAP) has also recommended that doctors administer the IPV when parents have a strong preference for that form of the vaccine.

As of late 1991, the U.S. Department of Health and Human Services was recommending the following schedule, roughly the same as that recommended by the AAP:

age of child	vaccinations
2 months old	DTP, polio, and Hib
4 months old	DTP, polio, and Hib
6 months old	DTP, Hib (as the doctor recommends)
12 months old	Hib (as the doctor recommends)
15 months old	DTP, polio, MMR (measles-mumps-rubella), Hib (as the doctor recommends)
5 years old	DTP, polio, MMR
15 years old	tetanus, diphtheria

Parents should check with their doctor or clinic for the latest immunization schedules. A Public Health Service (PHS) committee on immunization in June 1991 recommended that all children be given the Hepatitis B vaccine, which is at least 90 percent effective and judged to be one of the safest known, to help lessen risk of cancer and other liver diseases later in life. As of March 1992, recommended dosages or schedules of Hepatitis B vaccine for children had not been published, but the PHS's advisory committee recommended a series of three injections, to be given with the DTP vaccine at ages 2 months, 4 months, and 6 months. In developing countries, a tuberculosis vaccine is also commonly given; it may become common in industrialized countries as well, especially if the new drug-resistant strain of tuberculosis continues its ominous spread.

Most children are required to have certain basic vaccinations in order to enter school, but many younger children lack adequate protection against childhood diseases. A Centers for Disease Control survey released in early 1992 revealed that fewer than half of the children in nine major cities had received recommended vaccinations by age 2; of these cities, Houston was the worst, with only 10 percent, and El Paso the best, but still with only 42 percent. The result has been resurgent epidemics of such diseases as whooping cough and measles (which public health workers once thought was a target for complete eradication, like smallpox). Parents should be aware that this is a special problem in nursery schools and day-care centers, which generally have no immunization requirements.

In areas of measles outbreaks, some local public health authorities have been recommending additional and earlier shots for infants, sometimes at 6 months, 12 months, and then again before entering school. Measles can be a very serious disease for young children, ages 1 to 4 years old, because they have small airways in the respiratory system and can develop life-threatening dehydration; most vulnerable are children who were born prematurely and so have received less than the normal amount of antibodies from their mothers, and especially those who spent some time on respirators. Unfortunately, the earlier measles shots are given, the less reliable they are, since the antibodies the child receives from the mother counteract the effect of the vaccination. Measles can also be very serious for adults, leaving them vulnerable to dangerous and sometimes life-threatening bacterial infections; many adults who are now contracting measles were vaccinated in the 1960s and 1970s, when measles vaccines were sometimes ineffective or effective for a shorter time than anticipated. Parents who have not themselves had measles should check with their own doctors to see that they are properly protected against the disease.

Parents traveling out of the country should also be careful to have themselves and their children vaccinated—and should plan well ahead of time, since most vaccinations take at least some days to take effect. If you are visting Central or South America, or Western or Central

Africa, for example, a vaccination for yellow fever is obligatory and must be taken at least 10 days before departure; travelers need to carry an international certificate of vaccination. For the same areas, gamma globulin and vaccinations for polio, tetanus, and typhoid are optional but strongly recommended. For current information on immunization requirements, parents can contact the International Traveler's Hotline, Centers for Disease Control, 1600 Clifton Road, Atlanta, GA 30333; 404-639-2572 or 404-332-4559; or the Traveler's Medical Service, 2141 K Street NW, Suite 48, Washington, DC 20037; 202-466-8109. The brochure "Health Information for International Travelers" can be purchased from the Superintendent of Documents, U.S. Government Printing Office, Washington, DC 20402; 202-783-3238.

For any visit, no matter how short, to countries where malaria is considered a danger, all travelers should take the appropriate medications before, during, and *after* the visit. For information on malaria prevention, travelers can call the Centers for Disease Control hotline (404-639-1610), and be prepared to write down the names and dosages of drugs recommended.

Travelers should, of course, contact their family doctor before such a trip; the state or local health department also offers information on current recommendations. In early 1992, for example, an outbreak of a type of bacterial meningitis prompted a recommendation that U.S. children ages 2 to 19 traveling to Canada should be vaccinated against the disease (this particular vaccine has not been demonstrated as effective in children under age 2).

Vaccination costs have dropped significantly since the passage of the 1986 Childhood Vaccine Injury Act (see "Injury from Vaccinations? What to Do" on page 93), but expense is a continuing problem, especially where health-care personnel require a physical examination before giving a vaccination. Parents are increasingly turning to public health clinics for low-cost vaccinations, especially at convenient, walk-in centers where no appointments are required. Many clinics, however, complain of chronic shortages in government-supplied vaccines; others are overcrowded, with some requiring appointments weeks in advance, and some now charge for what used to be free vaccinations. The result is a partial breakdown in the vaccination system, which is likely to lead to more epidemics of childhood diseases. (For more information, contact: National Institute of Child Health and Human Development [NICHD], 9000 Rockville Pike, Building 31, Room 2A32, Bethesda, MD 20892; 301-496-5133.)

Vaccines: Looking to the Future

Research is being carried out on a number of new vaccines that hold promise for protecting children against disease, among them:

• A vaccine for chicken pox and shingles, both caused by the same *herpes zoster* virus (HZV). The HZV lies dormant after chicken pox infection and then years later can trigger the painful rash called shingles, usually in adulthood but also in children with leukemia. Developed in Japan, the vaccine is being used in Japan and Korea, and in Europe on children with impaired immune systems, but has not yet been approved in the United States, where tests are being conducted on its safety and long-term effectiveness.

• A vaccine to protect young children against three strains of bacteria that cause the brain and spinal cord inflammation called meningitis (*Escherichia coli K1* and *Meningococcus*, groups B and C). The combined vaccine, which also protects against tetanus, has been successfully tested on mice. (Young children can already be protected from some other forms of meningitis; see "Protecting Children Against Disease: Immunization" on page 87.)

• A new vaccine to protect against meningitis and urinary tract infections, which has been developed by the National Institutes of Health. As of late 1991, the NIH was taking applications from commercial drug companies to market the vaccine.

• A tetanus vaccine to be given to a pregnant woman, so her baby would be protected from tetanus at birth.

• A vaccine against AIDS (acquired immunodeficiency syndrome). Made from a harmless copy of the AIDS virus, rather than the virus itself, a vaccine has shown promising effectiveness in tests on monkeys with a simian form of AIDS. During 1991, an experimental human vaccine was being tested on humans, including many in several developing countries, where AIDS is spreading especially quickly. A human vaccine for general use is considered to be years away. The problem is especially complicated, since the AIDS virus exists in many different strains.

• A vaccine against Lyme disease. In 1991, a Lyme vaccine was approved for use with dogs, though some researchers are unsure that the vaccine approach will work against the tick-borne disease.

• A specialized cancer vaccine, made from genetically engineered versions of a cancer patient's actual tumor cells, designed to cause the body to attack the cancer.

• A "super vaccine" that in a single dose would protect children against all major childhood infections, possibly employing some timed-release mechanism within the body.

(For more information, contact: Food and Drug Administration, 301-443-3170 or 301-443-2410.)

Are Whooping Cough and Rubella Vaccines Safe?

An 11-member committee of the National Academy of Science's Institute of Medicine, formed in response to the public's safety concerns, conducted a 20-month review of all studies relating to the *rubella* (German measles) vaccine, normally given in a combined *measles-mumps-rubella (MMR) vaccine,* and the whooping cough (*pertussis*) vaccine, normally given in a combined *diphtheria-tetanus-pertussis (DTP)* shot. In a major 1991 report, they found that, in a small minority of children, the rubella shot triggered acute and sometimes long-term arthritis; and that the pertussis vaccine was linked to some cases of allergic reactions, prolonged crying, seizures, and shock symptoms. They noted that life-threatening allergic reactions, which occur in about two cases per 100,000 vaccinations, might also be caused by the diptheria or tetanus portions of the DTP vaccine.

However, the panel found:

• little or no evidence that would connect either of the vaccines with adverse effects, such as learning disabilities, hyperactivity, anemia, or chronic nerve damage;

• no evidence linking the DTP vaccine with autism;

• little or no evidence linking the DTP vaccine to infantile spasms, Reye syndrome, and sudden infant death syndrome;

• insufficient evidence of a link between the DTP vaccine and juvenile diabetes, severe skin rashes, low blood platelet cell counts, and Guillain-Barré syndrome and other nerve illnesses.

• insufficient evidence linking the rubella vaccine to nerve disorders (such as radiculoneuritis) or low blood platelet cell counts.

The committee noted that many of these possible adverse effects "occur in the absence of vaccination, are clinically ill-defined, and are generally of unknown causation in the general population." They urged more research in many areas on which there was insufficient information. Since early 1991, the federal government has been monitoring serious side effects of childhood vaccinations through its Vaccine Adverse Events Reporting System (800-822-7967), which requires physicians to report adverse reactions.

Panel members concluded that the rubella and diphtheria-tetanuspertussis vaccines are effective in protecting children against these diseases—and that the diseases themselves present greater dangers than the possible adverse reactions considered.

Partly in response to the above reports, the Public Health Service (PHS) in late 1991 modified its position relating to the DTP vaccine, when a child has any of the following reactions after being given a DTP shot:

- a temperature of 105° F within 48 hours of vaccination
- collapse or shock-like state within 48 hours of vaccination
- persistent, inconsolable crying lasting three hours, and occurring within 48 hours of vaccination
- convulsions, with or without fever, occurring within three days of vaccination

Previously the PHS had regarded any of the above reactions as "absolute reasons" for dropping the pertussis portion of the DTP shot in future shots. But in late 1991, the PHS indicated that these reactions are now to be regarded only as precautions, or warning signs. Under their new guidelines, physicians have more leeway in deciding whether to discontinue the pertussis component of future shots, or continue with the full DTP vaccine. (For more information on vaccine safety, contact: Food and Drug Administration, 301-443-3170 or 301-443-2410. For a critical view on safety concerns, contact: Dissatisfied Parents Together, 128 Branch Road, Vienna, VA 22180; 703-938-3783.) Parents may also wish to consult *The Immunization Decision—A Guide for Parents*, by Randall Neustaedter (North Atlantic, 1991), part of the "Family Health" series. (See also "Injury from Vaccinations? What to Do" below.)

Injury from Vaccinations? What to Do

If a child is injured or dies due to certain kinds of vaccinations, parents seeking financial compensation have in recent years had an alternative to costly civil lawsuits. The National Vaccine Injury Compensation Program, established under the Childhood Vaccine Injury Act of 1986, provides no-fault payment to parents in cases that fit within certain guidelines. The program's aim is to provide parents of affected children with compensation, without the necessity of costly and burdensome litigation, and at the same time to relieve doctors and vaccine manufacturers from legal action, which was causing many companies to stop making vaccines. Though problems remain, the program has indeed had the effect of stabilizing somewhat both the availability and cost of vaccines, which had temporarily threatened the country's vaccine supply system.

Vaccines covered under the program are the polio vaccine, the measles-mumps-rubella (MMR) vaccine, and the diphtheria-tetanus-pertussis (whooping cough) vaccine, abbreviated as DTP. For eligibility, over $1000 in expenses must have been incurred as a result of a child's injury or death that is deemed related to one of these vaccines. Claims must be filed with the U.S. Claims Court in Washington, DC (with two copies to the Secretary of Health and Human Services) within three years of the first symptoms and two years of death.

In evaluating a claim, officials use a vaccine injury table to assess whether the case meets certain criteria, regarding links between administration of a vaccine and injury or death. For example, the first seizure must occur within three days of vaccination for a child's seizure disorder to be considered linked to the DTP vaccine. Similarly, claims that the MMR vaccine caused encephalitis will meet the court's criteria only if the symptoms of the disease occurred within 15 days of receiving MMR. For a severe anaphylactic reaction or shock to be considered caused by either the DTP or MMR vaccine, the reaction must have taken place within 24 hours of immunization.

If the court rules favorably on a claim, the family is eligible for up to $250,000 for (as described in the *FDA Consumer*) "present and future pain and suffering. This includes past and future unreimbursed medical expenses, residential and custodial care and rehabilitation costs, and projected lost earnings from age 18. Attorney's fees may also be awarded, even if the petition is denied. . . . $250,000 is awarded in the event of death." If parents are not offered payment from the program— or if they reject it—they still have the alternative of bringing a civil suit.

The lightly funded program has received little publicity, but even so has had many more claims than originally expected—so much so that the government launched a reevaluation of vaccine safety (see "Are

Whooping Cough and Rubella Vaccines Safe?" on page 92). By 1991, the program had an enormous backlog of unconsidered claims and seemed to be running out of funds. Continuing support for the program lay in the lap of Congress. (For more information, contact: Food and Drug Administration, 301-443-3170 or 301-443-2410; also Dissatisfied Parents Together, 128 Branch Road, Vienna, VA 22180; 703-938-3783; see also *FDA Consumer*, September 1990.)

Taking Temperatures: A New Approach

A child is sick and feverish. Does she have a temperature? To find out, parents have for decades resorted to the old standby, the mercury-in-glass thermometer. But many have had problems in trying to get the child to stay still for several minutes, as is necessary with a thermometer, whether used orally, rectally, or under the arm. Many parents are also afraid of the thermometer breaking and injuring the child. Some have tried temperature "strips" placed against the child's forehead, but these may not be as accurate and reliable as desired. Now parents have a new alternative: Thermoscan™, a battery-powered hand-held instant thermometer, placed in the patient's ear, that gives a reading in just one second.

The procedure is simple: The child's outer ear is pulled back slightly to straighten the ear canal; the blunt "nose" of the Thermoscan is placed in the child's outer ear. After waiting two seconds, the parent pushes and holds a button; one second later, the temperature is displayed. Basically, the Thermoscan takes a "snapshot" of the infrared (heat) waves given off by the tissue surrounding the eardrum, and then converts the reading into an oral or rectal equivalent temperature (as the user chooses) on a display dial. The Thermoscan is less vulnerable to environmental influences than the mercury thermometer, since the area of the eardrum shares its blood supply with the hypothalamus, the brain's temperature control center.

The Thermoscan can be used on patients of any age, from infants to the elderly, with changes in appropriate settings. For parents, its main advantages are its speed, safety, lack of discomfort, and elimination of the struggle to keep children still long enough to take their temperature. It can even be used with a sleeping child, and in a dimly lit room, since the digital display reading is large and lighted. Its manufacturers say it is specially designed so that it cannot damage the eardrum, no

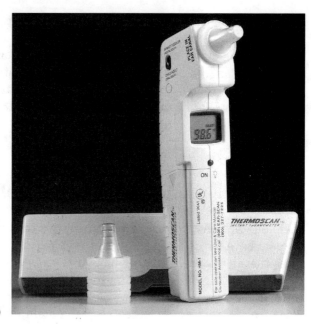

Thermoscan™
(THERMOSCAN, INC.)

matter what the patient's age; to be sure with their child, however, parents will want to consult with their doctor before purchasing and using a Thermoscan.

Thermoscan's developers suggest that parents take the temperature of all family members, when healthy, several times a day for a few days, to find the normal temperature range for each person. That is good advice in general, whatever temperature-taking device is used, since body temperature changes throughout the day, and both the average temperature and range of temperatures vary widely from one person to another. Doing this will also help parents become accustomed to using the new Thermoscan before sickness strikes. (For more information, contact: Thermoscan, Inc., 6295 Ferris Square, Suite G, San Diego, CA 92121; 800-EAR-SCAN™ [327-7226] or 619-535-9600.)

Is the Cure Worse Than the Disease?

Many infants and young children have febrile seizures—twitching or jerking and loss of consciousness associated with high fever. For decades, doctors have routinely given children daily doses of phenobarbital to prevent recurrence of such seizures. But a study by the National Institute of Neurological Disorders and Stroke (NINDS) indicates that the drug is ineffective as an anticonvulsant, since children who took the drug had as many seizures as those who did not. Worse, those who took phenobarbital had significantly lower scores on intelligence tests, effects that lasted for at least some months after the drug was stopped. Continuing studies will examine longer-term effects. The lead author of the study, Dr. Jacqueline R. Farwell, commented: "I believe that phenobarbital is not indicated in febrile seizures. The treatment is worse than the disease." Though frightening to parents, febrile seizures are also, after a study in the early 1980s, believed to be less dangerous than previously thought. Some doctors are now questioning whether febrile seizures should be treated at all. (For more information, contact: National Institute of Neurological Disorders and Stroke, 9000 Rockville Pike, Building 31, Room 8A06, Bethesda, MD 20892; 301-496-5751.)

Overdosing Children with Over-the-Counter Medicines

In early 1992, the Food and Drug Administration (FDA) issued a warning that parents can easily overdose their children when administering over-the-counter liquid medicines to fight flus and colds. Problems generally occur when parents misread the markings on the "dose cups" often provided as caps for liquid medicine bottles, or when they do not properly understand and follow dose directions.

The FDA began investigating accidental overdosing on learning of a child who became ill after being given three times the recommended dose of a medicine. In that case, the parents had measured the liquid to the "two tablespoon" level marked on the dose cup packaged with the medicine; the recommended dose was actually two *teaspoons*, but the dose cup had no teaspoon markings. Even small overdoses of some medications, such as the painkiller acetaminophen (as in Tylenol and Tempra), can be dangerous to a child if given over a period of several days.

The FDA has undertaken a survey of liquid medicines to make sure dose cups are marked properly and has urged manufacturers also to review their labeling and packaging. FDA Commissioner David Kessler stressed, "If the label says to give two teaspoons every four hours, that's the amount the child should get at the prescribed intervals. . . . If the condition worsens or fails to improve, the child should be seen by a physician. If parents have any questions about the proper dose of a medication, they should consult their pharmacist or physician." He also urged parents to read medicine labels carefully, to make sure that two medications for different symptoms do not contain the same ingredients, resulting in an accidental overdose. (For more information, contact: Food and Drug Administration, 301-443-3170 or 301-443-2410.)

Asthma and Allergies

On asthma—potentially life-threatening attacks of wheezing, coughing, and breathing difficulty, often triggered by one or more allergies—there is bad news and good news for parents.

The bad news is that asthma cases are on the rise, most sharply among people under 18. As recently as 1980, fewer than 40 of every 1,000 people in that age group had asthma; by 1987, that figure was up to over 50. Asthma is also causing more fatalities overall, up from about 2,600 a year in 1979 to 4,600 in 1988. In that same period, the number of children under the age of 15 hospitalized with asthma almost doubled. Asthma is a particular problem for children, partly because their immature respiratory systems and narrow breathing passages make them especially vulnerable to an asthmatic attack. In addition, asthma is often not diagnosed in children; parents and doctors alike may attribute their wheezing to a respiratory infection or some other condition. Asthma experts have urged doctors to test the breathing capacity of all patients suspected of having asthma, using a device called a *spirometer*. Parents should be alert to the possibility of asthma and raise it with the child's pediatrician or the family doctor. At least one study has also suggested that sensitivity to allergens that cause asthma attacks is increased by ozone pollution (from automobile exhausts and industrial emissions), a major problem in cities.

The good news is that researchers have been developing new and promising treatments for asthma. Traditional asthma medications, called *bronchodilators*, focused on relaxing muscles, the idea being that constricted muscles were blocking air flow to the lungs. But in recent years asthma experts have come to understand that, several hours *after* the initial tightening, cells in the airways released chemicals that caused inflammation; new drugs have been developed to prevent damage from these chemicals, which if unchecked can lead to further, and more serious, attacks.

Among the new medications for countering inflammation of air passages are inhaled steroids. Such drugs have been used only for very severe cases over the years because of their adverse side effects (see "Anabolic Steroids and Their Substitutes: Controlled Substances" on page 110), but in recent years researchers have learned how to administer steroids safely in inhaled form. This can ease asthmatic effects, but without (it is believed) affecting the whole body, though long-term effects are yet to be established. Certainly, patients must be carefully taught how to inhale the steroids safely.

Parents with asthma in the family should seek the best and most current information available from both government and private organizations. One study of asthma treatment, published in the January 1991 issue of the *New England Journal of Medicine*, strongly suggests that asthma patients are not being *over*treated, but rather *under*treated. Researchers found that many nonspecialist doctors were unaware of the shift in focus from bronchodilators to treating inflammation, which is often implicated in asthma deaths. However, *over*treatment can also be a problem. An August 1991 study indicates that overuse of other anti-inflammatory drugs, called beta-2 agonists, might increase the risk of fatal asthma attacks. All in all, effective asthma treatment involves vigilance and a careful balancing act. Some asthma experts suggest that asthma patients should use a spirometer every day, to test their breathing, to get timely therapy when needed, to prevent further attacks, and to help control chronic symptoms. (For more information, contact: National Asthma Education Program, 4733 Bethesda Avenue, Bethesda, MD 20815; 301-951-3260; or National Institute of Allergy and Infectious Diseases, 9000 Rockville Pike, Building 31, Room 7A32, Bethesda, MD 20892; 301-496-5717; or Asthma and Allergy Foundation of America, 1717 Massachusetts Avenue, NW, Suite 305, Washington, DC 20036; 202-265-0265.)

Parents with asthma in the family may find help from various recently published materials, among them:

For Parents

♦ *Is This Your Child? Discovering and Treating Unrecognized Allergies*, by Doris Rapp (Morrow, 1991).

* *How to Identify—and Control—Your Child's Food Allergies*, by Jane McNicol (Wiley, 1991). Advice from a research dietician.
* *Conquering Your Child's Allergies*, by M. Eric Gershwin, M.D., and Edwin L. Klingelhofer (Reading, MA: Addison-Wesley, 1990).

For Young Readers

* *The Lion Who Had Asthma*, by Jonathan London (Albert Whitman, 1992). A "Concept Book," for ages 2 to 6.
* *Living with Allergies*, by Dr. T. White (New York: Watts, 1990).
* *Allergies*, by Gerald Newman and Eleanor Newman Layfield (Watts, 1992). For children grades 9 through 12; describes allergies affecting the respiratory and gastrointestinal systems as well as the skin, ears, eyes, and mouth, and the medicines and other treatments available.

General Works for Adults

* *The Asthma Self-Help Book*, by Paul J. Hannaway, M.D. (Prime, 1992).
* *The Complete Guide to Food Allergy and Intolerance*, by Dr. Jonathan Brostoff and Linda Gamlin (Crown, 1992).
* *The Whole Way to Allergy Relief and Prevention: A Doctor's Complete Guide to Treatment and Self-care*, by Jacqueline Krohn and others (Hartley & Marks, 1991). (Contact: P.O. Box 147, Point Roberts, WA 98281.)

For some books on environmental health hazards that might trigger or aggravate allergies and asthmatic conditions, see "Children's Health—Parents' Guides" on page 103. See also "Free Information for Parents" on page 212.

When Is Fluoridation Safe?

A 1991 study involving over a dozen federal agencies, including the Public Health Service and the National Center for Toxicological Research, concluded that fluoridating drinking water poses no detectable risk of causing cancer in humans and is not linked with Down's syndrome, gastrointestinal problems, or diseases of the genital, urinary, and respiratory systems. The study also found that the benefits of fluoridated water outweigh any risks, cutting the number of cavities among children by two-thirds in the last 50 years.

However, researchers found that some people may be getting more fluoride than they need, which can cause discoloration of the teeth, called *dental fluorosis*. The report recommended that parents instruct their children to use only a pea-sized amount of fluoridated toothpaste and to rinse carefully after brushing; they should be taught not to swallow either toothpaste or fluoridated rinses, both of which have high fluoride concentrations.

The report also said that children should not be given additional fluoride when their home water supply has recommended amounts. The Food and Drug Administration (FDA) recommends that parents check with local health officials to find out the fluoride concentration in their water supply. The FDA notes that about 1 part per million (ppm) is ideal. Less than 0.7 ppm is not adequate to protect developing teeth; more than 1.5 to 2.0 ppm can lead to mild dental fluorosis. Where water is artificially fluoridated, the Environmental Protection Agency (EPA) standard is set at between 0.7 and 1.2 ppm, with the lower amount used in warmer regions, where people drink more water.

If the fluoride concentration is too low, children should receive fluoride supplements in the form of drops or chewable tablets. The American Dental Association and the American Academy of Pediatrics suggest that, where water has less than 0.3 ppm fluoride, children should receive full supplementation: 0.25 milligrams up to age 2, 0.5 mg for ages 2 to 3, and 1 mg after age 3 and until the teen years. Where water supplies have 0.3 to 0.7 ppm fluoride, supplementation should be adjusted accordingly to give the child the appropriate daily amount.

If the fluoride concentration level of the drinking water is in the optimum range, and the family physician or dentist still prescribes supplements, the FDA recommends that parents explore the matter of possible excess fluoride; exceptions would be breast-feeding babies, who drink little or no water, or babies given ready-to-drink formulas. If the water's fluoride concentration is too high, the FDA recommends that parents contact the local EPA office, as fluoride would then be considered a contaminant.

Families who drink only bottled water will have difficulty assessing the level of fluoride they are getting; despite advertising claims about "springs of remarkable purity," many bottled brands (perhaps 50 percent) obtain their water from municipal supplies, which may or may not be fluoridated, though some may have the fluoride content removed during the bottling process. In one 1989 test of popular bottled waters, all but three had less than 0.25 ppm fluoride; of the three, all imported carbonated waters, two were still below the optimum cavity-fighting range and one was above it.

Fluoridation is not a national requirement, so each locality makes its own decision on whether or not to fluoridate. Some parents remain concerned about possible links between fluoridation and cancer. A 1990 study with rats had found that 4 out of 50 had developed osteosarcoma, a rare form of bone cancer; but researchers noted that the 4 rats had been given amounts 30 to 170 times the amounts recommended for use in humans, and that none of the rats developed cancer at lower levels. More significantly, a 1991 study found no difference in the rate of osteosarcoma between people living in fluoridated areas of New York State and those in unfluoridated areas. Fluoridation is strongly endorsed by organizations such as the American Medical Association, the American Dental Association, the U.S. Public Health Service, and the National Research Council. The benefits are clear: In its 1986–87 survey, the Public Health Service found that over 65 percent of American 9-year-olds have never had a cavity in their permanent teeth. (For more information, contact: Food and Drug Administration, 301-443-3170 or 301-443-2410.)

Guides to Modern Dental Care

Two recent works focus on family dental concerns, giving special emphasis to the ongoing "revolution" in dental care. A visit to the dentist is changing from a fearful experience to one with a largely preventive stance, with the promise of much better dental health for today's children than for their parents. Today's parents may, in fact, need reeducation in this area, for modern dentistry is increasingly focused on painless prevention, as opposed to painful procedures.

• *Protecting Our Children's Teeth: A Guide to Quality Dental Care from Infancy through Age Twelve*, by Malcolm S. Foster (Plenum, 1992). Focuses specifically on children, starting with prenatal tooth development and going through what pregnant women and new parents should do to help their child develop healthy teeth. Foster discusses the main concerns parents have regarding teeth, such as the effects of breast-feeding, bottle-feeding, thumb sucking, and early loss of baby teeth, as well as what to expect and when; dental hygiene, including flossing and brushing; and dental examinations—including tips on how to inform and reassure children.

◆ *The Mount Sinai Medical Center Family Guide to Dental Health*, by Jack Klatell, D.D.S., Andrew S. Kaplan, D.M.D., and Gary Williams, Jr. (Macmillan, 1991). A comprehensive guide, which focuses on the collaboration between doctor and patients, ranging from the basics, such as choosing the right toothpaste, to advanced dental procedure and dental insurance, especially how to become better "dental consumers," and also covers dental phobias and first aid for dental emergencies.

Children's Health—Parents' Guides

Childhood health problems bring chills to the hearts of all parents. While no book can substitute for professional medical advice, a number of new books can provide reassurance by helping parents understand and deal with health questions facing their family.

For Parents

◆ *Your Child's Health: The Parents' Guide to Symptoms, Emergencies, Common Illnesses, Behavior, and School Problems*, rev. ed., by Barton D. Schmitt (Bantam, 1991). Covers major child-care topics, from medical emergencies to behavior problems, in an easy-to-follow outline fashion.

◆ *The New American Encyclopedia of Children's Health*, by Robert Hoekelman and others (NAL-Dutton, 1991).

◆ *The Parent's Desk Reference*, by Irene Franck and David Brownstone (Prentice Hall, 1991). Includes discussions of major types of health problems, treatments, resources for help, and works for parents and children.

◆ *Your Child's Medication: A Parent's Guide to Common Prescription and Over-the-Counter Medications*, by Karen S. Bond (Wiley, 1991). Advice from a pharmacist.

◆ *The Better Life Institute Family Health Plan*, by Steven M. Zifferblatt, Ph.D., Patricia M. Zifferblatt, and Norm Chandler Fox (Thomas Nelson, 1991). Described as "the first comprehensive family diet, exercise, and health plan for body, mind, and spirit."

• *Your Healthy Child: A Guide to Natural Health Care for Children*, by Alice Likowski [Duncan] (Tarcher, 1991). Reviews homeopathic, nutritional, herbal, and acupuncture treatments for common childhood illnesses.

Of special concern to many parents in these environmentally conscious times is protecting their children—and themselves—from possible toxic hazards in their home or neighborhood. Three recent books to help them do that are:

• *Healthy Homes, Healthy Kids: Protecting Your Children from Everyday Environmental Hazards*, by Joyce M. Schoemaker and Charity Y. Vitale (Island Press, 1991). Helps parents identify the most serious risks facing themselves and their children, including lead, asbestos, radon, and chemicals, and ways to reduce exposure or take remedial action. The authors are both parents and college biology professors.

• *The Nontoxic Home and Office: Protecting Yourself and Your Family from Everyday Toxics and Health Hazards*, by Debra Lynn Dadd (Tarcher, 1992). A revised edition of the 1986 book that focused on home environs, with wide-ranging coverage of dangers and alternatives, by a consumer advocate.

• *Your Health and the Indoor Environment: A Complete Guide to Better Health through Control of the Indoor Atmosphere*, by Randall Earl Dunford and Kevin G. May (NuDawn Publishing, 1991). Focuses on how common and unexpected toxins in the air can affect the health of the whole family, with specific recommendations on how to reduce indoor air pollution. (For more information, contact: NuDawn Publishing, 10819 Myrtice Drive, Dallas, TX 75228.)

Parents who have young children facing an operation may wish to take a look at *Once I Had an Operation*, a 17-minute film produced and directed by Laurie Wagman (1991), which introduces children (ages 5 through 9) to surgical procedures and hospital experiences in general. The film focuses on a group of children who pause in their play to tell about their operations, with flashbacks showing the preoperation visit to the surgeon, breathing and visualization exercises for relaxation, meeting the anesthesiologist, postoperative recovery and its discomforts, and final discharge. The work's upbeat approach should also be reassuring to parents.

AIDS—Don't Kid Yourself, Kids Get It, Too

That's the message that basketball star Earvin "Magic" Johnson has for kids in his new book, *What You Can Do to Avoid AIDS* (Times Books, 1992). His message is also for parents, for it is up to them to make sure their children know about HIV, the human immunodeficiency virus that causes the disease; about AIDS itself; about sexual responsibility in general; and—since there is no such thing as absolutely safe sex—at least, about safer sex. Faced with personal tragedy, Johnson is using his celebrity to help others, and parents may be able to use Johnson's plight and approach to reach kids on a life-and-death question. The American Medical Association put it succinctly: "Magic Johnson's message is straight-talking, honest, and accurate. This book could help save lives." In addition to its straight talk for kids, the book includes a directory of resources, for the United States and Canada. Agreeing with the importance of the opportunity and the urgency of the situation, many other people and organizations are supporting the spread of the word on AIDS through this book, providing free advertising and public service messages, in addition to the usual publicity, with both the publisher's and author's profits committed to the Magic Johnson Foundation for prevention, education, research, and care in the battle against AIDS. The work is also available in a Spanish-language edition and on audiocassette (Random House, 1992). (For more information, contact your local library or bookstore; or the Magic Johnson Foundation, 2029 Century Park East, Suite 810, Los Angeles, CA 90067; 310-785-0201.)

Among other recent books about AIDS and other sexually transmitted diseases (STDs) of interest to children, teens, or parents are:

For Young Readers

• *AIDS: How It Works in the Body*, by Lorna Greenberg (Watts, 1992). Explains how HIV (human immunodeficiency virus) attacks the body, how the immune system works to defend the body, and how AIDS shows itself; part of the "Full-Color First Books" series, for children in grades 3 through 6.

◆ *David Has AIDS*, by Doris Sanford (Multnomah, 1989). For children in kindergarten through grade 4, part of the "In Our Neighborhood" series. It tells the story from David's point of view; one of the few books for children who have AIDS or know someone who does. The book also contains two lists: one of how AIDS is transmitted; the other, how it is *not*.

◆ *What's a Virus Anyway? A Kid's Book about AIDS*, by David Fassler, M.D., and Kelly McQueen (Waterfront, 1990; Spanish edition, 1991). For children in preschool through grade 6.

◆ *Learning about AIDS*, by Alvin Silverstein and Sylvia Silverstein (Enslow, 1989). For children in grades 4 through 6.

◆ *AIDS: Deadly Threat*, rev. and enlarged ed., by Alvin Silverstein and Sylvia Silverstein (Enslow, 1991). Part of the "Issues in Force" series, for children in grades 6 and up.

◆ *Sexually Transmitted Diseases*, by Mark McCauslin (Crestwood/Macmillan, 1992). Part of the "Facts About" series for children in grades 5 and 6.

For Teens

◆ *STD: Sexually Transmitted Diseases*, by J. T. Daugirdas (Mac-Text, 1991). For grades 8 through 12; uses diagrams and cartoons to supplement the fact-filled text on the six most common STDs—syphilis, AIDS, gonorrhea, chlamydia, herpes, and human papilloma virus—and some other lesser known ones. (For more information, contact: 15W560 89th Street, Hinsdale, IL 60521.)

◆ *Sexually Transmitted Diseases*, by Alan E. Nourse, M.D. (Watts, 1991). Discusses gonorrhea, syphilis, herpes, chlamydia, hepatitis, and AIDS—how to recognize them, treat them, and prevent them. For children in grades 9 through 12.

◆ *Coping with Health Risks and Risky Behavior*, by Alan R. Bleich (Rosen, 1990). Part of the "Coping" series for children in grades 7 through 12.

◆ *Fighting Back: What Some People Are Doing About AIDS*, by Susan Kuklin (Putnam, 1989). For ages 13 and up; an American Library Association (ALA) Best Book for Young Adults that describes how volunteers help people with AIDS by offering support and help with daily chores, and portrays the daily lives of people with AIDS.

For Parents or Other Adults

* *AIDS-Proofing Your Kids: A Step-By-Step Guide*, by Loren E. Acker and others (Beyond Words Publishing, 1992). A guide to sex education that goes beyond simple information to stress the teaching of safe practices, including abstinence and the use of condoms.
* *How to Find Information About AIDS*, 2d ed., Jeffrey T. Huber, ed. (Haworth, 1991). A guide to organizations, institutions, and hotlines offering information about AIDS, as well as print, electronic, and audiovisual sources.
* *AIDS and the Law: A Basic Guide for the Non-Lawyer* (1992), by Allan H. Terl. Directed to parents and others who are not lawyers but who are interested or involved in legal questions regarding AIDS, in such areas as education, family law, housing, insurance, employment, and the military. (For more information, contact: Taylor & Francis Group, 1900 Frost Road, Suite 101, Bristol, PA 19007-15948; 800-821-8312.)

Sex Education—A Matter of Life and Death

One of the greatest changes for today's generation of parents is that with the arrival of AIDS on the scene, sex education has indeed become a matter of life or death. Unfortunately, most adults have no model for educating their children about sex, as that is a job that parents have traditionally abdicated. Most of today's adults learned about sex willy-nilly, picking up information—and a good deal of misinformation—any way they could, but with precious little help from parents or any knowledgeable adult.

But that is no longer good enough. Today, the price of misinformation and ignorance can be death. Many school systems have family-life programs that include sex education, but there is no substitute for parents teaching their own children about love, sex, and human relationships, and in the process trying not only to protect them but also to pass on their own values.

Fortunately for parents, there is also a wide range of new books on sex education, some intended for use directly by children of various ages, some oriented toward helping parents and other adults in the task of preparing their children for sexual lives. A selection of recent publications follows:

For Young Children

• *Girls Are Girls and Boys Are Boys: So What's the Difference?*, by Sol Gordon (Prometheus, 1991). Part of the "Books for Young Readers" series, for children ages 6 to 10.

• *Love and Sex and Growing Up*, by Eric W. Johnson (Bantam, 1990). For children in grades 4 through 8.

• *In the Beginning: Teaching Your Children about Sex—Ages 4–7* and *God's Good Gift: Teaching Your Kids about Sex—Ages 8 to 11*, both by Mary A. Mayo (Zondervan, 1991).

• The "Human Development" series from Steck-Vaughn for young readers, including *Childhood*, *Adolescence*, *Adulthood*, and *Advanced Years* (all 1992).

For Older Children

• *Tell It Like It Is: Straight Talk About Sex*, by Annamaria Formichella and others (Avon, 1991).

• *Teen Guide to Safe Sex*, by Alan E. Nourse (Watts, 1990).

• *Boys and Sex*, 3d ed., by Wardell B. Pomeroy (Doubleday/Dell, 1991). For children in grades 6 and up.

• *Sex Is Not a Four-Letter Word*, by James N. Watkins (Tyndale, 1991). For young adult readers.

• *Be Smart about Sex: Facts for Young People*, by Jean Fiedler and Hal Fiedler (Enslow, 1990). For children in grades 6 and up.

• *Focus on Sexuality*, by Elizabeth Poe (ABC-Clio, 1990). Part of the "Teenage Perspectives" series.

• *Adolescence*, by Rebecca Stefoff (Chelsea House, 1990). Part of the "Life Cycle" series, for children in grades 6 through 12.

• *The Dating Dilemma: Handling Sexual Pressures*, by Bob Stone and Bob Palmer (Baker Books, 1990).

• *Family Values and Sex Education*, by Terrance D. Olson and Christopher M. Wallace (Focus on the Family, 1990). For children in grades 7 through 9.

• *The Sex Education Dictionary for Today's Teens and Preteens*, by Dean Hoch and Nancy Hoch (Landmark, 1990). For children in grades 5 through 12.

• *The Sexual Dictionary: Terms and Expressions for Teens and Parents*, by Kathryn T. Johnson and others (Larksdale, 1992). Part of the "Life Management" series.

* *Coping with Your Sexual Orientation*, by Deborah A. Miller and Alex Waigandt (Rosen, 1990). Part of the "Coping" series, for children in grades 7 through 12.
* *Sex: A Christian Perspective* (Group Publishing, 1990). For children in grades 9 through 12.

For Use with Groups

* *Kerry's Thirteenth Birthday: Everything Your Parents and Their Friends Know about Sex but Are Too Polite to Talk About*, by Mary J. Rachner (Oxner Institute, 1991). For children in grade 8; a teacher's manual is available.
* *Sex and the Teenager: Choices and Decisions*, by Kieran Sawyer (Ave Maria, 1990). For children in grades 9 through 12; a director's manual is available.

For Parents

* *How to Teach the FACTS of Life*, by Rose Fuller, and *FACTS Parent Curriculum: A Sexuality Education Program*, by Rose Fuller and others (Northwest Family Services, 1991). Part of the "Family Accountability Communicating Teen Sexuality" series.
* *Talking to Your Children about Love and Sex*, by Leon Somers (NAL-Dutton, 1990).
* *Teaching Your Child about Sex*, by Terrance S. Drake and Marvia B. Drake (Deseret Books, 1990). A reprint of the 1983 edition.
* *Sex Education for Toddlers to Young Adults: A Guide for Parents*, by James Kenny (St. Anthony Mess. Press, 1990).
* *Sex Stuff for Parents: The Painless, Foolproof, "Really Works!" Way to Teach 7–17-Year-Olds about Sex So They Won't Get AIDS, a Disease or a Baby (and You Won't Get Embarrassed!)*, by Carole Marsh (Gallopade, 1990).
* *Raising Sexually Healthy Children*, by Lynn Leight (Avon, 1990).
* *Sexual Development of Young Children*, by Virginia Lively and Edwin Lively (Delmar, 1991). A teacher's guide is available.
* *Mom's a Bird, Dad's a Bee: Developing a Healthy Outlook on the Facts of Life*, by Maryann Mayo (Harvest House, 1991).
* *Healthy Sex Education in Your Schools: A Parent's Handbook*, by Anne Newman (Focus on the Family, 1990).

Background Works

• *Living Smart: Understanding Sexuality in the Teen Years*, by Pennie Core-Gebhart and others (University of Arkansas Press, 1991).

• *What's Wrong with Sex Education?: Preteen and Teenage Sexual Development and Environmental Influences*, by Melvin Anchell (Hoffman Center, 1991).

• *Has Sex Education Failed Our Teenagers?: A Research Report*, by Dinah Richard (Focus on the Family, 1990).

• *Sex Respect: The Option of True Sexual Freedom: A Public Health Guide for Parents*, rev. ed., by Coleen K. Mast (Respect, 1990).

• *The Myths of Sex Education: Startling Research that Deserves a Close Look from Parents and Teachers*, by Josh McDowell (Here's Life, 1990).

Many other works may be found in libraries or bookstores. Practical help is also available from various government organizations. The Public Health Service, for example, has a brochure on "Condoms and Sexually Transmitted Diseases." In some areas, schools are making condoms available to sexually active students, to help protect them from AIDS. Parents may also want to check out "AIDS—Don't Kid Yourself, Kids Get It, Too" on page 105.

Anabolic Steroids and Their Substitutes: Controlled Substances

Athletes, bodybuilders, and adolescents have for years been taking anabolic steroids—synthetic versions of the male sex hormone testosterone—to enhance their athletic performance or physical appearance. Such uses are not medically approved and can lead to severe health problems, including liver, heart, and kidney disease, personality changes, stunted growth, sterility, and even death. A 1991 study of 49 steroid-using weightlifters, sponsored by the National Institute of Alcohol Abuse and Alcoholism, confirmed that use of anabolic steroids can become addictive. In the report published in the *British Journal of Addiction*, Dr. Kirk Brower and others note that the best predictors of dependency are larger doses, more cycles of use, and dissatisfaction with body size, with more than 4 out of 5 participants experiencing withdrawal symptoms on ceasing use of steroids, along with a variety of other symptoms of dependence.

Despite warnings of such problems, the illegal use of anabolic steroids continued to grow, by 1989 becoming an estimated $300–400 million-a-year industry. In an attempt to control such illicit use, Congress in 1990 passed a law stipulating that beginning in February 1991, anabolic steroids would be classified as a "controlled substance," the same category as cocaine, heroin, LSD, and other habit-forming drugs. Such drugs can only be administered by people registered with and approved by the Drug Enforcement Administration (DEA). Anyone else retaining a supply of steroids risks, for a first offense of trafficking or illegal dispensing, five years in prison and a $250,000 fine.

Even while the DEA is attacking steroid use, however, the FDA has found that other substances were being sold to former steroid users. One such is gamma hydroxybutyrate (GHB), which is marketed for reducing fat; building muscle (by, it is claimed, releasing large amounts of "natural" human growth hormone); inducing sleep; and giving a "high." In fact, a report in *FDA Consumer* indicates that GHB can be poisonous and is potentially lethal, causing such symptoms as stomach and intestinal cramps, breathing difficulty, uncontrollable seizure-like movements, and coma. Sold in places such as bodybuilding gyms, fitness centers, health-food stores, and mail-order outlets in the form of granules, capsules, or powders, GHB may also be known as gamma hydroxybutyric acid, sodium oxybate, or gamma hydroxybutyrate sodium. GHB is being tested under FDA auspices for treatment of the rare sleeping disorder narcolepsy, but apart from that carefully controlled trial, the FDA recommends that anyone taking GHB should stop immediately, and anyone with symptoms should quickly seek medical attention and see that their physician reports the symptoms to the local poison-control center.

Another illicit drug marketed as a "steroid alternative" is clenbuterol, a drug not approved for any use in the United States, though it is used by veterinarians in some countries. Little is known about the effects of clenbuterol, but dozens of people in Spain became ill after eating beef liver that contained residues of the drug.

By conducting raids on the underground laboratories making GHB and other such substitutes, the DEA stressed that it will tolerate no such substitutes with a "false appearance of legality," but is "going after everything illegal in the anabolic steroid milieu." Another problem is that no buyers of illegal drugs, produced in uninspected, uncontrolled, unapproved settings, can be sure just *what* kind of drug they are getting. Parents of teenagers will want to be sure their children are aware of the dangers of using any anabolic steroids or substitutes. (For more information, contact: Food and Drug Administration, 301-443-3170 or 301-443-2410; and National Institute on Drug Abuse, 301-443-6245.)

Parents may also want to point their children in the direction of the following materials:

• *Steroids*, by Sarah Stevens (Macmillan/Crestwood, 1991). Part of the "Facts About" series, for children in grades 3 through 8.

• *Focus on Steroids*, by Katherine Talmadge (Twenty-First Century Books, 1991). Part of the "Drug-Alert" series, for children ages 8 to 12.

• *Steroids*, by Hank Nuwer (Watts, 1990). For children in grades 7 through 12.

• *Drugs in Sports*, rev. ed., by Edward F. Dolan (Watts, 1992). Describes the hazardous effects of such substances as steroids, amphetamines, blood boosting, cocaine, marijuana, and crack, which are used by some athletes to obtain a competitive edge. For children in grades 9 through 12.

• *Athletes and Addiction: It's Not a Game* (1991). A video produced by ABC Sports and hosted by television sports anchor Jim McKay on substance-abuse problems among athletes, including firsthand discussions with well-known athletes on their addiction-related problems. For ages 14 and up. (For purchase or rental, contact: MTI Film & Video, 108 Wilmot Road, Deerfield, IL 60015.)

Down with Fat!

In late 1990, the federal government for the first time made specific recommendations on the amount of fat Americans should eat daily. As part of new dietary guidelines for Americans, the government moved well beyond general advice to "avoid too much fat," and now recommends that no more than 30 percent of a person's daily calories should come from fat, and no more than one-third of that from saturated fats, which are high in cholesterol. And for the first time, these recommendations were extended to cover not just adults but also children, starting at 2 years of age. (A child's nutrition and dietary needs are quite different before age 2, and do not fall under the same guidelines.) That means that in a 2,000-calorie daily diet—as might be normal for a full-grown adult of medium build—fat should make up a maximum of 67 grams, with less than 22 grams of that from saturated fats, such as butter.

The problem is that Americans routinely have a far higher proportion of fat in their diet, an average of about 37 percent, according to some recent estimates. Many of the favorite foods of kids as well as adults— ice cream, hot dogs, hamburgers, grilled cheese sandwiches, fried chicken, potato chips, and the like—are extremely high in fat. For example, a child who eats one Kid Cuisine Fried Chicken frozen meal will get 28 grams of fat, or almost half of the fat a child 4 to 6 years old should have in a whole day, under these federal guidelines. A cup of whole milk contains about 10 grams of fat, and even milk with 1 percent fat has 2.5 grams per serving. However, advertising claims of "low fat" or "less fat" have been confusing and often deliberately misleading to consumers who seek to lower the fat in their diets. The federal government is trying to make the job easier with its new food labels and precise definitions of terms used in food advertising. (See "New Food Labels" on page 115.)

School lunches have also traditionally been very high in fat. Many nutritionists have complained that schools have not been required to meet any specific standards for fat (or other substances, such as cholesterol or sodium) and often resemble fast-food operations in their high-fat approaches. Whether or how quickly schools will begin to implement the government's low-fat guidelines in lunch programs depends partly on public pressure to do so. Children themselves are being taught about the new understanding of fat as part of a revised approach to nutrition (see "The New Food Guide Pyramid" page 114).

The focus has turned toward fat because recent research indicates that obesity may be linked more to the proportion of fat in the diet than to the number of calories consumed; in essence, researchers are finding that all calories are not equal. Calories from other types of food, such as carbohydrates and protein, are used by the body for fuel and only stored if the food contains more calories than the body needs at the moment. However, almost all fat calories are immediately stored in fat cells, which are used only when the body's other sources of energy are depleted or unavailable. Unfortunately for the overweight, the amount of fat that can be stored seems limitless; each fat cell can expand to more than 10 times its original size, and if the available fat cells become filled, new ones are developed for additional storage. Research—and the experience of millions of dieters—have also shown that it is extremely difficult to get rid of fat once it has been stored; in various ways, the body resists efforts to lose the weight. (For more information, see "Never Say Diet?", by Ruth Papazian, *FDA Consumer*, October 1991.)

The New Food Guide Pyramid

The old "four food groups" image used in nutrition education since the 1950s has yielded to a new approach for teaching the public, and especially children, about nutrition. After several years of analysis and debate, the federal government in early 1992 announced that its new main approach would be based on a Food Guide Pyramid. The pyramid is made up of five food groups—fruits and vegetables are now considered separately—with recommendations on the number of servings a person should have each day. "Serving" does not mean the normal amount a person might eat at one sitting, nor is it arbitrarily set by the manufacturer (as in the past), but is defined by the FDA according to the food group. The basic recommendations are:

• Grains (bread, cereal, rice, and pasta), 6 to 11 servings (such as one slice of bread or one ounce of cereal)
• Vegetables, 3 to 5 servings (such as one cup of raw leafy greens or one-half cup of other vegetables)
• Fruits, 2 to 4 servings (such as one medium banana, orange, or apple)
• Dairy products (milk, yogurt, and cheese), 2 to 3 servings (such as one cup of milk or 1.5 ounces of cheese)
• Meat, poultry, fish, eggs, nuts, and dry beans, 2 to 3 servings (such as 2 to 3 ounces of cooked lean beef or chicken)

At the top of the pyramid is a small category of fats, oils, and added sugars, with the recommendation to "use sparingly," as part of more general guidelines on reducing fat in the diet (see "Down with Fat!" on page 112). Unlike past decades, when dieters passed up bread while eating a hamburger, modern nutrition advice calls for having grain products provide a substantial part of a healthy daily diet, while avoid-

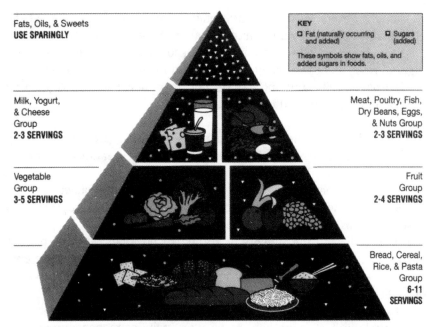

Food Guide Pyramid (*FDA Consumer*)

ing high-fat meats. To aid consumers in making food purchases, the federal government is calling for more useful information on food packages (see "New Food Labels" below), including what is considered an appropriate serving size for the particular food. (For more information on the Food Guide Pyramid, contact: Human Nutrition Information Service, Hyattsville, MD; 301-436-8498.)

New Food Labels

Parents—and all consumers—will soon have better information in their supermarkets. As mandated by the Nutrition Labeling and Education Act (NLEA), passed in 1990, the Food and Drug Administration (FDA) has developed new, more useful, more understandable, consumer-oriented food labels. The FDA is now charged with clarifying and regulating the use of health-related terms, to ensure that consumers obtain accurate nutritional information from food labels. Under the new program, virtually all packaged foods will contain nutrition information and information on conditions for their use. Testing and revision of the specific content and format of the labels continued through 1992 and into 1993, but in general the food-labeling program being reviewed requires that:

• Ingredients be listed in descending order of predominance by weight. Manufacturers who wish to declare ingredients by percent of content will follow an FDA-set uniform format.

• All sweeteners be grouped together under the collective term "sweeteners," with the various types being listed in parentheses in descending order of predominance by weight.

• Labels list all ingredients of standardized foods, such as peanut butter, bread, ketchup, mayonnaise and macaroni, for which the government has set standards (or recipes) since the 1930s, but whose ingredients may no longer be familiar to many shoppers.

• Color additives be listed on labels by name.

• Labels indicate whether the product includes monosodium glutamate (MSG) and protein hydrolysates (used as flavors or flavor enhancers), so consumers with special religious, medical, or cultural dietary requirements can identify the food source of the additive.

• Juice beverage labels state the percentage of actual fruit or vegetable juice in the drink, and the percentages of different types of juices, if the drink includes more than one.

• Caseinate be identified as a milk derivative when used in foods that are called "nondairy," such as coffee whiteners, since some people are allergic to milk.

• Sulfites be declared in those foods for which ingredients are standardized, since some people are allergic to sulfites.

• Serving sizes be defined by the FDA in accordance with everyday norms, not arbitrarily set by manufacturers.

• Terms such as "light" and "low-fat" be defined by the FDA, so they cannot be used misleadingly in advertising, as in the past.

The FDA is also offering guidance to shoppers by preparing materials for stores to display near counters that sell raw fruits, raw vegetables, and raw, minimally processed, or heat-treated fish and shellfish. These displays would initially be voluntary but would become mandatory if not in sufficient use by May 1993. The U.S. Department of

Agriculture (USDA) is making similar arrangements for the labeling of meat and poultry, which it regulates.

In addition, the new law has given the FDA for the first time the authority to allow food labels to carry claims relating food to specific health conditions; previously such claims were not allowed because the FDA regarded products making those claims as drugs. Among the food–health condition relationships now allowed to be shown on labels are:

+ calcium and osteoporosis
+ sodium and hypertension
+ fat and cardiovascular disease
+ fat and cancer

The FDA will explore other such claims of health relationships, such as fiber and heart disease, fiber and cancer, folic acid and neural tube defects (such as spina bifida), antioxidant vitamins and cancer, zinc and immune function in the elderly, and/or omega-3 fatty acids and heart disease. Foods making such health claims would also have to meet certain FDA guidelines. Specifically, those foods that contain more than 11.5 grams of total fat, 4 grams of saturated fat, 45 milligrams of cholesterol, or 360 milligrams of sodium per amount commonly consumed, per established serving size, and per 100 grams of the food would be barred from making any health claims.

One of the main areas of contention in the development of food labels is the FDA's attempt to make them more meaningful by indicating the maximum daily recommended amounts—called *daily reference values or DRVs*—of substances such as fat, saturated fat, cholesterol, protein, fiber, sodium, potassium, and carbohydrates. The idea is to help consumers make nutritionally wise shopping decisions by allowing them to compare the amount of nutrients in the food with the maximum amount an "average" person should consume. What the FDA came up with was an "average" diet of 2,350 calories a day, broken down into the maximum amounts of various nutrients. However, many consumer advocacy groups say that the 2,350-calorie figure is far too unrepresentative to be used as a guideline across the board for the whole population, and that the resulting DRVs are far too high for most women, children, and men over 50, and too low for many men ages 25 to 50. They stress that it would be especially difficult for parents to use in assessing nutritional values of food for their children and might cause them to give their families meals too heavy in fats or sodium, for example. Manufacturers, however, point out that food labels have limited space in which to include all the information that will now be required, so an "average" is necessary. The FDA is gathering reactions and comments to the proposed plans from all interested parties to be used in developing the final food-labeling rules. (For more information, contact: Food and Drug Administration, 301-443-3170 or 301-443-2410.)

Kids Are Cooking

Part of independence is knowing your way around a kitchen. For latchkey kids—those who spend a great deal of time at home on their own, while their parents are working—knowing how to prepare food is not a luxury, but a necessity. Several books have recently been published to meet their needs, among them:

• *Betty Crocker's Boys and Girls Microwave Cookbook*, by the Betty Crocker Editors (Prentice Hall, 1992). Provides "complete instructions for fast, safe microwave cooking," including more than 100 "kid-tested" recipes for breakfasts, lunches, dinners, snacks, and desserts, with an easy-to-follow, step-by-step format, clarified further by 60 line drawings and over 30 full-color photographs showing finished dishes and serving ideas. Microwave safety information is stressed, and "special safety signals" indicate "when adult assistance is a good idea." This is a companion to *Betty Crocker's New Boys and Girls Cookbook* (Prentice Hall, 1990), designed for kids 8 to 12, but often used by even younger children.

• *The Guaranteed Goof-Proof Microwave Cookbook for Kids*, by Margie Kreschollek (Bantam, 1992). Presents relatively simple dishes that children can prepare on their own, including such kids' favorites as hot dogs and fudge, along with microwaving basics and important safety tips. Tested with a class of eighth graders, the book is intended for children 14 and older, but reviewers suggest that it may also be used by younger children who have already developed skills at using a microwave or have parental supervision.

• *Kids Cook! Fabulous Food for the Whole Family*, by Sarah Williamson and Zachary Williamson (Williamson, 1992). Includes 150 recipes from "two kids who found they were fending for themselves (and their working parents) in the kitchen." (For more information, contact: Box 185, Charlotte, VT 05445.)

♦ *Kitchen Fun for Kids: Healthy Recipes and Nutrition Facts for 7-to-12-Year-Old Cooks*, by Michael Jacobson and Laura Hill (Holt, 1991). For children in grades 3 through 6; offers over 50 recipes, for main meals or snacks, using healthful ingredients, plus much practical general advice on diet and nutrition. It provides a difficulty rating for each recipe.

Parents should, however, make sure their children are aware of the hazards in cooking. Most children are well aware of the dangers posed by burners and boiling water, but many parents let very young children use the microwave, thinking it is safe. The U.S. Department of Agriculture (USDA), however, warns that:

> . . . **severe burns can and do occur from improper microwave use.** Special packaging for kids' favorite foods like popcorn, pizza, and french fries can get too hot for kids to handle. Steam from popcorn bags can burn the eyes, face, arms, and hands. Jelly donuts, pastries, hot dogs, and other foods can reach *scalding* temperatures in seconds. The U.S. Consumer Product Safety Commission estimates that nearly 1,300 children under the age of 15 suffered microwave-related burns in 1990.

The USDA recommends that only children who can read be allowed to use the microwave, and that, if you give permission for your child to use the microwave, you should start by holding a training session with the child. The USDA offers these tips for kids on safe microwaving:

♦ Never turn on an empty oven. This can cause the oven to break.
♦ Read package directions carefully. Make sure you know how to set the microwave oven controls (for example, 10 seconds, rather than 10 minutes).
♦ Use only microwave-safe cookware. Mark specific utensils and containers for microwave use and keep them in a certain place. Never reuse cold-storage containers such as margarine tubs.
♦ Rotate food in the microwave and stir halfway through cooking if possible.
♦ Use pot holders to remove items from the microwave. Microwavable dishes get hot from cooked food. Do not use the microwave if you have to reach up to remove food from the oven.
♦ If a dish is covered with plastic wrap or wax paper, turn up one corner to let excess steam escape. Pull plastic wrap off foods so steam escapes away from hands and face. Steam can burn.

+ Never pop any food right from the microwave into your mouth. Allow the food to cool for several minutes before eating.

Specific Tips for Kids' Favorite Foods:

+ Hotdogs and Baked Potatoes: Pierce before cooking. This keeps them from exploding.
+ Jelly Donuts and Fruit Pastries: Break open before eating. The jelly or fruit inside can get very hot and burn your mouth.
+ Popcorn: Let the bag sit for several minutes before opening. Steam from the bag can burn the face, eyes, arms, and hands.

(For more information, see "Before Parents Get Home—Food Safety After School," by Pat Moriarty, from the Winter 1992 *Food News for Consumers*; see also "Free Information for Parents" on page 212.)

Eating Disorders and Body Image

Eating disorders continue to be a significant problem, especially among teenage girls and young women, and to a much smaller extent among boys. Anorexia, with its self-starvation, and bulimia, with its binge-purge cycles, have at least become widely known, so that many people—friends, family, and other adults—are more alert to the signs and can try to get help before the disorder has produced irreversible damage.

Recently some specialists in the field have been pressing for recognition of compulsive eating as a distinct type of problem, the *binge eating disorder*. This is characterized by recurrent episodes of excessive, out-of-control eating, often lasting hours at a time and involving large amounts of food, frequently way over 2,000 calories—more than an adult should need for an entire day. Unlike the occasional "splurge" that most people have—gobbling a container of ice cream, for example—the pattern of behavior associated with binge eating disorder is characterized by phases of compulsive eating that often involve:

+ Eating far more rapidly than usual
+ Eating until uncomfortably full
+ Eating large amounts of food even when not physically hungry
+ Eating large amounts throughout the day, not in distinct meals

   • Eating alone because of feeling embarrassed over the amount being consumed

   • A feeling of being unable to stop eating or control consumption, once a binge starts

   • Feelings of distress, disgust, guilt, or depression about the over-eating.

People with this type of disorder do not attempt to purge their bodies of excess calories, as in bulimia, but simply gain weight from their compulsive eating. In 1992 Dr. Robert Spitzer proposed to the Society of Behavioral Medicine in New York that "binge eating disorder" be made an official diagnosis, so that specific therapies might be developed for it, and so that patients would more likely be eligible for insurance coverage of their weight-control treatment.

   Of much wider concern is the question of body image, for teenagers as well as for adults. It is true that over one-quarter of all American children are considered medically obese—that is, 20 percent over the normal weight for their height. This poses long-term health risks for them and calls for a rational approach to weight control and fitness. However, many people who diet strenuously, including most of those with anorexia and bulimia, are not overweight, but only *think* themselves to be so: They have an unrealistic image of what is an "ideal" weight, for people in general and for themselves in particular. Often these are fostered by social images, such as the unrealistic figures of the Barbie® and other fashion dolls (see "Happy To Be Me" on page 13). Children also exaggerate or even imagine defects in themselves, as part of a general fear of being unattractive. This is especially true in adolescence, notably among girls, some of whom fight the normal and healthy changes in their body proportions, as they seek to emulate the svelte, skinny, and often downright anorexic figures in the media. Interestingly, one recent study of 3,000 adolescents found that while most teenage boys were trying to *gain* weight, to have a body shape more like an adult's, approximately two-thirds of the teenage girls were attempting to *lose* weight; these were typically girls who were already of normal weight. Some other studies have suggested that girls with eating disorders are often copying their mothers' behavior toward dieting and eating, and view of bodily perfection. The eating disorders bulimia and anorexia are found only among 2 to 4 percent of teenage girls (and a much smaller percentage of boys), but clearly the concerns about distorted body image are far wider than that.

One spot of good news about nutrition is that most children—99 percent, according to a 1991 Gallup poll—know about the major food groups; the importance of eating fruits, vegetables, and high-fiber foods, and avoiding too much fat and sugar; and the role of exercise in good health. Parents of teens interested in healthful eating and weight management may want to point them in the direction of a new book by Charles A. Salter: *Looking Good, Eating Right: A Sensible Guide to Proper Nutrition and Weight Loss for Teens* (1991), published by Millbrook Press, for children in grades 7 through 10. Those who prefer vegetarian diets may also be interested in Salter's *The Vegetarian Teen: A Teen Nutrition Book* (Millbrook, 1991).

For parents with more specific concerns about eating disorders, here is a selection of recent publications, many of which not only describe the causes and courses of such disorders but also point readers toward sources of help:

For Young Readers

• *About Weight Problems and Eating Disorders*, by Joy Berry (Childrens, 1990). Part of the "Good Answers to Tough Questions" series, for grades 3 and up.

• *Eating Disorders*, by Don Nardo (Lucent Books, 1991). Part of the "Overview" series, for grades 5 through 8.

For Teens

• *Straight Talk about Eating Disorders*, by Michael Maloney and Rachel Kranz (Facts on File, 1991). Part of the "Straight Talk" series, for grades 7 through 12.

• *Everything You Need to Know about Eating Disorders*, by Rachel Kubersky (Rosen, 1991). Part of the "Need to Know" series, for grades 7 through 12.

• *Coping with Eating Disorders*, by Barbara Moe (Rosen Group, 1991). Part of the "Coping" series for grades 7 through 12; serves as an introduction to destructive eating patterns, with many illustrative cases.

• *Eating Disorders*, by John R. Mathews (Facts on File, 1990). Part of the "Library in a Book" series, for grades 9 through 12.

• *Living with Anorexia and Bulimia*, by James Moorey (St. Martin's, 1991). Part of the "Living With" series.

◆ *Weight: A Teenage Concern*, by Elaine Landau (Lodestar, 1991). Gives a nonjudgmental overview of topics related to weight control. For children ages 12 and up.

◆ *So You Think You're Fat*, by Alvin Silverstein and Sylvia Silverstein (HarperCollins, 1991).

Guides for Families and Other Adults

◆ *A Parent's Guide to Eating Disorders and Obesity*, by Martha Jablow (Delacorte, 1992).

◆ *A Parent's Guide to Eating Disorders: Prevention and Treatment of Anorexia Nervosa and Bulimia*, by Brett Valette (Avon, 1990).

◆ *Anorexia, Bulimia, and Compulsive Overeating: A Practical Guide for Counselors and Families*, by David Swift and Kathleen Zraly (Continuum, 1990). Part of "The Counseling" series.

◆ *Eating Disorders and Athletes: A Handbook for Coaches*, by AAHPERD Staff (Kendall-Hunt, 1991).

◆ *Bulimia: A Guide for Family and Friends*, by Robert T. Shermand and Ron A. Thompson (Free Press, 1990). A question-and-answer approach.

◆ *Overweight Children: Helping Your Child Achieve Lifetime Weight Control*, by Michael D. LeBow (Plenum, 1991).

◆ *Beyond Baby Fat: Weight-Loss Plans for Children and Teenagers*, by Frances S. Goulart (Berkley, 1991).

◆ *Helping Obese Children: Weight Control Groups That Really Work*, by Roselyn Marin (Learning, 1990).

Personal Accounts

◆ *My Fight for Life: I Am a Teenage Anorexic*, by Kitty L. Scott (Vantage, 1991).

◆ *Hope and Recovery: A Mother-Daughter Story about Anorexia Nervosa, Bulimia, and Manic Depression*, by Becky Thayne Markosian and Emma Lou Thayne (Watts, 1992). For children in grades 9 through 12.

◆ *Debbie Gibson, Electric Star: A Guide to Understanding and Overcoming Bulimia*, by Randi Reisfeld (Bantam, 1990).

◆ *Set Free: A Woman's Victory over Eating Disorders*, by Linda McGrath (Japan Publications USA, 1992).

◆ *Life-Size*, by Jenefer Shute (Houghton Mifflin, 1992). A fictional but frighteningly real view of an anorexic's life from the inside.

Other General and Background Works

◆ *Eating Disorders: The Facts*, 3d ed., by Suzanne Abraham and Derek Llewellyn-Jones (Oxford University Press, 1992). Part of "The Facts" series.

◆ *Controlling Eating Disorders with Facts, Advice, and Resources*, Raymond Lemberg, ed. (Oryx Press, 1992).

◆ *No More Black Days: Complete Freedom from Depression, Eating Disorders and Compulsive Behaviors*, by Lauri A. Mallord (White Stone, 1992).

◆ *Bulimia: A Guide to Recovery*, rev. ed., by Lindsey Hall and Leigh Cohn (Gurze Books, 1992).

◆ *It's Not Your Fault: Overcoming Anorexia and Bulimia Through Biopsychiatry*, by Russell Marx (Random, 1991; NAL-Dutton, 1992).

◆ *Eating Disorders*, by Steven Spotts (Rapha, 1991).

◆ *Rapha's 12-Step Program for Overcoming Eating Disorders*, by Robert S. McGee and William Drew Mountcastle (Rapha, 1991). Part of the "Rapha Recovery" series.

◆ *Obesity and Anorexia Nervosa: A Question of Shape*, by Peter Dally and Joan Gomez (Faber and Faber, 1991).

◆ *The Beauty Myth*, by Naomi Wold (Morrow, 1991). Charges that America has a "cult of the anorexic."

◆ *Anorexia and Bulimia: Anatomy of a Social Epidemic*, by Richard A. Gordon (Blackwell, 1990).

◆ *Eating without Fear: A Guide to Understanding and Overcoming Bulimia*, by Lindsey Hall (Bantam, 1990).

Parents may also want to look at "Down with Fat!" on page 112. (For more information, see "Never Say Diet?" by Ruth Papazian, *FDA Consumer*, October 1991.)

What's *New* in Learning and Education

Preschool Power

That's the title—and the promise—of an award-winning video for children published by Concept Videos. *Preschool Power* (1990) is a 30-minute music video for kids ages 1 to 6. Featuring nine preschoolers as teacher-demonstraters, and based on Montessori educational methods, the video shows kids "how to button, buckle, zip, wash their hands, put on their own jackets, tidy their room, make snacks, even pour without spilling a drop." But it does this with jokes, music, dancing, and (as the video's subtitle says) "Jacket Flips and Other Tips." *Preschool Power* won the Gold Medal from the New York Film and TV Festival and received the highest rating (4 stars) from *Video Review*.

Concept Videos followed this with *More Preschool Power!* (1991), a 30-minute sequel, with more preschoolers teaching their peers such skills as tying shoes, brushing teeth, and even making fruit salad, along with such play activities as shadow puppets, tongue-twisters, and "silly walks," and how to help even younger children, again all in the context of songs, music, and jokes. *More Preschool Power!* won the 1991 Gold Medal from *Parent's Choice* (see "Best Reading for Kids" on page 133) and was also honored by the 1991 California Children's Video Awards. Third in the series is *Preschool Power 3!* (1992), again using songs, music, and jokes, as preschoolers teach others how to put on gloves, fold paper, sweep up spills, make French bread, make giant bubbles, set up "domino knockdowns," and play with scarves, as well as helping around the house and cooperating with others. (For more information, contact: Concept Videos, P.O. Box 30408, Bethesda, MD 20814; 800-333-8252 or 301-986-4144 in MD or outside the USA.)

Preschool Power (CONCEPT VIDEOS)

More Preschool Power! (CONCEPT VIDEOS)

Preschool Power 3! (CONCEPT VIDEOS)

Parents interested in learning more about the Montessori approach might consult these recent books:

♦ *Montessori at Home: A Complete Guide to Teaching Your Preschooler at Home Using the Montessori Method* (1991), rev. and exp. ed.; *Modern Montessori at Home: A Creative Teaching Guide for Parents of Children 6 through 9 Years of Age* (1991); and *Modern Montessori at Home, No. II: A Creative Teaching Guide for Parents of Children 10 through 12 Years of Age* (1991), all by Heidi A. Spietz (American Montessori Consulting).

♦ *Michael Olaf's Essential Montessori: A Guide and Catalogue for Montessori Education from Birth—at Home and at School*, by Susan Stephenson and Jim Stephenson, ed. (M. Olaf, 1990).
(For more information, contact: American Montessori Consulting, P.O. Box 5062, Rossmoor, CA 90721-5062.)

For some other approaches to developing learning skills in their young children, parents may also want to look at some of the following recent publications:

♦ *The Ready-to-Read, Ready-to-Count Handbook: A School Readiness Guide for Parents and Preschoolers*, by Teresa Savage (Newmarket Press, 1991). Offers lesson plans, games, assignments, and cartoons to help parents get their preschoolers ready for school.

♦ *Games for Learning: Ten Minutes a Day to Help Your Child Do Well in School from Kindergarten to Third Grade*, by Peggy Kaye (Farrar, Straus & Giroux, 1991). Offers 70 simple, enjoyable games to enhance children's skills in logical thinking, reading and writing, mathematics, and science and social sciences. Most games require only paper and pencil, pen, or crayon, and have notes on suggested grade levels.

♦ *Is Your Bed Still There When You Close the Door? . . . And Other Playful Ponderings*, by Jane M. Healy (Doubleday, 1992). Shows parents how to stimulate creativity, thinking, and communication in their young children.

♦ *Teaching Children to Think: New Strategies for Parents and Teachers*, by David Perkins (Free Press, 1992). Suggests ways that adults can increase understanding in children.

♦ *Nurturing Your Child's Natural Literacy*, by William Cole Cliett and H. Thomas Filmer (Maupin House, 1992). Offers techniques for parents, caregivers, and preschool teachers.

• *Nathan's Day at Preschool*, by Susan Conlin and Susan Friedman (Parenting Press, 1991). For ages 3 to 5; presents brief episodes during a day at preschool for parents and children to discuss, or at least for the child to relate to. (For more information, contact: Parenting Press, 11065 Fifth Avenue, NE, #F, Seattle, WA 98125.)

Listening for Language Development

Researchers are finding that babies learn language sounds far earlier than was previously thought. A 1992 study, for example, suggests that by the age of 6 months, babies have learned the basic sounds of the language spoken by the people around them. The finding was surprising because previous studies had indicated that it is normally *another* 6 months before babies understand that sounds are used to convey word meanings. In the study, Dr. Patricia Kuhl led a team of researchers in testing 64 babies in the United States and Sweden. Sitting on its mother's lap, each baby listened to pairs of sounds, notably an "i" and a "y," that in Sweden are two distinct sounds, but which to Americans are the same sound. The babies were trained to ignore paired sounds that were alike, but to look over their left shoulders if the sounds were different (where they would see a little puppet bang a drum). Researchers found that the American babies ignored the paired "i" and "y" sounds, but the Swedish babies looked over their shoulders, indicating that they registered a difference between them.

Such studies have several practical implications. They underline the importance of recognizing and treating quickly chronic ear infections in babies, since otherwise these may hinder language development. They also highlight the role of parents and caregivers as early language tutors of their children, and emphasize the importance of communicating with hospitalized infants, such as premature babies or those with severe health problems. Such studies also confirm the usefulness of talking to babies—as so many parents and other adults do—with a relatively high-pitched voice, clear pronunciation, and marked intonation. By doing so, researchers suggest, they are providing their babies with the basics of language. Even nonsense sounds such as "goo-goo" have value, since infants are learning sounds even if they do not yet recognize that a meaning may be attached to them. (For more information, see "Linguistic experience alters phonetic perception in infants by 6 months of age," by Dr. Patricia Kuhl et al., *Science*, January 31, 1992.)

Parents and caregivers who deliberately want to stimulate language development in preschoolers may wish to buy or rent the video *Talking from Infancy: How to Nurture and Cultivate Early Language Development* (Brookline Books, 1991), and its accompanying paperback book, by psychologist William Fowler. This nontechnical presentation reviews the stages of language development—vocalization, words, sentences, themes—and discusses how to use picture books, storytelling, daily routines, and toys such as dolls, trucks, and boxes to encourage children's development at every stage. (For more information, contact: Brookline Books, P.O. Box 1046, Cambridge, MA 02238.)

For children 8 to 10 who are curious about language, there is *Why Do We Speak As We Do: A Guide to Learning About Language*, by Kay Cooper (Walker, 1992). To give their children an early taste of foreign languages, parents can turn to Penton Overseas, which has developed the new "Lyric Language" series of audiotapes for children 4 to 8. Each 30-minute audiocassette features 11 songs, the alphabet, and topics, such as days of the week, recorded in one of several language pairs; the first three are French/English, German/English, and Spanish/English. Each audiotape is accompanied by a songbook illustrated by Family Circus cartoonist Bil Keane. Another approach is the "Fun to Learn" series by John Grisewood, for grades K through 4, with *Fun to Learn French* and *Fun to Learn Spanish* (Watts, both 1992), with color illustrations and dual-language vocabulary lists.

Make Reading Time Family Time

That's the message of the free brochure "Barbara Bush's Family Reading Tips." The brochure includes pointers on ways for parents to enrich reading aloud and to fill the home with opportunities for reading, as part of an effort to encourage reading at all age levels. It was initially published in late 1991, to coincide with the premiere of Barbara Bush's weekly ABC Radio broadcast, "Mrs. Bush's Story Time." (For a copy, contact: Barbara Bush Foundation for Family Literacy, 1002 Wisconsin Avenue, NW, Washington, DC 20007.)

Parents who want to join with others to encourage family reading may want to join with others to show in their community *While We Are*

Very Young: You Are Never Too Young to Enjoy Reading Activities, a film produced by the Marion County School System (1990; released 1991) and available for public rental, showing parents how to support reading-readiness skills taught in schools, with examples of books, games, and other materials. (For more information, contact: GPN, P.O. Box 80669, Lincoln, NE 68501.)

Several recent books also aim to help parents enhance their children's reading skills, among them:

* *Read for the Fun of It*, by Caroline Feller Bauer (H. W. Wilson, 1992). Provides parents, teachers, and librarians with ideas, resources, and sample programs introducing children to the wonders and pleasures of the printed word.
* *From Curiosity to Confidence: Help to Build Self-Esteem through Early Reading by Using Home Computers*, by Roger Young (Ten Speed/Celestial Arts, 1992). Offers a new approach to early childhood education through home computers.
* *Get Ready to Read: A Practical Guide to Teaching Young Children at Home and in School*, by Toni S. Gould (Walker, 1991).

For suggestions on *what* to read, see "Best Reading for Kids" on page 133.

Your Child Writes the Great American Novel

Well, perhaps not quite. But one of the finest, and most widely used, of children's writing programs has been updated. It's the *Bank Street Writer*, which has been used by elementary and middle-school students in classrooms and homes for over a decade. The new version, *Bank Street Writer for the Macintosh*, is described as a "full featured word processor," which means that it allows children to do basically what adult programs do—to write, correct, save their writing on a disk, and print out their work—and also provides numerous "extras," including:

* A spelling checker
* A thesaurus, for exposure to a wider range of words
* A writing guide and a punctuation guide, offering child-oriented guidance

• The ability to use charts and columns in written documents
• Multiple type fonts, which children can use for flyers, newsletters, or for fun
• The option of including sound with their document.

In fact, the *Bank Street Writer* is so flexible that some reviewers have recommended it as a sensible choice for the whole family.

The publisher also includes some special features intended for classroom use but that are perhaps equally applicable at home. For example, an adult can write a message to appear on the screen when the child starts the program, such as a description of the week's activities. Adults can also use special instructions to prevent—or at least *try* to prevent—documents from being erased by others. A 250-page manual for teachers is composed of three sections: Getting Started, a Reference Section, and Teaching Guide, with suggestions both for general use and use in specific areas of study, including word-play games. Again, parents may find it equally useful. The *Bank Street Writer for the Macintosh* works on any Macintosh computer from the Mac Plus on; it requires at least one megabyte (MB) of working memory, and a hard disk is recommended. Versions are also available for Apple computers and for IBM or IBM-compatible computers. For "publication," this and other writing programs require a printer, of course. (For more information on the Macintosh version, contact: Scholastic Software, Inquiry Department, P.O. Box 7502, 2931 East McCarty Street, Jefferson City, MO 65102; 800-541-5513. For information on the *Bank Street Writer* consumer editions for IBM or Apple computers, contact: Broderbund Software-Direct, P.O. Box 6125, Novato, CA 94948-6125; 800-521-6263 or 415-492-3500.)

Another children's writing classic widely used in schools has also been revised and upgraded. This is *The Writing Center*, an enhanced Macintosh version of the earlier *The Children's Writing and Publishing Center*, which was for IBM (or IBM-compatible) and Apple II computers. Designed for children in grades 2 through 12, The Writing Center is a desktop publishing program that allows kids to write and custom-design a report, letter, newsletter, or other document. The program comes with 200 picture files that (along with graphics from other programs) can be put into the text and cropped, enlarged, or flipped, with text automatically wrapping around them. The program also includes a spelling checker, a thesaurus, suggestions for activities, and templates for standard format and designs; and it can accept files developed using the Apple II program and other Macintosh word processing programs. *The Writing Center* requires a Macintosh with a hard disk and 1 megabyte of memory. (For more information on the new Macintosh version, as well as the earlier IBM and Apple versions, contact: The Learning Company, 6493 Kaiser Drive, Fremont, CA 94555; 510-792-2101.)

A different approach is taken by the *Children's Newspaper Maker* (1990), which allows children to create their own newspapers. The youngest children work largely by modifying ready-made sections, such as school news, world news, and a weather report. At the middle level, children use "story starters" and clip art from the disk to help them along. Older, more experienced children write their own stories, which are saved on disk, and add graphics of their own to illustrate their printed pages. Reviewers found it more structured than *The Writing Center*, and a good introduction to desktop publishing and the writing process in general. The program is intended for children ages 8 to 12 and requires an Apple IIGS computer with 1 megabyte of memory. (For more information, contact Orange Cherry Talking Schoolhouse Software, Box 390, Westchester Avenue, Pound Ridge, NY 10576.)

Budding writers who have learning disabilities may benefit greatly by using a new computer software program from Interactive Learning Materials: *Write This Way for the Learning Disabled Student* (1991). For students in grades 4 through 12 who need extra help, the program offers such features as a spelling checker (with an expandable 40,000-word dictionary), flagging of nine main types of grammatical errors, and three font sizes for printouts. A user's guide provides useful ideas and instructions for teachers or parents trying to teach writing and word-processing skills to young people. The program requires a Macintosh computer, with 1 megabyte of memory. (For more information, contact: Interactive Learning Materials, 150 Croton Lake Road, Katonah, NY 10536.)

For young writers who want some additional help, or who don't have access to a family or school computer, Troll Associates has published a new series of books for children in grades 5 through 9, written by Elizabeth A. Ryan: *How to Be a Better Writer, How to Build a Better Vocabulary, How to Make Grammar Fun—(And Easy!)*, and *How to Write Better Book Reports* (all 1991). Reviewers found the books helpful and readable, especially for insecure or reluctant writers. For middle-schoolers, there is *What's Your Story: A Young Person's Guide to Writing Fiction*, by Marion Dane Bauer (Clarion, 1992). For older children

12 and up eyeing a possible writing career, there is *Young Person's Guide to Becoming a Writer*, by Janet E. Grant (Shoe Tree Press, 1991). (For more information, contact your local library or bookstore.)

Best Reading for Kids

How do parents wade through the enormous flood of books to find those that are the best for their children? There's no one simple answer but many ways to deal with the problem.

One approach is to subscribe to a publication that regularly reviews children's publications. A classic in that field is the quarterly *Parent's Choice*, which has for over 16 years been providing information to parents and educators about books, as well as movies, television, toys, games, records, videos, and computer software for kids. (For more information, contact: Parent's Choice Foundation, P.O. Box 185, Newton, MA 02168; 617-965-5913.) Also useful to parents is the quarterly *RIF Newsletter* and parent guides for encouraging reading, published by Reading Is Fundamental (RIF), an organization of educators, librarians, parents, community leaders, and others who encourage home reading and community reading programs. (For more information contact: Reading Is Fundamental [RIF], 600 Maryland Avenue, SW, Suite 500, Washington, DC 20560; 202-287-3220; for ordering brochures: Publications Department, Smithsonian Institution, 600 Maryland Avenue, SW, Suite 500, Washington, DC 20024.)

In addition, many major city newspapers review children's books in their Sunday editions, and parenting magazines have at least occasional book reviews and often annual "best books" lists. The American Library Association issues an annual "best books" list (see your local library); so does the Library of Congress (see "Free Information for Parents" on page 212). There are also a number of children's book clubs; though parents make the selections, these often send the books directly to the children, a winning approach. People who subscribe to parents' or children's magazines are likely to see ads for several such book clubs and to be solicited for membership by mail.

In early 1992, the American Library Association (ALA)/Children's Book Council Joint Committee selected some recent books, both paperbacks and hardcovers, that they felt should form the core of a home library. Under the title "Building a Home Library," these recommendations were published in four separate lists: Preschool, Early School,

Middle Grades, and Young Adult. They appeared first in the ALA publication *Booklist* (available at most libraries) in the March 1, April 1, May 1, and June 1, 1992 issues, and were also made available in brochure form. With the ALA's permission, these four lists are also reprinted at the back of this book, starting on page 218. Note that the lists do not include older classic works, which they felt were well covered in reference books (such as those below). (For more information, including prices for bulk orders, contact: ALA Graphics, American Library Association, 50 East Huron Street, Chicago, IL 60611; 312-944-6780 or 800-545-2433, press 8.)

Many reference books describe recent or classic books for children, often categorizing them by age, type of work (fiction, nonfiction, or picture book), and theme or area of interest. Several of these publications focus on books for reading aloud or playacting, not only with young children but also with teens. Among the recent offerings are:

♦ *Classics to Read Aloud to Your Children*, by William F. Russell (Crown, 1992).

♦ *Alleyside Book of Flannelboard Stories: 20 Read-to-Tell Flannelboard Stories with Easy Patterns*, by Jeannette Graham Bay (Freline/Alleyside Press, 1991). A collection of 20 flannelboard tales, including one for each month of the year and others about animals, colors, shapes, community helpers (such as nurses or bus drivers), and holidays, such as Christmas and Easter, for use with preschoolers. (For more information, contact: Freline/Alleyside Press, P.O. Box 889, Hagerstown, MD 21741).

♦ *Multicultural Folktales: Stories to Tell Young Children*, by Judy Siera and Robert Kaminski (Oryx, 1991). A collection of 25 folktales for children ages 2 to 7, with directions for making flannelboard figures or puppets to use with some stories. Drawn from various continents, countries, and ethnic traditions, the stories are grouped by ages (2 to 5 and 5 to 7) and include suggestions for presentation techniques and audience participation. Three folktales are also given in Spanish translation.

♦ *Fantastic Theater: Puppets and Plays for Young Performers and Young Audiences*, by Judy Siera (Wilson, 1991). A work on puppet theater, which includes practical tips on construction and rehearsal and over 30 plays from folklore, fairy tales, songs, and myths.

♦ *Books Kids Will Sit Still For: The Complete Read-Aloud Guide*, 2d ed., by Judy Freeman (Bowker, 1990).

♦ *Storytelling for Young Adults: Techniques and Treasury*, by Gail de Vos (Libraries Unlimited, 1991). Intended for librarians and teachers, but may also be useful to parents as a guide to folktales, urban legends, horror, humor, romance, and other types of stories attractive to young adult audiences.

Several other general publications describe books for young children. The one written directly for use by parents or other caregivers is listed first; the others are expensive professional publications and are best checked in the library:

* *The ALA Best of the Best for Children*, by the American Library Association (Random House, 1992). A guide for parents to the best books for children.
* *Children's Catalog*, 16th ed. (H. W. Wilson, 1991). A basic librarians' guide to "the best new and established fiction and non-fiction titles written for children from pre-school through the sixth grade."
* *Play, Learn, and Grow: An Annotated Guide to the Best Books and Materials for Very Young Children*, by James L. Thomas (Bowker, 1991). For work with children up to age 6.
* *Picture Books for Children*, 3d ed., by Patricia J. Cianciolo (American Library Association, 1990). Another standard resource.
* *Books, Babies, and Libraries: Serving Infants, Toddlers, Their Parents, and Caregivers*, by Ellin Greene (American Library Association, 1991). A book intended for librarians, but including lists of useful books, magazines, films, and videotapes for parents and their children.
* *Best Books for Children: Preschool through Grade 6*, 4th ed., by John T. Gillespie and Corinne J. Naden (Bowker, 1990). The standard reference book, available in many child-oriented libraries, which can be a useful resource for parents seeking reading material for a particular age group or on a certain topic.
* *The Best in Children's Books: The University of Chicago Guide to Children's Literature, 1985–1990*, by Zena Sutherland, Betsy Hearne, and Roger Sutton (University of Chicago Press, 1991). Selects about 1,500 reviews that appeared in the *Bulletin of the Center for Children's Books* between 1985 and 1990 to help parents, teachers, librarians, and others choose the best in recent children's literature. Sutherland also edited the previous *Best in Children's Books*, covering 1966–72 (1976), 1973–78 (1980), and 1979–84 (1986).
* *Children's Book Awards International: A Directory of Awards and Winners, from Inception through 1990*, by Laura Smith (McFarland, 1992). An index of award-winning titles.

 • *Our Family, Our Friends, Our World: An Annotated Guide to Significant Multicultural Books for Children and Teenagers*, by Lyn Miller-Lachmann (Bowker, 1991).

For middle, junior, and high school readers, recent works include:

 • *Read for Your Life: Turning Teens into Readers*, by Gladys Hunt and Barbara Hampton (Zondervan, 1992). Advice on how to do just that, with a list of 300 suggested books.
 • *Your Reading: A Booklist for Junior High and Middle School Students*, 8th ed., Alleen Pace Nilsen, ed. (National Council of Teachers of English, 1991). A standard resource published in rotation with books for other age groups, which offers descriptions of titles published between 1988 and 1990, grouped into sections, such as "Understanding Competition: Sports" or "Books to Help with Schoolwork." It and other books from the NCTE will be useful to parents and to students themselves, as well as teachers and librarians, in finding the right books in their areas of interest.

For a list of "Timeless Classics," children's books published before 1960, see "Free Information for Parents" on page 212. Parents may also want to look at "Make Reading Time Family Time" on page 129, "Children's Magazines—New and Booming" on page 1, and "TESS: A Guide to Computer Software" on page 182.

National Standards and Testing: Right for America's Schools?

Virtually everyone agrees that the educational system needs to be reformed. But how to change it? One new suggestion has split the educational community and is likely to spark considerable controversy in the coming months and years. That is the idea of national standards and testing.

In April 1991, President Bush called for a voluntary system of national examinations, called American Achievement Tests, at grades 4, 8, and 12, in five key areas: English, mathematics, science, geography, and history. In January 1992, the National Council on Education Standards and Testing (NCEST)—a bipartisan advisory panel of educators and political leaders, created by Congress in June 1991—recommended the establishment of national educational standards and of tests to see how well those standards are met. Within a week over 50 prominent educators and testing experts released a statement opposing such national tests, saying that they would end up penalizing students from poor schools and depriving local communities of control over their children's learning. The lines were drawn on what will be a deeply divisive, wide-ranging discussion that receives its urgency from the well-recognized crisis facing American education. What do parents need to know about the pros and cons of the issue?

Most basically, nationwide standards and testing would be a revolutionary change. American education has traditionally stressed local control, the result being a patchwork of widely differing courses, requirements, tests, and results, established to meet the needs and desires of the local states and communities. One basic question is whether Americans want to give up a good deal of local control for a national standard. It is proposed that local school boards would retain autonomy and have some leeway on content, teaching, and testing. But there is still widespread uneasiness about creating another level of federal bureaucracy, and fear that it would stifle teacher creativity.

Proponents of the new approach say that, with American education in such a sorry state, especially in inner-city and poor rural schools, national standards and testing are the only way to produce across-the-board educational reforms and bring all students up to clearly defined high standards. They point out that national standards would help parents know how their children compare with other children across the country, not just in a locality; would allow localities to evaluate their teachers and school systems properly; and would make post-secondary schools and employers better able to assess the meaning and value of a student's record and diploma.

Critics of the approach are concerned that national testing may be counterproductive, hurting some of the students it is intended to help, and in the process diverting attention *away from* basic educational reform. They stress that there is no evidence that national standards and tests will lead to better instruction—in fact, recent experience of wide-scale testing suggests quite the contrary. Rather, when test results are used as standards of school accountability, schools often raise their test averages artificially by excluding low-scoring students. One commentator suggested that to expect a test to improve education is like expecting a new thermometer to take the chill off a cold room. Critics also say that American students are already overtested, more than in any other country in the world, an emphasis that sometimes seems to have turned schools into test-coaching centers, and that what students really need is better teaching and schools that are better funded.

Critics are also concerned that, as in some parts of Europe and in Japan, national testing would result in a kind of tracking system, determining who will be in line for elite careers, with tests being used as barriers, not gateways, for poorer students. Ironically, this comes at a time when traditional tracking, or ability grouping, has come under widespread criticism for not improving educational achievement, but in fact worsening the school experience for many students (see "Tracking: Beginning of the End?" on page 145). Significantly, what would happen to students who failed the national tests has so far been left unclear.

Some people have proposed that a single test be given for high school graduation; but most educators have concluded that no single test could be developed that would be good enough and fair enough, nor would it be feasible for such a high-stakes decision about a student's life and future. Many people are also concerned that any national test would be biased against minorities, as most standardized tests are, since many questions draw largely on the content of experiences of the *majority*. The National Council on Education Standards and Testing proposed not a single national test, however, but tests developed by states and regions under a plan—so far vaguely defined—that would allow the results to be compared to a national standard.

Proponents of national testing point out that they are not proposing to use standardized, multiple-choice tests, which are so familiar from recent decades and which many feel have so distorted education, as schools overemphasize rote learning for the tests. Rather, the Council proposes a testing approach that is open-ended, forcing students to think, and with questions often related to the kinds of tasks they will need to perform once they leave school and enter the work force. Follow so-called "performance standards," many questions will not have a single right or wrong answer, but will call for an evaluation of various aspects of a problem, resulting in a reasoned answer, often given in essay form. Various groups are at work preparing models for such tests; they are also seeking ways for regions to be able to devise their own tests and still have the results be compared with national standards. Some people are concerned that such performance-oriented nationwide testing may reflect a vision of education tailored to the commercial world, which may not reflect what the entire community wants from its schools, for example, by undercutting traditional emphasis on the humanities or liberal arts. An additional concern is that performance testing is far more sophisticated than standardized testing and requires more teacher training, and therefore is more expensive; but no sources of new funding have yet been proposed to cover the much larger costs anticipated.

The Council's report stresses that it is not recommending a single national curriculum, but instead advising that the proposed standards be broad and general descriptions of core knowledge and skills. Such standards and tests do not yet exist, however, and would probably take far longer to develop than most politicians recognize, even if it were clear that Americans wanted and could agree on what skills and knowledge students should have in all academic subjects. While that would be relatively easy in mathematics, considerable controversy exists over content and approaches to history and aspects of science, such as evolution. Even if agreement could be reached, many critics are concerned that the standards would be a lowest common denominator, and so might lower the level of instruction in many schools.

More than that, simply mandating national standards—without providing poorer schools with the funds necessary to meet those standards—makes the promise of educational reform impossible to realize, and offers no solution to the "savage inequalities" in educational opportunity that Jonathan Kozol wrote of in his recent best-selling book (see page 101). The ambivalence of concerned educators and policymakers toward the national testing proposals was made clear in 1991 comments by Phyllis McClure of the NAACP Legal Defense and Education Fund:

> One of the worst things about American schooling now for poor and disadvantaged kids is that they are held to few and sometimes no standards at all. The thing that attracts me about this proposal is that it establishes a common, high standard for all kids. But how do you expect high standards of kids who go to the worst possible schools? There's got to be some kind of leverage to force the system to provide the resources that these kids need.

Proponents say that national standards for students are needed if America is to keep up with its international competitors, noting that the United States is the only industrialized country without minimum standards for what children should know at various grade levels, in core subjects such as mathematics, science, history, and geography. Critics point out, however, that none of these competitor countries has a national examination system of the sort proposed; and most have no government-mandated testing in the higher grades, nor do they use tests to hold schools accountable.

As presently conceived, adoption of national standards and testing would be voluntary, but the Council recommended offering incentives for states and local school districts to adopt them, such as linking federal scholarships to test results, or penalizing schools with many failing students.

Instead of a top-down federal mandate, critics of nationwide testing favor programs to reform ways of teaching and of evaluating learning in an integrated way, at the local level, from the classroom up. One approach being employed in a number of schools and states is basing performance assessments on portfolios of student work (see "The Portfolio Approach in Education" on page 146). (For more information, contact: National Committee for Citizens in Education [NCCE], 10840 Little Patuxent Parkway, Suite 301, Columbia, MD 21044; 800-NET-WORK [638-9675] or in Maryland 301-997-9300; or the U.S. Department of Education, Office of Educational Research and Improvement, 555 New Jersey Avenue, NW, Washington, DC 20208; 202-401-3032; or the National Education Association (NEA), 1201 16th Street, NW, Washington, DC 20036; 202-822-7200.)

Whatever decisions are made in the coming years on the federal level regarding nationwide testing and curriculum, parents will find many changes occurring on the local level. More than ever before, children will benefit from parental involvement in improving the local schools. A number of recently published books have been designed to help parents help their children, at different levels of the educational system. Among them are:

Guides on Enhancing Learning

• *The Giftedness in Your Child: Unlocking Every Child's Unique Talents, Strengths, and Potential,* by Rita Dunn, Kenneth Dunn, and Donald Treffinger (Wiley, 1992). Attempts to give substance to the idea that every child is "special," by helping parents recognize their children's individual ways of learning and enhance their special talents and abilities, as through games and techniques designed to encourage imagination and self-esteem. The book also includes checklists for parents to use in assessing television shows, school programs, and their child's development.

◆ *Growing Up Confident: How to Make Your Child's Early Years Learning Years*, by Melitte Cutright (Doubleday, 1992). A parents' guide to providing their children with "roots and wings" (according to a Chinese proverb); reviews the range of opinion and expert answers to the main concerns, theories, and questions of parents of school-age children. By the former director of communications and programs of the National PTA and author of *The National PTA Talks to Parents* (Doubleday, 1989), the book includes many checklists and guidelines, such as books without gender stereotypes.

◆ *More Parents Are Teachers, Too: Encouraging Your 6 to 12-Year-Old*, by Claudia Jones (Williamson, 1991). Offers goal-directed activities in math, language, science, geography, art, music, and physical education, for parents to use with their children. Jones also authored *Parents Are Teachers, Too: Enriching Your Child's First Six Years* (1988).

◆ *Boosting the Underachiever: How Busy Parents Can Unlock Their Child's Potential*, by Victor Cogen (Plenum, 1990; Berkley, 1992). Shows parents how they can help "normal children whose academic performance is significantly below their potential."

◆ *What's Best for Kids: A Guide to Developmentally Appropriate Practices for Teachers and Parents of Children Age 4–8*, by Anthony Coletta (Modern Learning Press [Rosemont, NJ], 1991). Stresses understanding the stages of children's development, and the importance of making discipline and education decisions based on the needs of the children, not adults. It includes checklists for assessing preschoolers' readiness for kindergarten and evaluating children's learning in both school and home.

◆ *The Confident Learner: Help Your Child Succeed in School*, by Marjorie R. Simic and others (Grayson Bernard, 1992). Offers advice on parental involvement with schools and homework, and other more general questions such as building self-esteem, reducing stress, and providing adult role models, all buttressed by useful annotated bibliographies of books for parents, books for children in various age groups, activities, and read-aloud suggestions.

◆ *The Passionate Mind: Bringing Up an Intelligent and Creative Child*, by Michael Schulman (Free Press, 1991). A professional-level guide for maximizing a child's learning potential; illustrates teaching techniques for illuminating the information basics a child seeks: who, what, and why, and how to organize that information meaningfully.

• *Games for Learning: Ten Minutes a Day to Help Your Child Do Well in School—from Kindergarten to Third Grade*, by Peggy Kaye (Farrar, Straus & Giroux, 1991). Offers 85 brief learning games for parents to play with children ages 5 to 10 to improve vocabulary, math, handwriting, phonics, and science, using materials such as cards, dice, or pennies. Kaye also wrote *Games for Reading: Playful Ways to Help Your Child Read* (Pantheon, 1984) and *Games for Math: Playful Ways to Help Your Child Do Math* (Pantheon, 1988).

• *Help Your Child Excel in Math: Easy, Practical Methods That Make Learning Fun*, by Margaret Berge and Philip Gibins (Lifetime Books, 1992). Shows how to help preschoolers understand basic math concepts and motivate students to memorize math facts, reinforcing the elementary school curriculum with enjoyable home activities and math games—and in the process perhaps easing math anxiety among parents as well!

• *Awakening Your Child's Natural Genius: Enhancing Curiosity, Creativity and Learning Ability*, by Thomas Armstrong (Tarcher, 1991).

See also "Make Reading Time Family Time" on page 129, "Preschool Power" on page 125, and "Kids and Science" on page 157.

Guides on Schools and School-Related Problems

• *Your Child's First School: A Handbook for Parents*, by Diana Townsend-Butterworth (Walker, 1992). Covers educational concerns from preschool to later years, including how to evaluate curriculum and staff, and the pros and cons of private and public schools. Written by an experienced school director and parent counselor, the book stresses the importance of continuing parental involvement in their child's school life.

• *The School Book: Everything Parents Must Know about Their Child's Education, from Preschool through Eighth Grade*, by Mary Susan Miller (St. Martin's, 1991). A wide-ranging guide in question-and-answer format; advises parents on everyday problems, such as homework, as well as such difficult concerns as drugs and sex.

• *Helping Parents Cope with the Bewildering World of Public Schools*, by Bill Sanders (Wynwood, 1992). Designed to help parents and children better communicate with each other, and to get parents more involved in their children's schools, stressing the importance of "Judeo-Christian values."

 • *How to Get the Best Public School Education for Your Child: A Parent's Guide for the Nineties*, by Carol A. Ryan and others (Walker, 1991).

 • *Making Schools Better: What Parents, Teachers, and Communities Can Do to Breathe New Life into America's Classrooms*, by Larry Martz (Times Books, 1992). Discusses a variety of programs to suit different communities, on all grade levels.

 • *Parenting Our Schools: A Hands-On Guide to Education Reform*, by Jill Bloom (Little, Brown, 1992).

 • *1,001 Ways to Improve Your Child's Schoolwork: An Easy-to-Use Reference Book of Common School Problems and Practical Solutions*, by Lawrence J. Greene (Dell, 1991).

 • *Common and Uncommon School Problems: A Parent's Guide*, by David Gross and Irl Extein (Berkley, 1990), a paperback edition of *The Parent's Guide to Common and Uncommon School Problems* (PIA Press, 1989). Shows how to spot signals of problems, how to handle some, and how to get help for others.

 • *Taming the Homework Monster: How to Stop Fighting with Your Kids Over Homework*, by Ellen Klavan (Poseidon, 1992). Suggests how parents can resolve problems with their children over schoolwork.

 • *Ending the Homework Hassle: How to Help Your Child Succeed Independently in School*, by John K. Rosemond (Andrews & McMeel, 1990). The author is a psychologist and syndicated columnist and the author of *Six Point Plan for Raising Happy, Healthy Children* (Andrews & McMeel, 1989) and *Parent Power! A Common-Sense Approach to Parenting in the 80s* (Globe Pequot, 1981; Pocketbook, 1983), which is being updated for the 90s.

 • *The Homework Solution: Getting Kids to Do Their Homework*, by Linda Agler Sonna (Williamson, 1990).

 • *Erasing the Guilt: Play an Active Role in Your Child's Education No Matter How Busy You Are*, by Nancy S. Haug and Nancy D. Wright (Career Press, 1991). Seeks to allay parents' guilt at not being sufficiently involved in their children's education by outlining ways to develop efficient, limited, quality involvement in school, in the midst of busy lives.

See also "Confused about Dyslexia and Learning Disabilities?" on page 150.

For Parents of Gifted Children

• *The Joys and Challenges of Raising a Gifted Child,* by Susan K. Golant (Prentice Hall, 1991). Offers personal advice, with many anecdotes for and about families with gifted children, and includes a bibliography, a list of math and word books for gifted children, and discussion of sensitive issues such as elitism, sibling rivalry, testing, relations with peers, and parental stress. Golant was a gifted child herself and has two gifted daughters.

• *The Survival Guide for Parents of Gifted Kids: How to Understand, Live with, and Stick Up for Your Gifted Child,* by Sally Yahnke Walker (Free Spirit, 1991). Gives basic advice to parents of gifted children, including how to gain support for gifted programs from educators and politicians, as well as practical suggestions for "How Not to Raise a Nerd" and how parents can deal with the stress of a perpetually inquisitive child. (For more information, contact: Free Spirit, 400 First Avenue North, #616, Minneapolis, MN 55401.)

See also "Something New Under the SAT" on page 182.

Background Works

• *Savage Inequalities: Children in America's Schools,* by Jonathan Kozol (Crown, 1991). A slashing report on the two-tier educational system that crushes the hopes and aspirations of many disadvantaged children in American society, with firsthand comments from many children and teachers.

• *Smart Schools, Smart Kids: Why Do Some Schools Work?,* by Edward B. Fiske (Simon & Schuster, 1991). An overview of alternatives to what Fiske called the outmoded "factory model" of public school education, focusing on schools with decentralized management, shared decision-making, rearranged schedules, new technology, and new ways of evaluating learning, with anecdotal descriptions of their practical use in schools today.

• *Schools That Work: America's Most Innovative Public Education Programs,* by George H. Wood (Dutton, 1992). A journey through schools across the country that are encouraging both learning and personal development in students, many of whom (along with their teachers) are quoted, as part of an exploration of new approaches to education.

+ *Educating for the 21st Century: The Challenge for Parents and Teachers*, by Mark H. Mullin (Madison, 1991). Focuses on educational reform in the crucial high school years, stressing the need to offer not simply useful education but also moral education.

+ *The Unschooled Mind: How Children Think and How Schools Should Teach*, by Howard Gardner (Basic, 1991). A Harvard educational psychologist's analysis of how—even when they appear to succeed—schools fail to achieve their real goal of "genuine understanding," settling for (at best) acceptable mastery, and in the process blunting or destroying most students' enthusiasm; he offers concrete proposals for school restructuring and reform.

+ *Why Children Reject School: Views From Seven Countries*, Colette Chiland and J. Gerald Young, eds. (Yale University Press, 1990). Offers perspectives from mental health professionals around the world.

+ *Why Our Schools Are Failing and What We Can Learn from Japanese and Chinese Education*, by Harold W. Stevenson and James W. Stigler (Summit, 1992). Presents these two child development specialists' critique of those characteristics of East Asian education that might be useful in America; reviewers found the book free of "culture-bashing" in either direction.

Tracking: The Beginning of the End?

In many schools, children are routinely divided into groups based on their presumed ability and previous marks. Once placed in such a "track," however, children are often unable to move out of it, being labeled as "fast," "slow," or "average" by their teachers and, increasingly, by themselves. Many parents and educators have come to realize that the damage posed by such labeling far outweighs the supposed benefits of tracking. The National Education Association, the nation's largest teachers' organization, is among the groups tolling the bell for tracking. In a report issued in July 1990, they called for the gradual end of tracking and proposed that teachers and schools work together to develop more effective strategies for class groupings (see "The Portfolio Approach" page 146). The NEA report also found tracking—whether deliberately or accidentally—often segregates students into racially identifiable groups. In particular, they found that minorities are underrepresented in "gatekeeper classes," such as algebra and geometry, courses that must be completed before students can enter more advanced courses.

In the same month, the National Governors' Association's Education Task Force—the group assigned to monitor how well state and federal governments are fulfilling commitments made at the 1989 "education summit"—also called for an end to ability grouping and tracking of students. Their report said that ability grouping makes "low expectations become self-fulfilling prophecies" among students in the early grades and that tracking leaves far too many high school graduates "unprepared for either work or post-secondary education." A report by the Quality Education for Minorities Project also drew similar conclusions, charging that the damage caused by tracking "lasts a lifetime." (For more information, contact: National Committee for Citizens in Education [NCCE], 10840 Little Patuxent Parkway, Suite 301, Columbia, MD 21044; 800-NETWORK [638-9675] or in Maryland 301-997-9300; or the National Education Association [NEA], 1201 16th Street, NW, Washington, DC 20036; 202-822-7200.)

The Portfolio Approach

Parents, educators, politicians, and other concerned citizens who are dissatisfied with the proliferation of standardized testing, its distortion of education, and its burden on students are looking toward new and better ways of evaluating student progress in learning. One of the most interesting new approaches is portfolio evaluation. In education, a portfolio is a systematic collection of representative samples of a child's work from throughout a whole school year in a range of areas. A portfolio for an English class, for example, would include essays, poems, stories, plays, and other kinds of writing done during the year. In a mathematics class, it might include maps, scale drawings, graphs, analyses of graphic data, and geometric designs made from string, as well as solutions to homework problems, with written explanations of how the answer was reached. Such homework problems are often more varied and open-ended than questions commonly found in classrooms and on standardized tests; they may call for a judgment based on a variety of facts, with no single right answer, or they may have a single right answer, but one that can be reached in several different ways.

Among the many advantages of portfolio evaluation are that it fosters independent, creative thinking and problem solving; encourages the student's unique learning pattern; stimulates learning because it is both more interesting and more gratifying; and gives a far better indication of a child's abilities than do standardized tests. Proponents of portfolio evaluation hope that it will supplement—and, some hope, perhaps eventually replace—standardized test assessments. The new kinds of evaluation also call for new ways of teaching, the aim being to move away from the repetitive "skill-and-drill" approach that has predominated, especially with standardized, multiple-choice testing, and toward a more innovative and stimulating type of teaching and learning. Many school districts are experimenting with the portfolio approach and one state, Vermont, has since the 1990–91 school year been using portfolio evaluation statewide, at first experimentally in 138 schools, in mathematics and English. Many supporters of nationwide testing also support portfolio evaluation (see "National Standards and Testing: Right for America's Schools?" on page 136), as do many opponents of tracking (see "Tracking: Beginning of the End?" on page 145). The portfolio approach has drawn enthusiastic support from many educators, parents, and children involved. One of the not-inconsiderable side benefits is that, as students become engaged in doing their own work, and in sharing that work with others, classroom discipline problems diminish sharply. Portfolios also give parents a far better idea of their children's educational progress; in some districts, portfolios are eventually turned over to the family, often to be valued as part of a child's "archive."

Portfolio evaluation is not without problems, however. Teachers worry that on a busy school day with crowded classrooms, they do not have the time to give students the intensive help portfolios require; some are also concerned about how well they will be able to shift from conventional classroom patterns to new ways of teaching, and how portfolio evaluation may reflect on their own teaching abilities. Many people are concerned that portfolios cannot be graded in the conventional way and that comparing grades among students in the same or different schools is difficult. Parents, especially, worry that their child may suffer from an "impressionistic" evaluation. (One of the advantages of standardized tests, after all, is precisely that their grading is objective—even to the extent of sometimes being done by computer—and does not depend on the subjective evaluation of any single person.)

Educators are responding to some such concerns. For example, Vermont has developed a mixed-assessment approach, in which the final grade in a subject will be determined by evaluation of the student's portfolio in general and of the student's choice of his or her single "best piece" of the year, with the student's reasons for the choice, as well as of performance on a uniform test, which requires the student to write on a particular topic or complete a mathematical problem in a certain period of time. During the experimental period, at least, a sampling of portfolios will be independently assessed by teams of two teachers; if their assessments differ substantially, the portfolio will be reviewed by another two-person team, in an effort to refine evaluation standards. Some colleges are also beginning to offer training in portfolio evaluation.

Parents who want to learn more about portfolios, as well as other alternative ways of assessing learning, can look at the new book *Testing for Learning: How New Approaches to Evaluation Can Improve American Schools*, (Free Press, 1992), by Ruth Mitchell, associate director for the Council for Basic Education. Intended for parents and other concerned people, the book outlines the problems with standardized multiple-choice tests, and explores a variety of alternatives, with descriptions of programs currently in place across the United States.

What's Wrong with Today's History Textbooks?

According to 1991 news reports, plenty. A review of 10 junior and senior high school history textbooks being considered for adoption in Texas showed almost 5,200 errors. Among the most glaring mistakes uncovered were the wrong date for the Japanese attack on Pearl Harbor and the assertion that U.S. President Harry Truman had "easily settled" the Korean War by dropping an atomic bomb. Red faces were found at several major textbook houses. The textbooks were later approved by the Texas Education Agency, with the stipulation that corrections be made before they reached Texas classrooms. Many such textbooks today are not written by authors who are subject experts, but rather are put together to publishers' specifications by "development houses"; unfortunately, not all people working on the books are qualified to deal with the subject matter. So if children complain that a textbook is wrong, check it out! They just might be right.

Moving? How to Choose a New School District

For many parents who are planning to move—whether across the county or across the country—the first decision is: Which school district is best for the children? One recent book offers parents some guidance in answering that question. *Public Schools USA: A Comparative Guide to School Districts*, 2d ed., by Charles Harrison (Peterson's Guides, 1991), evaluates over 400 school districts in major metropolitan areas of 26 states (states without a big city are not included). Listed alphabetically, from Albany to Washington, districts included have over 2,500 students, are within 25 miles of the core city, and are generally organized K through 12. For each district, the book presents key statistics, such as enrollment, attendance, expense per student, teacher/student ratio, dropout rate, average teacher's salary, number of advanced-placement courses offered, and scores on such tests as the Scholastic Aptitude Test (SAT) and the American College Test (ACT). These are compared with state and national averages, resulting in an Effective Schools Index (ESI) for each. Reviewers caution that statistics were provided by the districts themselves, that many relate to expenditure rather than educational results, and that some of the ESIs appear to have been calculated incorrectly. Keeping those caveats in mind, parents may still find the work useful in summarizing data on the major school districts. The book also includes average statistics for each state; further information on districts, such as addresses and phone numbers; and suggestions and charts for use in evaluating elementary and secondary schools. Parents may also want to check out *The College Board Guide to High Schools* (1990), which provides data, though not ratings, on 25,000 secondary schools.

Another approach is to consult the SchoolMatch® educational database, which covers information on "all U.S. public school systems, metro areas, small cities and towns, rural areas . . . [and] accredited private schools," giving key school ratings such as school size, pupil/teacher ratio, test scores, commuting distance, local home values, resident income levels, and special school programs. Users complete a Family Profile Guide, and the SchoolMatch system finds up to 15 school systems to meet their needs, anywhere in America. The service also provides a SchoolMatch Report Card, to tell parents how their child's present—or future—school system stacks up. (For more information, contact: SchoolMatch, 5027 Pine Creek Drive, Westerville, OH 43081; 614-890-1573.)

Confused about Dyslexia and Learning Disabilities?

If so, you're not alone. Recent studies have thrown into question some long-accepted assumptions about dyslexia—reading difficulty that is often classified under the more general term "learning disabilities." Dyslexia has long been thought to have a biological basis and to be a permanent disability. But a major new study, published in the *New England Journal of Medicine* in January 1992, suggests that dyslexia may not be permanent, but instead may change during a child's development. Dr. Sally Shaywitz of the Yale University School of Medicine directed a team that studied 414 children in a Connecticut school for nine years, from their entry into kindergarten in 1983. What they found astonished the experts, notably:

  ♦ That children classified as borderline dyslexics moved in and out of the dyslexic group over the years.
  ♦ That most children who were diagnosed as dyslexic in the early grades were not classified so in later years. Specifically, fewer than one in three labeled dyslexic in the first grade remained so in the third grade; by sixth grade the ratio was one in six.
  ♦ That other children who were not considered dyslexic in the early years came to be considered so later on.

The meaning and implications of these findings are just beginning to be explored.

Certainly the study has raised questions about what dyslexia is and how it is identified. One widely used definition, from the World Federation of Neurology, is that dyslexia is "difficulty in learning to read despite conventional instruction, adequate intelligence, and socio-cultural opportunity." Children are generally given various tests, assessing their ability to receive information accurately (input), transmit it accurately (output), put pieces of information together (integration), as in matching sounds with the written word, and remember pieces of information (memory). These tests focus on the various areas in which children have trouble, such as in reversing letters (for example, b and d) or transposing letters (was for saw). Children who score low on such tests are considered dyslexic. But students are sometimes classified as dyslexic or learning disabled simply if their IQ scores are substantially higher than their reading achievement scores.

Among the questions raised by the new study are:

• Can we distinguish between children with dyslexia and those who, for a variety of other reasons, are poor readers? Some people have suggested that, even if dyslexia has a biological basis, the term has been too broadly and imprecisely defined, becoming a catchall. The Yale study also suggests the possibility that some students, though they seem able to read normally, actually have dyslexia, which may become apparent only later. Shaywitz suggested that dyslexia may be like high blood pressure or obesity, in that the lines between normal and abnormal vary, as does the severity of the condition, and that children move in and out of the "abnormal" group.

• Are we able to identify dyslexia and learning disabilities in very young children? Many experts have long felt that dyslexia and other learning disabilities could not be identified in preschool children because early reading and learning problems may result from other causes, such as unfamiliarity with structured learning, cultural differences, social or emotional problems (as when a family is homeless or in the process of breaking up), or language differences (as when a language other than English is spoken in the home). More important, children develop at widely different rates, so it is possible that those labeled as dyslexic early in school are simply developing more slowly than average.

• More generally, are children being properly identified as dyslexic or learning disabled? Some people have suggested that both parents and schools have too readily applied the notion of dyslexia and learning disabilities, regarding these categories as convenient, socially acceptable explanations of educational problems—and one that may relieve parents and teachers from feeling responsible for a child's failure to learn. Others believe that dyslexia and learning disabilities are to some extent "socially created" categories, reflecting the priorities of a high-pressure society, as well as the lower status accorded to nonacademic skills, such as woodworking or dancing. In addition, some people have charged that, because the category of learning disabilities falls under the Education for All Handicapped Children Act, therefore qualifying for special aid, schools have more readily classified children as learning disabled, not always with sufficient cause.

◆ Do dyslexia and learning disabilities have a biological basis? Educators, psychologists, neurologists, and other experts have long assumed that such disabilities are permanent and so have sought specific biological defects common among dyslexic children. In 1991 a team of neurologists, under Ranjan Duara of the University of Miami (Florida) School of Medicine, scanned the brains of 21 people with dyslexia and 29 normal readers, and reported significant differences in one area of the left half of the brain; such results are yet to be confirmed, however, and their implications explored.

◆ Can children "outgrow" dyslexia or learning disabilities? The Yale study suggests that we need to know much more about how children with dyslexia fare over time. Can they, for example, learn how to overcome their disabilities, so they can read and learn normally? Or might some parts of the brain develop in such a way as to compensate for the original problem, as was suggested by some findings in the 1991 Miami study? Or were many people mislabeled as dyslexic, having only a slower-than-normal development in some areas?

◆ Do specific treatments and therapies help children with dyslexia and learning disabilities? Indeed, does that explain the children who moved out of the "dyslexic" category during the study? In the past, any child who was able to move out of a reading disability group was regarded as a success for whatever teaching or therapy approach was being employed. But if, as the Yale study showed, children move in and out of the dyslexic group for other, as yet unknown reasons, treatments and therapies will need to be generally reevaluated.

◆ Are the study's results caused by a fluke? What we do not yet know is whether or not there were some special circumstances in the school and community used in the Yale study that would have caused the results obtained. It remains for other researchers to confirm, expand on, modify, or contradict the results of this single study.

(For more information, contact: National Institute of Child Health and Human Development, 301-496-5133; or Orton Dyslexia Society (ODS), 724 York Road, Baltimore, MD 21204; 800-ABCD-123 [222-3123] or 301-296-0232).

In a different study, a team of brain researchers reported finding a physical basis for dyslexia; specifically, they found indications that dyslexia was not purely a language problem but may result from unsynchronized timing in the visual system's circuits, where information is not received in the proper sequence for ready processing by the brain. The visual system involves two major pathways: one for seeing motion, depth perception, stereoscopic vision, low contrast, and spatial orientation; the other for seeing color, detailed forms, high contrast, and stationary images. The study found that, in people with dyslexia, the first system worked "sluggishly," and that in autopsies on brains of dyslexics, the first system seemed to be more disorganized and to involve smaller cells. As described in the Proceedings of the National Academy of Sciences in 1991, this study, by Dr. Margaret Livingstone and others, involved only a small group of subjects, but, if confirmed, offered the possibility of identifying dyslexia in very young children, even infants, and of providing help early, when it presumably would do the most good. One of the authors stressed that such a slightly sluggish visual system should not be viewed as a disorder, but may in fact be part of the normal variation of the human brain, often in people otherwise highly gifted. Observers note that the findings give support to one approach to treating dyslexia, which involves using colored filters in reading (see *Reading by the Colors*, listed on page 154), and may suggest new ways to help people with dyslexia. Other studies suggest that hearing and touch may be involved in a similar way. Also, researchers have found that animals can form antibodies that destroy proteins found only in the first visual pathway, which suggests the possibility that dyslexia may be an autoimmune disease (in which the body mistakenly attacks and damages part of itself) that is acquired or triggered before or shortly after birth.

Meanwhile, parents of children who have reading or general learning difficulties—whether or not they have been labeled as "dyslexic" or "learning disabled"—must make practical day-to-day decisions on how to give and get help. In general, experts recommend that parents in this situation keep in mind several guidelines:

• Try to clear aside any anger at the school or at yourself as having somehow "failed"; such judgments are generally counterproductive and often damaging to the child.

• Encourage and support your child, rather than trying to drive your child to succeed, and placing disproportionate emphasis on academic performance.

• Focus on what the child does well, not on failures.

• Understand that your child has not an *in*ability, but a *dis*ability, making learning more difficult, not impossible.

• Recognize that there are various ways of learning, and be alert and open to ways of learning that may be easiest for your child.

♦ Communicate your love and acceptance of the child, and your understanding of his or her frustration at having to work so hard at some things.

A number of recent books offer more specific help and guidance to parents and others, among them:

General Works and Practical Guides for Parents

♦ *The Misunderstood Child: A Guide for Parents of Learning Disabled Children*, rev. ed., by Dr. Larry B. Silver (TAB–McGraw-Hill, 1992).

♦ *Reading by the Colors: Overcoming Dyslexia and Other Reading Disabilities Through the Irlen Method*, by Helen Irlen (Avery, 1991).

♦ *Why Is My Child Having Trouble at School?: A Parent's Guide to Learning Disabilities*, by Barbara Novick and Maureen Arnold (Random, 1991).

♦ *Help Me to Help My Child: A Sourcebook for Parents of Learning Disabled Children*, by Jill Bloom (Little, Brown, 1991).

♦ *Understanding Dyslexia: A Practical Handbook for Parents and Teachers*, by Anne M. Huston (Madison Bks UPA, 1991).

♦ *Can Anyone Help My Child?: Therapies and Treatment for Attention Deficit and Other Learning and Behavioral Disorders in Children, Adolescents, and Adults*, rev. ed., by Guy D. Ogan (Faith Publications & Media, 1991).

♦ *A Parent's Guide to Attention Deficit Disorders*, by Lisa J. Bain (Delta, 1991). Part of a series of books written with the Children's Hospital of Philadelphia.

♦ *Mothers Talk about Learning Disabilities: Personal Feelings, Practical Advice*, by Elizabeth Weiss (Prentice Hall, 1991).

♦ *Upside-down Kids*, by Harold N. Levinson (M. Evans, 1991).

Books for Kids

♦ *The School Survival Guide for Kids with LD (Learning Differences): Ways to Make Learning Easier and More Fun*, by Rhoda Cummings and Gary Fisher (Free Spirit, 1991). For grades 3 and up; with an optional audiocassette.

♦ *What Do You Mean I Have a Learning Disability?*, by Kathleen M. Dwyer (Walker, 1991). For grades 3 through 6; presents the story of a 10-year-old boy who learns why he's having trouble in school and who is able to succeed, with a tutor's help.

♦ *Dyslexia*, by Elaine Landau (Watts, 1991). For children in grades 3 through 5, or for reading aloud with younger children.

♦ *Learning Disabilities*, by Paul Almonte and Theresa Desmond (Crestwood/Macmillan, 1992). Part of the "Facts About" series, for children in grades 5 and 6.

Personal Experiences

♦ *Succeeding Against the Odds: Strategies and Insights from the Learning-Disabled*, by Sally L. Smith (Tarcher, 1992). Smith, the founder of the Lab School in Washington, D.C., draws on her experiences with learning-disabled students (including her own child).

♦ *An Autobiography of a Dyslexic*, by Abraham Schmitt, as told to Mary Lou Hartzler Clemens (Good Books, 1992).

♦ *Reversals: A Personal Account of Victory over Dyslexia*, by Eileen Simpson (Farrar, Straus and Giroux, 1991).

Professional Works (for parents who want to dig deeper)

♦ *The Learning Disabled Child*, by Silvia Farnham-Diggory (Harvard University Press, 1992).

♦ *Learning Disabilities: What To Do after Diagnosis: A Survival Guide*, in 4 vols., by Jill Smith and Howard Diller (Apodixis, 1991). *Vol. 1: Kindergarten Through Third Grade, Vol. 2: Fourth Through Sixth Grade; Vol. 3: Seventh Through Twelfth Grade; Vol. 4: College and the Workplace.*

♦ *Learning about Learning Disabilities*, Bernice Y. Wong, ed. (Academic Press, 1991).

♦ *The Reading Brain: The Biological Basis of Dyslexia*, Drake D. Duane and David B. Gray, eds. (York Press, 1991).

♦ *Strategies for Teaching Students with Learning and Behavior Disorders*, 2d ed., by Candace S. Box and Sharon Vaughn (Allyn, 1991).

♦ *Learning Difficulties*, by Richard I. Fisher (Kendall-Hunt, 1991).

♦ *Language-Related Learning Disabilities: Their Nature and Treatment*, by Adele Gerber (P. H. Brookes, 1992).

Reference Works

♦ *A National Directory of Four Year Colleges, Two Year Colleges, and Post High School Training Programs for Young People with*

Learning Disabilities, 7th ed., P. M. Fielding and John R. Moss, eds., (PIP, 1992).

  ♦ *Directory of Facilities and Services for the Learning Disabled, 1991–92* (Academic Therapy, 1991).

Parents might also want to refer to *The Parent's Desk Reference*, by Irene Franck and David Brownstone (Prentice Hall, 1991), which includes a lengthy write-up on learning disabilities in general, including an observational checklist, extensive book list, and many activities useful for children with learning disabilities.

No Smart Drugs

Some people have been persuaded that there are so-called "smart drugs" that can improve memory, concentration, or intelligence; elevate the normal brain to a higher-than-normal state; and even correct brain dysfunctions, such as epilepsy. But the Food and Drug Administration (FDA) warns that no drugs or other products have been approved for these purposes.

The products in question vary widely and may be made from a wide variety of ingredients, including herbs; vitamins; amino acids (the body's basic building blocks), especially phenylalanine and alanine; other substances such as choline (derived from lecithin); prescription drugs; and unapproved drugs. Sometimes these are sold as powdered nutrient supplements, which are then mixed with liquids and sold as "smart drinks" at "health bars." The drugs may also be purchased through pharmacies or mail-order firms from abroad, or from health-food stores in the United States.

The FDA cautions, however, that claims for these smart drugs have not been submitted to controlled scientific testing and that no data supporting these claims have been submitted to the government. The FDA warns that using such drugs can be dangerous for several reasons:

  ♦ Imported drugs are not manufactured under the quality-control standards of the United States, perhaps the strictest in the world.

  ♦ People are placing themselves at risk when they take prescription drugs without a doctor's supervision and when no evidence has shown that the drugs are either safe or effective.

• Even "healthful" and vital nutrients, such as vitamins and amino acids, can be harmful and sometimes toxic when taken in excessive amounts.

Parents should not be misled by marketing claims and should alert their children to the possibility of misleading or misguided sales pitches. (See also "Countering TV Advertising" on page 15.) The FDA has warned that any product associated with smart-drug claims, regardless of its composition, is illegal and subject to seizure and other actions. (For more information, contact: Food and Drug Administration, 301-443-3170 or 301-443-2410.)

Kids and Science

Parents who want to enhance the scientific and technological "literacy" of their children have many new books and series to help them do so, at various stages in their children's education. Many of these books include not just presentations of concepts, developments, and inventions, but also many projects for kids themselves to carry out, often using materials available in the home. Parents should keep in mind—as the books themselves generally stress—that students should have adult supervision and guidance, especially where chemicals are involved. Some experiments, especially for older children, require specialized equipment and call for particular safety precautions, as is generally outlined in the books; some may call on community resources. In addition, a few titles focus specifically on projects for science fairs and competitions, an area of increasing interest to scientifically oriented kids.

Below is a sampling of the recent publications in these areas; some of these are parts of continuing series, to which new titles are added year by year. Though intended for use by children, many of these books are sold primarily to libraries and bookstores; parents often find them hard to come by since libraries buy them and bookstores stock them spottily, especially in times of economic recession. If the book is *not* available locally, parents can generally call for it through the interlibrary loan system (see your local library). Books can also be ordered, either through a local independent bookstore—most of these take special orders, though many "chain" bookstores do not—or directly from the publisher (ordering information is available at your local library, in standard reference works such as *Books in Print*).

The works below are organized roughly by the age groups for which they are intended. Note also that most kids' books focusing on nature and the environment are listed in a separate section, "Kids Go Green, Too" on page 165.

For Preschoolers and Kindergarteners—and Up

• The "Rookie Read-About Science Big Books" series, by Allan Fowler, published by Children's Press. For children in preschool through grade 2. It includes these recent titles: *How Do You Know It's Fall?* (1992), *How Do You Know It's Summer?* (1992), *Frogs and Toads and Tadpoles, Too!* (1992), *Horses, Horses, Horses* (1992), *It's Best to Leave a Snake Alone* (1992), *Thanks to Cows* (1992), *How Do You Know It's Spring?* (1991), *How Do You Know It's Winter?* (1991), *Please Don't Feed the Bears* (1991), *So That's How the Moon Changes Shape!* (1991), *What's the Weather Today?* (1991), *The Sun Is Always Shining Somewhere Big Book* (1991), *Cubs and Colts and Calves and Kittens* (1991), *Hearing Things Big Book* (1991), *Seeing Things Big Book* (1991), *Smelling Things Big Book* (1991), and *Tasting Things Big Book* (1991). Titles are published in either the "Big Book" format—15- by 17½ inches—or a smaller 6- by 7-inch format, both with full-color illustrations; many are also available in paperback, some in Spanish.

• The "What's Inside?" series, from Dorling Kindersley (1992). For children in preschool through grade 3. It includes *Baby, Plants, Insects,* and *Boats*.

• *Science for Me*, by Linda Diebert (Good Apple, 1991). For children in preschool through grade 2.

• *Child's Play 6–12: 160 Instant Activities, Crafts and Science Projects*, by Leslie Hamilton (Crown, 1992). For children in kindergarten and up.

For Young Readers

• The "Step into Science™" series of science activity books for new readers, ages 7 to 10, published by Random House. It includes *Green Thumbs Up! The Science of Growing Plants* (1992), *More Power to You! The Science of Batteries and Magnets* (1992), *Over the Rainbow! The Science of Color and Light* (1992), and *Up, Up and Away! The Science of Flight* (1992).

* The "Simple Science Projects" series, by John Williams, published by Gareth Stevens, for children in grades 2 through 4. Titles, all beginning *Simple Science Projects with*, include: *Air*, *Color and Light*, *Electricity*, *Flight*, *Machines*, *Time*, *Water*, and *Wheels* (all 1992).
* The "Science Book of" series with experiments and projects for children ages 7 to 10, by Neil Ardley, published by Harcourt Brace Jovanovich. Titles, which all begin with *Science Book of*, include *Energy*, *Hot and Cold*, *Machines*, and *The Senses* (all 1992); and *Water*, *Color*, *Light*, *Sound*, *Magnets*, *Electricity*, *Air*, and *Things That Grow* (all 1991).
* The "Fun with Simple Science" series, by Barbara Taylor, published by Warwick Press, for children in kindergarten through grade 4. Titles include *Air Flight*, *Batteries and Magnets*, *Color and Light*, and *Growing Plants* (all 1991); and *Liquid and Buoyancy*, *Machines and Movement*, *Shadows and Reflections*, and *Sound and Music* (all 1990).
* *Science Activities*, by H. Edom (EDC, 1992). For children in grades 1 through 4.
* *Wonders of Science*, by Melvin Berger (Scholastic Inc, 1991). For children in grades 2 through 5.
* *Mindtwisters*, by Godfrey Hall (Random, 1992). For children in grades 3 through 6.
* *Fun and Games: Stories Science Photos Tell*, by Vicki Cobb (Lothrop, 1991). For children in grades 3 and up.
* The "Science Dictionary" series, by James Richardson, published by Troll, for children in grades 3 through 7, which provides definitions of things and concepts. Titles all begin with *Science Dictionary of*, and include *Animals* (1991), *Dinosaurs* (1991), *Space* (1991), and *The Human Body* (1991).

For Middle Readers

* The "Experiment!" series, by David Darling, published by Dillon/ Macmillan, for children in grades 4 and up. Titles include: *From Glasses to Gases: The Science of Matter* (1992), *Between Fire and Ice: The Science of Heat* (1992), *Making Light Work: The Science of Optics* (1991), *Sounds Interesting: The Science of Acoustics* (1991), *Spiderwebs to Skyscrapers: The Science of Structures* (1991), and *Up, Up, and Away: The Science of Flight* (1991).
* The "Science Starters" series, by Barbara Taylor, published by Watts, for children in grades 5 through 8. Titles include *Electricity and*

Magnets (1990), *Energy and Power* (1990), *Force and Movement* (1990), and *Weight and Balance* (1990).

◆ The "Weather Watch" series, by Philip Steele, published by Watts, for children in grades 5 through 8, is illustrated with full-color photographs. Titles are all subtitled *Causes and Effects* and include *Frost* (1991), *Heatwave* (1991), *Storms* (1991), *Wind* (1991), *Rain* (1991), and *Snow* (1991).

◆ *Science in a Nanosecond: Illustrated Answers to 100 Basic Science Questions*, by James A. Haught (Prometheus Books, 1991). For children in grades 4 and up.

◆ *175 Amazing Nature Experiments*, by Rosie Harlow and Gareth Morgan (Random, 1992). For children ages 9 to 12.

◆ *175 More Science Experiments to Amuse and Amaze Your Friends*, by Terry Casn and Barbara Taylor (Random, 1991). For children in grades 4 through 7; a sequel to *175 Science Experiments to Amuse and Amaze Your Friends*, by Brenda Walpole (Random House, 1988).

◆ The "Hands on Science" series, published by Watts. For children in grades 5 through 8; includes *Earthquakes to Volcanoes: Projects with Geography* (1992) and *Mining to Minerals: Projects with Geography* (1992), both by John Clark; *Feeding to Digestion: Projects with Biology* (1992), *Fins to Wings: Projects with Biology* (1992), and *Jellyfish to Insects: Projects with Biology*, all by William Hemsley; *Rain to Dams: Projects with Water* (1991) and *Reproduction to Birth: Projects with Biology* (1991), both by Clint Twist; *Seeds to Plants: Projects with Biology* (1991), by Jeffrey Bates; *Weather and Climate: Projects with Geography* (1991), by David Flint; *Nerves to Senses: Projects with Biology* (1991), by Steve Parker; *Measuring and Maps: Projects with Geography* (1991), by Keith Lye; *Burning and Melting: Projects with Heat* (1990), by Peter Lafferty; *Sound Waves to Music: Projects with Sound* (1990) and *Muscles to Machines: Projects with Movement*, (1990), both by Neil Ardley.

◆ The "Technology in Action" series, for children in grades 5 through 9, published by Watts. Titles include *Food Technology* (1992), *Building Technology* (1991), *Energy Technology* (1991), *Information Technology* (1991), *Aircraft Technology* (1990), *Car Technology* (1990), *TV and Video Technology* (1990), *Ship Technology* (1990), *Train Technology* (1990), and *Farming Technology* (1990), all by Mark Lambert; *Houses and Home* (1992) and *Water Transportation* (1992), both by Alistair Hamilton-MacLaren; *Machines* (1991), by Lambert and Hamilton-MacLaren; *Sports Technology* (1992), by Neil Duncanson; *Medical Technology* (1991), by Jenny Bryan; *Military Technology* (1991), by

Chris Smith and Bernard Harbor; *Camera Technology* (1991), by Alastair Jervis; *Undersea Technology* (1990), by Ralph Rayner; and *Spacecraft Technology* (1990), by John Mason.

◆ *Science Through Art*, by Hilary Devonshire, published by Watts, for children in grades 5 through 8. Titles include *Light* and *Water* (both 1992).

◆ *Great Science Fair Projects*, by Phyllis Katz and Janet Frekko (Watts, 1992). For children in grades 5 through 8.

◆ The "Fun With Science" series, published by Warwick Press, for children in grades 5 through 8. Titles include *Cycles and Seasons* (1991), *Energy and Growth* (1991), *Observing Minibeasts* (1991), and *Trees and Leaves* (1991), all by Rosie Harlow and Gareth Morgan; and *Chemistry* (1990) and *Weather* (1990), both by Steve Parker.

◆ The "World Around Us" series, published by Warwick Press, includes *The Human Body*, by Michael Gabb; *Nature*, by Jennifer Cochrane; *The Sea*, by Brian Williams; and *Space*, by Ian Ridpath (all 1991).

◆ The "Way It Works" series, for children in grades 6 and up, published by New Discovery Books/Macmillan. Illustrated in full color; titles include *Heat* (1992), *Electricity* (1992), and *Light* (1992), all by Neil Ardley; and *Water* (1992), *Motion* (1992), and *Air* (1992), all by Philip Sauvain.

◆ *How Do You Know It's True?: Discovering the Difference Between Science and Superstition*, by Hy Ruchlis (Prometheus Books, 1991). Part of the "Young Readers" series.

◆ *Physics for Every Kid: 101 Easy Experiments in Motion, Heat, Light, Machines, and Sound*, by Janice Vancleave (Wiley, 1991).

◆ *Simon and Schuster Young Readers Book of Science*, by Robin Kerrod (Simon & Schuster, 1991).

◆ *How to Make a Chemical Volcano and Other Mysterious Experiments*, by Alan Kramer (Watts, 1991). For children in grades 5 and up.

◆ *Aviation and Space Science Projects*, by Ben Millspaugh (TAB Books, 1991).

For Older Readers

◆ The "Projects for Young Scientists" series, for students in grades 9 through 12, published by Watts. Titles include *Science—Technology—Society Projects for Young Scientists* (1991) and *Consumer Chemistry Projects for Young Scientists* (1991), both by David E. Newton; *Electronics Projects for Young Scientists* (1991), by George D. Leon; and *Physics Projects for Young Scientists* (1991), by Peter Goodwin. Books in this series offer pointers for developing projects, ranging from step-by-step approaches to general guidelines, which students develop and modify according to their interests and skills.

  • *How to Excel in Science Competitions*, by Melanie Jacobs Krieger (Watts, 1991). A work for high school students who want to pursue independent scientific research projects. It gives an overview of the major science competitions, profiles student researchers, and offers guidelines for approaching an independent project. The author, who has coached students in such competitions, includes rules, entry forms, and sources of more information. Part of the "Experimental Science" series.

  • *Tomorrow's Technology: Experimenting with the Science of the Future*, by Irwin Math (Scribner's, 1992). Gives an overview of the promise of today's technological advances, with instructions for science projects based on them. For ages 12 and up.

  • *1001 Ideas for Science Projects*, by Marion A. Brisk (Prentice Hall, 1992).

  • *Complete Handbook of Science Fair Projects*, by Julianne B. Bochinski (Wiley, 1991).

  • *Space Science Projects: A Source Guide* (Gordon Press, 1991).

Why . . . ?

Kids love to ask questions. While no parents will have the answers to all their children's questions, they can get a head start with the new "Questions and Answers About Animals" series, for children ages 4 to 6. Written by Anita Ganeri and published by Barron's, each book asks and answers questions such as "Why do fireflies glow in the dark?" or "Which animals often eat with a 'fork'?" Titles include *Animal Behavior* (1992), *Animal Families* (1992), *Animal Food* (1992), *Animal Records* (1992), *Animal Babies* (1991), *Animal Camouflage* (1991), *Animal Movement* (1991), and *Animal Talk* (1991). For kids ages 8 to 12, Barron's has also published *Why Is the Sky Blue? And Answers to Questions You Always Wanted to Ask*, by David West (1992).

Meanwhile, Random House has weighed in on the Q & A front with *The Random House Book of 1001 Questions and Answers About Animals*, by Michele Staple and Linda Gamlin (1990), for children in grades 3 through 7. This is a big, beautiful, to browsing book; one reviewer called it a "giant natural science smorgasbord . . . jam-packed . . . with oddities, facts, and figures about the animal world." The work is organized around questions such as "What is the difference between horns and antlers?" and "How big is a giant earthworm?" Answers are often supplemented by a full-color illustration. (For older kids, parents should check out "Kids and Science" on page 157.)

Can't We Help It Get Well?

Parents of nature-loving children often hear that question when confronted with a wounded wild bird or animal, but—apart from health professionals—few have any idea of what to do or how to proceed. But now there is a medical manual for laypeople treating animals: *Care of the Wild: First Aid for Wild Creatures* (University of Wisconsin, 1991). Written by W. J. Jordan, a veterinarian, and the late John Hughes, a wildlife casualty expert, the book covers a range of animals from bats and badgers to wildfowl and wolves, with advice on approaching and capturing the injured creature, transporting it, initial care and feeding, symptoms, diagnosis, treatment, and the like. Reviewers caution that, although written for nonprofessionals, many techniques may be beyond the capabilities of untrained caretakers, but parents facing a wounded bird or animal, with nowhere else to turn, will be glad for the practical advice and counsel.

Talking Dinosaur

Given the near-universal children's passion for anything related to dinosaurs, almost all parents will at some time in their parenting lives temporarily need to become dinosaur experts. A new book has just the answer to a parent's prayers on the subject: *How to Talk Dinosaur with Your Child*, by Q. L. Pearce (Lowell House, 1992). It provides parents with an overview of dinosaurdom and answers to the most common children's questions about dinosaurs. Along the way it provides tips on how parents can help their children think scientifically, and how to prepare for a museum visit, family fossil hunts, or even a dinosaur party.

For young dinosaur devotees themselves, there are also several new books at hand. Perhaps the most outstanding are:

* *Living with Dinosaurs*, by Patricia Lauber (Bradbury/Macmillan, 1991). For children in grades 1 through 5, it gives readers a view of life 75 million years ago from the dinosaur's perspective, including the sights, smells, sounds, and also the other animals and plants in their habitats. Lauber is also the author of *The News about Dinosaurs* (1989) and *Dinosaurs Walked Here and Other Stories Fossils Tell* (1987), both also published by Bradbury. *Living* also includes a "How We Know What We Know" section explaining how scientists investigate fossil remains.

* *A Dinosaur Named after Me*, by Bernard Most (Harcourt Brace Jovanovich, 1991). For children in preschool through grade 3, it has a child introducing 25 dinosaurs and having fun with their names—especially showing other kids how to find their name within a dinosaur's name, often by changing a letter or finding a rhyme (such as "Pat" in "Apatasaurus" or "Stegosaurus" being renamed "Gregosaurus"). Scientific names and their pronunciations are also provided.

* *Dinosaur Island*, by Max Haynes (Lothrop, 1991). For children in preschool and up; this is a picture book in which young readers find hidden dinosaurs that the two boys in the book miss on their visit to the island. The guide includes a key to the dinosaurs pictured in the book, including names and phonetic spellings.

Other new dinosaur-oriented books include:
* *Flying Dinosaurs—Pterodactyls*, by Michael Berenstain (Western, 1991). Part of the "Golden Look-Look Books" series, for children in preschool through grade 3.

* *Let's Look at Dinosaurs*, by Gina Ingoglia (Putnam, 1991). Part of the "Poke and Look Learning Books" series, for children in preschool through grade 1.

* *Dinosaurs* (Ladybird, 1991). Part of the "Ladybird Learners" series, for children in grades 1 through 4.

* *Discovering Dinosaur Babies*, by Miriam Schlein (Four Winds/Macmillan, 1991). For children in grades 1 through 5.

* *Dinosaur Dinners*, by Sharon Cosner (Watts, 1991). Part of the "First Books" series, for children in grades 2 through 4.

* *All You Need to Know about Dinosaurs*, by Mark Norell (Sterling, 1991). For children in grades 2 through 9.

Dino-roars™ (FISHER-PRICE)

◆ *The Science Dictionary of Dinosaurs*, by James Richardson (Troll, 1991). For children in grades 3 through 7.

◆ *The National Wildlife Federation's Book of Dinosaurs and Other Pre-Historic Animals* (Earthbooks, 1991). For children in grades 4 and up.

(For more information, check your local library or bookstore.)

For the age 2 and up dino-loving crowd, the well-known toy and child product manufacturer Fisher-Price introduced a new line of stuffed animals in 1992: the Dino-roars™. These three soft, brightly colored dinosaurs give a fun roar when kids squeeze them. (See local toy stores, or contact: Fisher-Price, 620 Girard Avenue, East Aurora, NY 14052; 800-433-5437 or 716-687-3000.)

Kids Go Green, Too

Big as the environmental movement has been among adults, it is even bigger among children, who in fact often come to educate the adults in their families on ways to help save the earth. A number of green-oriented books have been published that are specifically directed to children. The smash hit among them—and inspiration for many others—is *50 Simple Things Kids Can Do to Save the Earth*, by the Earth Works Group (Andrews & McMeel, 1990), published to coincide with the twentieth anniversary of Earth Day; in less than two years it sold over 787,000 copies.

Below is a sampling of recent environmental publications relating to kids' concerns. These works are organized roughly by the age group for which they are intended. Note that some other nature-oriented science and project books are listed under "Kids and Science" on page 157; and that many of these are continuing series, with new titles added year by year.

For Preschoolers and Kindergarteners—and Up

• *I Can Help*, by Merry Fleming Thomasson (Thomasson-Grant, 1992). Shows how children (ages 2 to 7) can help save the environment. Part of the "Hey, Look at Me!" series, in which a child's photo is placed in the back cover, making him or her the "star" of the book.

• *The Berenstain Bears Don't Pollute (Anymore)*, by Stan and Jan Berenstain (Random House, 1991). For children in preschool through grade 1.

• *Dinosaurs to the Rescue!: A Guide to Protecting Our Planet*, by Laurie Krasny Brown and Marc Brown (Little, Brown, 1992). Features the polluting "Slobosaurus" and gives examples of positive actions. For children in preschool through grade 3.

• *Grover's 10 Terrific Ways to Help Our Wonderful World* (Random House, 1992). For children in preschool and kindergarten.

• *Teenage Mutant Ninja Turtles ABC's for a Better Planet* (Random House, 1991). For children in preschool through grade 3.

• *Here Comes the Recycling Truck!*, by Meyer Seltzer (Albert Whitman, 1992). For children ages 3 to 7.

For Young Readers

• The "Wildlife at Risk" series, published by Bookwright/Watts, for children in kindergarten through grade 4. Titles include *Gorillas* (1991) and *Elephants* (1990), both by Ian Redmond; *Wolves* (1992) and *Pandas* (1991), both by Gillian Standring; *Bears* (1991) and *Rhinos* (1991), both by Malcolm Penny; *Monkeys* (1992), by Tess Lemmon; and *Seals and Sea Lions* (1992), *Turtles and Tortoises* (1992), and *Whales and Dolphins* (1991), all by Vassili Papastavrou.

♦ The "Look Closer" series, published by Dorling Kindersley, for children in grades 1 through 4. It gives a "close-up view" of life in a particular setting, including *River Life, Meadow, Tree Life, Tide Pool, Pond Life, Rainforest, Desert Life*, and *Coral Reef* (all 1992).

♦ The "World About Us" series, from Gloucester Press/Franklin Watts, for children in grades 2 through 4. Titles include *Toxic Waste* (1992), by Margaret Spence; *Nuclear Waste* (1992), by Brian Gardiner; *Polluting the Oceans* (1991), *Acid Rain* (1991), *The Greenhouse Effect* (1991), *The Ozone Layer* (1991), *Tropical Rainforest* (1991), and *Traffic Pollution* (1991), all by Michael Bright; and *Recycling* (1991) and *Vanishing Habitats* (1991), both by Tony Hare.

♦ The "Tell Me About Books" series, published by Random House, for children in grades 2 through 5. Titles include *Desert Animals* (1992), by Michael Chinery; and *Grassland Animals* (1992), *Ocean Animals* (1992), *Rainforest Animals* (1992), and *The World of Animals* (1991), by Tom Stacy.

♦ "Lighter Look Books" (Millbrook Press, 1991). A series on environmental and related subjects for children in grades 2 through 6, all with a light tone. Titles include *Poison! Beware! Be an Expert Poison Spotter* (1991) and *What a Load of Trash! Rescue Your Household Waste* (1991), both by Steve Skidmore; *Buy Now, Pay Later!: Smart Shopping Counts* (1992), *Make A Splash!: Care about the Ocean* (1992), and *Down the Drain: Explore Your Plumbing* (1991), all by Thompson Yardley; and *Worm's Eye View: Make Your Own Wildlife Refuge* (1991), by Kipchak Johnson.

♦ *The Big Green Book*, by Fred Pearce (Grosset & Dunlap, 1991). Presents an environmental view of the earth and problems such as the greenhouse effect, disappearing rain forests, the thinning ozone layer, and the trash crisis in ways understandable and attractive to young children, ages 7 to 10.

♦ The "What We Can Do about" series, published by Watts, for children in grades 3 through 5. The titles begin with *What We Can Do about* and include *Conserving Energy* (1992) and *Protecting Nature* (1992).

♦ The "SOS Planet Earth" series, by Mary O'Neill, published by Troll Associates, for children in grades 3 to 6. Titles include *Air Scare* (1991), *Nature in Danger* (1991), and *Power Failure* (1991).

♦ *Endangered Plants*, by Elaine Landau (Watts, 1992). It is about some of the 3,000 types of plants at risk in the United States alone and efforts to save them, and is part of the "Full-Color First Books" series, for children in grades 3 through 5.

• The "Earth Keepers" series, from Twenty-First Century Books. For children in grades 3 through 7. Titles include *Jacques Cousteau: Champion of the Sea* (1992), *Henry David Thoreau: A Neighbor to Nature* (1991), and *Rachel Carson: The Wonder of Nature* (1991), all by Catherine Reef; *Marjory Stoneman Douglas: Voice of the Everglades* (1992), by Jennifer Bryant; *Jane Goodall: Living with the Chimps* (1992), by Julie Fromer; *George Washington Carver: Nature's Trailblazer* (1992), by Teresa Rogers; *Chico Mendes: Fight for the Forest* (1991), by Susan DeStefano; and *Gaylord Nelson: A Day for the Earth* (1991), by Jeffrey Shulman and Teresa Rogers.

• The "Vanishing Culture" series, by Jan Reynolds. Each title focuses on a culture that is the human equivalent of an endangered species and on a particular child of that culture, using color photographs. Published by Harcourt Brace Jovanovich for children in grades 2 and up, the first titles in the photo-essay series were *Sahara Vanishing Cultures* (1991) and *Himalaya Vanishing Cultures* (1991). A wide-ranging traveler who worked for *National Geographic*, Reynolds expects to round out the series with culture books about Australia, the Far North, the Amazon, Mongolia, and Native Americans.

For Readers in Middle Grades

• The "Saving Planet Earth" series, published by Children's Press, for children in grades 4 through 8. Titles include *Acid Rain* (1991) and *Water: A Resource in Crisis* (1991), by Eileen Lucas; *Hazardous Wastes* (1991), by Allen Stenstrup; *Too Many People?* (1992), *Global Warming* (1991), *Recycling* (1991), and *Oil Spills* (1991), all by Jean F. Blashfield and Wallace B. Black; and *Disappearing Wetlands* (1992) and *Vanishing Forests* (1991), both by Helen Challand.

• The "Save Our Earth" series by Tony Hare, from Gloucester Press/Watts. For children in grades 4 through 8. Titles include *Polluting the Air* (1992), *Domestic Waste* (1992), *Habitat Destruction* (1991), *Nuclear Waste Disposal* (1991), *Polluting the Sea* (1991), *Toxic Waste* (1991), *Acid Rain* (1990), and *Rainforest Destruction* (1990).

• The "Extinct" series, by Philip Steele, published by Watts, for children in grades 4 through 7. The titles follow the format *Extinct . . . : And Those in Danger of Extinction*, and include *Land Mammals* (1992), *Underwater Creatures* (1992), *Insects* (1992), *Amphibians* (1992), *Birds* (1991), and *Reptiles* (1991).

• The "Ecology Watch" series, from Dillon/Macmillan, for children in grades 5 and up. Titles include *Rivers, Ponds and Lakes* (1992), by Anita Ganeri; *Grasslands* (1992) and *Mountains* (1992), both by Alan Collinson; *Towns and Cities* (1992), *Polar Lands* (1992), and *Rainforests* (1991), all by Rodney Aldis; and *Deserts* (1991) and *Seas and Oceans* (1991), both by Clint Twist.

 • The "Green Issues" series, from Gloucester Press, for children in grades 5 through 8. Titles include *Vanishing Species* (1991), by Miles Barton; *Waste Disposal and Recycling* (1991), by Sue Becklake; and *Food and Farming* (1991), by John Becklake and Sue Becklake.

 • *Environmental America*, published by Millbrook Press, for children in grades 4 through 6. Environmental issues, problems, and concerns in the United States are treated by region: *The North Central States, The Northeastern States, The Northwestern States, The South Central States, The Southeastern States*, and *The Southwestern States* (all 1991).

 • *Save the Earth: An Action Handbook for Kids*, by Betty Miles (Knopf, 1991; revision of the 1974 edition). For children in grades 5 and up.

For Older Readers

 • The "Earth at Risk" series, from Chelsea House, for children in grades 9 through 12. Titles include *Global Warming* (1992), by Burkhard Bilger; *Acid Rain* (1991), by Peter Tyson; and *Overpopulation* (1992), *Extinction* (1992), and *Recycling* (1991), by Rebecca Stefoff.

 • *Environmental Science Projects: A Source Guide* (Gordon Press, 1991).

 • *The American Wilderness and Its Future: Conservation Versus Use*, by Edward F. Dolan (Watts, 1991). Presents the debate between conservationists and people supporting multiple use to children in grades 9 through 12.

 • *The Student Environmental Action Guide*, by the Student Environmental Action Coalition (SEAC) (Earth Works Press, 1991). This work by the new campus-based environmental network stresses environmentally useful activities in the campus environment.

For Parents and Teachers

 • *This Planet Is Mine: Teaching Environmental Awareness and Appreciation to Children*, by Mary Metzger and Cinthya P. Whittaker

(Simon & Schuster, 1991). Helps parents and teachers who want to involve children in environmental issues, with chapters on various topics, activities, and suggestions for working with young people.

• *The Green Encyclopedia*, by Irene Franck and David Brownstone (Prentice Hall/Simon & Schuster, 1992). Offers not only discussions of concepts, people, events, and issues, but also descriptions of many organizations working on various environmental issues, including some with special projects for families or young people.

• *E For Environment: An Annotated Bibliography of Children's Books with Environmental Themes*, by Patti Sinclair (Bowker, 1992).

(For advice on ordering or locating these books, see "Kids and Science" on page 157.)

Volunteering to Help the World

While parents strive hard to teach their young children social values, in older children it is sometimes the other way around: Preteens and teens can sometimes become the "conscience" of their families and communities, as they try to create a world that meets the ideals presented to them as children. In our own time, much of this idealistic energy has been channeled toward environmental issues (see "Kids Go Green, Too" on page 165), but some kids take a wider view of social goals. Two new books can be useful guides for them:

• *150 Ways Teens Can Make a Difference: A Handbook for Action*, by Marian Salzman, Teresa Reisgies, and many teenage contributors (Peterson's Guides, 1991). This is a practical guide for young people (grades 8 through 12) who want to "do good" in a wide range of human concerns, from health and the environment to education and politics, including numerous quotes from teen volunteers, discussion of how to find volunteer work that is right for their individual personality, and a list of associations to contact, by state.

• *The Kid's Guide to Social Action: How to Solve the Social Problems You Choose—and Turn Creative Thinking into Positive Action*, by Barbara A. Lewis (Free Spirit, 1991). This offers a step-by-step guide for children in grades 3 through 8. Lewis is an elementary school teacher whose students have effected changes; their experiences are used to illustrate the kid-oriented approaches described. (For more information, contact: Free Spirit, 400 First Avenue, North, Suite 616, Minneapolis, MN 55401.)

In some areas, community service has even become a policy, with every teenager being slated to perform some kind of social work, such as teaching a retarded child or helping run a day-care center for elders, before graduating from school.

Peace for Kids, Kids for Peace

The Big Book of Peace (Dutton, 1990), edited by Ann Durell and Marilyn Sachs, is a best-selling collection of stories, fables, poems, memoirs, and illustrations donated by some favorite authors and artists in children's literature, all to pass on this important message to kids in grades 7 through 12: Peace begins with us. The book, about the origins of conflict and the importance of peace, was inspired by a librarian unhappy with the number of books on war. Later, various celebrity narrators donated their talents for the production of a 90-minute audiocassette version of the book (The Publishing Mills, 1992). Royalties for the original book were donated to various organizations that urge world peace, as was a "significant portion" of the publisher's proceeds from the sale of the audiobook. (For more information on the audiocassette, contact Publishers Group West, 800-788-3123.)

Another book, taking a more personal approach, is *Peace on the Playground: Nonviolent Ways of Problem-Solving*, by Eileen Lucas (Watts, 1991), part of the "Full-Color First Books" series for children in grades 5 through 8. Some educational systems are, in fact, even adding programs on creative conflict resolution to their curriculum. By demonstrating to children how to deal with anger, frustration, and other such feelings, they are attempting to teach "emotional literacy" and seeking a commitment to peace that they hope will have a wide effect, not least on violence in the schools.

Yet another approach to peace stresses multicultural awareness: *Hands Around the World: 365 Creative Ways to Build Cultural Awareness and Global Respect*, by Susan Milord (Williamson, 1992). This invites children to experience, taste, and embrace daily lives from around the globe. (For more information, contact: Williamson, Box 185, Charlotte, VT 05445.)

A related work focusing on often-inadvertent social support for violent attitudes is *Boys Will Be Boys: How We Encourage Violence in Our Sons and What We Can Do to Stop It*, by Myriam Miedzian (Doubleday, 1991). This book develops the thesis that a "masculine mystique" of toughness, dominance, and competitiveness—fostered by television violence, war toys, and sports machismo—contributes to criminal and domestic violence; the author proposes child-rearing alternatives.

Children's Encyclopedias: What's New? What's Not?

All parents concerned with their child's education sooner or later face the question of which encyclopedia to get for home use. The choices are varied—not only are there a number of encyclopedias available, but some also now appear in a variety of formats, including electronic editions.

For most parents, the word "encyclopedia" calls to mind the large multivolume sets that they grew up with, on their home, school, or library shelves. These print-on-paper sets still dominate the world of encyclopedias, not just because they are familiar but also because they are enormously convenient. No nonprint form can quite match the convenience of being able to have several volumes open at once; to refer back and forth among articles; to have maps, photographs, and drawings available alongside text, and in different volumes at the same time; and to be able to put slips of paper or Post-It™-style notes in place to mark points of interest. At the most basic level, you can simply reach out, open a volume, and answer a question at any time, without needing to start up a computer to do so. Perhaps most important in a family setting, more than one person can use a print encyclopedia at one time—unlike electronic forms, which are limited to one person per computer.

But electronic editions of encyclopedias are becoming increasingly available and have their own distinct advantages and disadvantages, though these vary widely among formats and particular encyclopedias. For children accustomed to television and computers, the screen forms are often more familiar and less off-putting than a book, however unfamiliar computers may be to some parents. Children may enjoy being able to "bounce around" from one topic to another on screen, preferring the interaction with the computer program to simply reading, which seems (at least to some) more passive. Although access to text articles is sometimes more cumbersome, in many electronic editions specific articles can be printed out for off-screen reference if desired.

Parents should realize that electronic editions are not identical to the print versions. Sometimes the electronic edition has less—maps and illustrations may be left out in some formats, for example—while sometimes it may have more, perhaps adding more illustrations, graphics, dictionaries, atlases, even moving images, and sound, sometimes music and voices of notable figures, such as John F. Kennedy. Such "bells and whistles" features are attractive to children, especially to those of the MTV generation. Whether these electronic forms are as convenient to use for basic reference—the main aim of an encyclopedia, after all—remains to be seen.

Encyclopedias available in the CD-ROM format (a compact disc with a read-only format, similar to the CD used for music) allow more varied types of searching than print encyclopedias. In *Information Finder* (see *World Book*, below), for example, users can search for a particular topic, as in a print encyclopedia. But they can also do something they could not do with a print-on-paper encyclopedia: search for particular key words. While that sounds attractive, in practice it can produce far too many (and many irrelevant) references. Users must then refine the search by using various qualifiers (such as "and," "or," or "not"); such searching techniques require a sophistication beyond most young children and many older ones, except the most "computer literate," without some experience and training. Some electronic encyclopedias also offer features meant to mimic the convenience of the print form, such as "electronic bookmarks" or an "electronic notepad." Note that in addition to the cost of the encyclopedia itself, families must also purchase a CD-ROM machine, a substantial expense, though it may be used for other purposes as well.

Some electronic encyclopedias are available on-line—that is, reached using a computer and a data-transmitting device called a *modem*—generally as part of a much larger collection of information sources known as a *database*. Instead of buying an encyclopedia to keep and use in the home, families buy the ability to consult an encyclopedia at any time, paying by the use. Costs are figured in various ways. To reach many databases, you dial a phone number, which connects you to an electronic network, which in turn connects you to the electronic database. The costs for consulting the encyclopedia would include per-minute charges for the phone call to the network (often local), network time, and database time. For commercial services, these costs can mount up quickly; for consumer-oriented services, the per-minute costs are much less, but will need to be watched. Some databases take an alternative approach: For a flat, monthly fee, they provide unlimited access to the encyclopedia, with phone charges being the only per-minute cost. That is the approach used by services like Prodigy (see "Is There a Prodigy in Your Future?" on page 39). One advantage to on-line services is that they often have a wide variety of references available, not just a single encyclopedia.

On-line encyclopedias offer the potential for greater currency than print forms. This can be an illusion, however. Every encyclopedia is continually being updated in minor and major ways. An on-line ency-clopedia may be updated frequently; for example, the *Academic American Encyclopedia* (see page 175) is updated quarterly. But this updating is necessarily of a minor nature—filling in death dates, falls from power, or recent discoveries. The same kind of updating is carried on in annual editions and subsequent printings by print encyclopedias. For example, in the second printing of their 1991 edition, *The World Book Encyclopedia* (see below) included numerous revisions taking into account the massive political changes in Eastern Europe and the former Soviet Union at the end of 1990. But no encyclopedia—print or electronic—can possibly do a major overhaul of its contents quarterly. The real question is how thoroughly the encyclopedia revises its mate-rials to keep the *whole work* up-to-date. In their annual editions, some encyclopedias may update entries with new population figures or death dates but leave the basic articles unchanged for years, even though the work is labeled as that year's edition; others are extremely good at doing substantial revisions for currency. That being said, an on-line encyclopedia *is* being updated, while an encyclopedia that is fixed in form after you buy it—whether in book, CD-ROM, or other electronic form—gradually goes out of date, though they may be kept up-to-date by purchase of annual yearbooks or updating CD-ROMs.

Beyond the question of currency, on-line encyclopedias generally do not have the same convenience as other forms, print or electronic, and can be cumbersome to use. Because not all family members will be comfortable with electronic forms, an on-line encyclopedia may be most useful as a supplement to a print encyclopedia, especially for families that already subscribe to a computer information database.

The main question for parents choosing a general family encyclope-dia is: Which one is best suited for the age, reading level, and interests of the children and adults in your family? The comments below are intended to help parents choose, from among the currently available general encyclopedias, which is best for their family.

♦ *Academic American Encyclopedia* (Grolier). Intended for middle school through adult readers. First published in 1980, the *AAE* is the newest general English-language encyclopedia, though the smallest, with generally shorter entries. Topics are arranged alphabetically, with an extensive index and many cross-references for easy use; about one-third of the space is devoted to illustrations, over three-quarters of which are in color. Reviewers have lauded *AAE*'s coverage of science, technology, and Third World countries, and its up-to-date treatment of current events, including pop culture and international affairs. The American Library Association's *Booklist* described it as "an excellent home purchase." The *AAE* comes in 21 volumes, has approximately 28,900 entries in 9,800 pages, with about 16,900 illustrations. Modified versions of the *AAE* are sold in retail stores as *The Grolier International Encyclopedia* or the *Barnes & Noble New American Encyclopedia*; supermarkets sell a condensed version as *The Grolier Encyclopedia of Knowledge*. The on-line version of *AAE*, available from various sources such as Prodigy (see page 39) and Compu Serve, is updated quarterly. The AAE is also available in other electronic formats, including a tape version to be put into a private computer system. The CD-ROM version, called the *New Grolier Multimedia Encyclopedia*, has numerous illustrations, maps, and even sound. A

Academic American Encyclopedia on Prodigy® (PRODIGY SERVICES COMPANY)

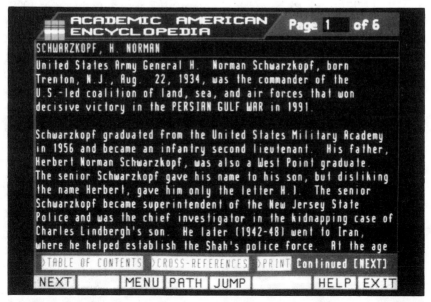

special "Links" feature eases access to thousands of cross-referenced articles; users can search not only article text, but also titles, map features, picture captions, bibliographies, and fact boxes. "Notepad" and "bookmark" features allow users to save, "cut and paste," and retrieve stored information. (For more information, contact: Grolier Electronic Publishing, Sherman Turnpike, Danbury, CT 06816; 800-356-5590 or in CT 203-797-3500.)

• *Children's Britannica* (Encyclopaedia Britannica), intended primarily for upper elementary school readers. First published in Britain in 1960, then Americanized in 1988, the *Children's Britannica's* first 18 volumes hold its A to Z articles, while volume 19 is an atlas, and volume 20 is an index, with references not just to the articles, but also to illustrations (about half in color), maps, and tables. In addition, the index volume includes "capsule fact" entries for topics not covered separately in the A to Z entries. Not surprisingly, given its origins, the *Children's Britannica* is especially strong in covering British Commonwealth countries. The encyclopedia uses relatively few internal cross-references to point readers to related articles; has few bibliographic references; and does not indicate pronunciation. The American Library Association's *Booklist* found it lacking in "overall flair in appearance," but "basically sound in coverage, accurate, and current," and "reasonably priced." In its 20 volumes, the *Children's Britannica* has about 9,900 entries (4,200 in the main text and 5,700 in the capsule index) and 6,200 illustrations, in 6,770 pages. Unlike the other major encyclopedias, The *Children's Britannica* did not issue a revised edition in 1992. (For more information, contact: Encyclopaedia Britannica, 310 South Michigan Avenue, Chicago, IL 60604; 800-554-9862 or 312-347-7000.)

• *Collier's Encyclopedia* (Macmillan). Intended for high school through adult readers. First published in 1950–51, *Collier's* is a standard general encyclopedia that in its A to Z coverage focuses on more general information, with fewer cross-references, than some other general encyclopedias, but has an excellent index, not only to articles but also to illustrations, bibliographies, and places on maps. While noting some unevenness in updating, the ALA's *Booklist* pronounced it "well-designed, attractive, and reasonably authoritative," and "useful in the home for teenagers and adults." *Collier's* comes in 24 volumes with approximately 25,000 entries and over 14,000 illustrations (28 percent in color) in 19,700 pages. (For more information, contact: Macmillan Publishing Co., 866 Third Avenue, New York, NY 10022; 800-257-5755 or 212-702-2000.)

◆ *Compton's Encyclopedia and Fact-Index* (Encyclopaedia Britannica). For upper elementary school through high school readers. First published in 1922, *Compton's* seeks to provide "pleasurable and stimulating reading experiences for young people." The volumes are made up of two parts: a general A to Z encyclopedia with cross-references, and a master fact index volume (Editions before 1992 had fact indexes also in individual volumes.) While heavily illustrated, these books have fewer four-color pictures than most others for children. The ALA's *Booklist* found it an "accurate, concise, and reasonably attractive encyclopedia whose updating is generally adequate," recommending it for school, library, or home use by children. *Compton's* comes in 26 volumes containing approximately 33,970 entries (5,230 in the main text and 28,740 in the *Fact-Index*) and 22,500 illustrations in 11,280 pages. An electronic version of *Compton's* is available through the computer service America Online; entries can be searched and articles printed out (downloaded) into the user's computer and printer. (For more information, contact: Encyclopaedia Britannica, 310 South Michigan Avenue, Chicago, IL 60604; 800-554-9862 or 312-347-7000; or America Online, 8619 Westwood Center Drive, Vienna, VA 22182; 800-827-6364 or 703-448-8700.)

◆ *The Encyclopedia Americana* (Grolier). For high school through adult readers. Published since 1829, the *Americana*, the second-largest general encyclopedia, seeks to "serve as a bridge between the worlds of the specialist and the general reader." Its particular strengths are in its biographies, geography, and United States history; a comprehensive index volume provides easy access. Updating has been slow and uneven, leaving many sections no longer as current as they should be, but *Booklist* still found that "*Americana* remains one of the most comprehensive sets for adults and high school and college students." The *Americana* comes in 30 volumes, containing approximately 52,000 entries and 22,860 illustrations in 26,740 pages. (For more information, contact: Grolier Electronic Publishing, Sherman Turnpike, Danbury, CT 06816; 800-356-5590 or in CT 203-797-3500.)

◆ *Funk & Wagnalls New Encyclopedia* (Funk & Wagnalls). For junior high school through adult readers. First published in 1912, under the present title since 1971, *Funk & Wagnalls* is designed primarily for home use by junior and senior high school students and nonspecialist adult readers. It follows the usual A to Z format, with a separate index volume, but without references to illustrations and bibliographies. Only about one-third of the illustrations are in color, though that proportion has been increasing, and it does not provide pronunciation for unfamiliar words. The ALA's *Booklist* noted that it "provides clear, up-to-date, worldwide coverage in a readable style," that "gives good value for the price," though it is not as detailed or scholarly as the major multivolume encyclopedias. *Funk & Wagnall's* comes in 29 volumes, containing approximately 25,000 entries and 9,450 illustrations in 13,020 pages. (For more information, contact: Funk & Wagnalls, Inc., 70 Hilltop Drive, Ramsey, NJ 07446; 201-934-7500.)

• *The New Book of Knowledge* (Grolier). For elementary through junior high school students. It has been published since 1910, from 1966 under this title and in an A to Z format, rather than in the earlier thematic approach. Articles are pitched to appropriate reading levels, with articles of interest to young children written at a lower reading level than more technical ones likely to be read by older children. Traditionally each volume contained its own Dictionary Index; these are gradually being phased out and their contents incorporated in the articles. The set also has a separate index volume, and entries contain many cross-references for ease of use. The set is attractively illustrated, with 90 percent of the illustrations in color. It also comes with a *Home and School Reading and Study Guide*, including a list of projects and "Wonder Questions." The ALA's *Booklist* judged it a "good choice," noting that "with its excellent illustrations and many extra features, it is sure to be attractive to children." *The New Book of Knowledge* comes in 21 volumes, with approximately 8,890 entries (4,240 in the main text and 4,650 in the dictionary index) and 23,000 illustrations in 10,570 pages. (For more information, contact: Grolier Electronic Publishing, Sherman Turnpike, Danbury, CT 06816; 800-356-5590 or in CT 203-797-3500.)

• *The New Encyclopaedia Britannica* (Encyclopaedia Britannica). For high school through adult readers. The largest general English-language encyclopedia, *Britannica* is also the oldest, published in America since 1901, wholly reorganized into a three-part arrangement in 1974. The 12-volume *Micropaedia* includes brief articles; the 17-volume *Macropaedia* includes lengthy articles, where more information is desired; the one-volume *Propaedia* gives a topical guide to the whole; and (since 1985) an extensive two-volume index allows ease of access. Illustrations are often rather small, about 30 percent of them in color. First-time purchasers also receive the *Britannica World Data Annual*, updates of which are bound into their *Britannica Book of the Year* updates. The ALA's *Booklist* judged that *Britannica's* "unparalleled strength is its historical treatment of world knowledge," providing a "wealth of information" presented with "outstanding scholarship and balanced coverage," and recommended it for home use by "adults, college students, and some high school students." The *New Britannica's* 32 volumes contain approximately 65,340 entries (64,670 in the *Micropaedia* and 670 in the *Macropaedia*) and 23,600 illustrations in 31,930 pages. (For more information, contact: Encyclopaedia Britannica, 310 South Michigan Avenue, Chicago, IL 60604; 800-554-9862 or 312-347-7000.)

♦ *New Standard Encyclopedia* (Standard Educational Corp.). For middle school through adult readers. Published since 1910, the *New Standard* aims to "provide as much information of interest to the general reader as is possible within an illustrated set selling for a modest price." Entries in the A to Z format are concise, with pronunciation guides for difficult or foreign words, with many cross-references for ease of use, as well as a separate index volume, including maps, illustrations, and bibliographies. About 28 percent of the illustrations are four-color, with the rest in two-color or black-and-white, some dated. The ALA's *Booklist* found that the *New Standard* "provides basic factual information on many topics, and students and adults will find that it usually satisfies their curiosity within the limitations of a set its size." The *New Standard* comes in 20 volumes with approximately 17,430 entries and 12,000 illustrations in 11,300 pages. (For more information, contact: Standard Educational Corp., 200 West Monroe, Chicago, IL 60606; 312-346-7440.)

♦ *Oxford Children's Encyclopedia* (Oxford University Press). For children ages 8 to 13. The seven-volume import became a best seller in Britain on its 1991 release. Topics are arranged alphabetically in five volumes, with biographies and indexes each in a separate volume. The set is heavily illustrated to appeal to the children of the television era, with approximately 3,000 illustrations, diagrams, and maps, many in full color. It also has numerous special features, such as timelines; "flashbacks" giving more historical information on certain subjects; "things-to-do" boxes with activities and experiments using easy-to-find materials; and special information and "see also" panels in the margin for research on related topics. Children 8 to 13 were involved in the development of the encyclopedia, giving information over several months on what they wanted to look up and what they expected to find, and making suggestions as to how the material should be presented for *their* needs, not those of adults—though some reviewers have recommended it for use by the whole family. United States buyers should be aware, however, that this encyclopedia is a British import, and spellings have not been Americanized. The *Oxford Children's* 7 volumes contain approximately 2,150 entries (1,500 articles and 650 biographies) and 3,000 illustrations in 1,648 pages. (For more information, contact: Oxford University Press, 200 Madison Avenue, New York, NY 10016; 212-679-7300.)

♦ *The World Book Encyclopedia* (World Book). For elementary and secondary school readers. The strengths of the *World Book*, first published in 1917, are in its excellent illustrations, 80 percent in color, its attractive layout, and its up-to-date coverage, especially of world events, scientific discoveries, current issues, and statistics, such as for population or economics. Arranged in an A to Z format, articles are written at various levels. Short, general articles are pitched at the lowest reading level; longer, more technical articles start out at the lowest reading level, for young users, but become more complex to meet the needs of older readers. Numerous cross-references are also provided in entries, and a separate volume is an index and research guide. For its attractiveness, up-to-date coverage, readability, and ease of use, the ALA's *Booklist* found it an "excellent source for elementary and secondary school students," and an "outstanding general encyclopedia for adults as well," recommending it as a "general reference tool for . . . families." The *World Book* has 22 volumes containing approximately 17,500 entries and 29,000 illustrations in 14,050 pages. The CD-ROM version of the *World Book* is called the *Information Finder*®, which also includes *The World Book Dictionary* and various additional features, such as keyword searching, "GoTo" cross-references, electronic bookmarks, an electronic notepad, on-screen help, the ability to print out all or part of articles, and special advanced searching techniques. It won the 1990–91 Technology and Learning Software Award of Excellence. (For more information, contact: World Book, Inc., 510 Merchandise Mart Plaza, Chicago, IL 60654; 800-621-8202 or 312-245-3456.)

Depending on their family's ages, needs, and desires, parents may also want to consider two other encyclopedias:

♦ *The Random House Children's Encyclopedia* (Random House). Intended for children ages 7 to 12. Originally prepared in Britain by Dorling Kindersley and published in Americanized form in 1991, this is one of the largest single-volume encyclopedias for children. It contains about 400 main entries in over 640 pages, and has over 3,500 color illustrations; many topics are covered in spreads of one, two, or more pages. At the back of the book is a 25-page Fact Finder, including a timeline, star maps, a chart classifying living things, the periodic table, and lists of such things as the largest deserts or longest bridges. *The Random House Children's Encyclopedia* retains the emphases of its British origins, with many American topics covered lightly or not at all, and no separate treatment of individual American states. The book includes a table of contents and an index, but given the book's organization, young readers may still have difficulty finding specific topics. However, it presents information attractively and concisely, and *Booklist* suggested that it may be especially appealing to children "resistant to reading," and as a supplement to standard multivolume children's encyclopedias. Random House also publishes the one-volume *Random House Encyclopedia*, intended for older and adult readers; it includes about 25,000 entries in the A to Z "Alphapedia" portion, about 900 double-page thematic articles in the "Colorpedia" portion, and an 80-page atlas. This encyclopedia is also published in an electronic edition, containing 20,000 entries, mostly from the "Alphapedia," but without illustrations; it comes on floppy disks and is designed to be placed on the hard disk of either an IBM, IBM-type, or Macintosh computer. Users can search the encyclopedia's text in various ways, leaving "bookmarks" in up to 30 places. (For more information, contact: Random House, 201 East 50th Street, New York, NY 10022; 800-638-6460 or 212-751-2600.)

• *The Doubleday Children's Encyclopedia*, John Paton and Roberta Wiener, eds. (Doubleday). A 4-volume set for children ages 7 to 11, originally published in Britain in 1989 and published in Americanized form in 1990. Most of the entries are arranged in A to Z order, often supplemented by boxes containing capsule facts, and with cross-references to other entries; the set also contains two dozen double-page "Special Feature" entries on such topics as "Space Exploration" and "Middle Ages," which themselves have fact panels, cross-references, and suggestions for projects. Entries are tagged with one of 16 subject symbols in the margin (such as a dog symbol for animals), and each volume contains an index by subject symbol; Volume 4 also contains a general index. The set has over 2,000 illustrations, mostly in color, but has therefore much less space for text. *Booklist* judged that it would "have limited value as a reference set for school assignments," but found it an "attractive and readable browsing set for primary and elementary-aged children," for a "general introduction to a subject and for quick reference." (For more information, contact: Doubleday, Inc., 666 Fifth Avenue, New York, NY 10103; 800-223-6834 or 212-765-6500.)

Booklist is a standard library journal, which does an annual review of the current editions of encyclopedias and also of dictionaries. Interested parents should ask at their library's reference desk for the appropriate issues.

TESS: A Guide to Computer Software

TESS is The Educational Software Selector, a comprehensive database of educational computer programs for every level, from preschool through college, which describes over 10,000 educational programs, providing information about content, grade level, hardware compatibility, supplier, price information, review score, and citations to reviews. The database is primarily for professional librarians and educators, but information on approximately 2,400 of the most recent and highly rated educational software programs is now available in print form in *The Latest and Best of TESS* (1991–92 ed.). Parents who own or plan to buy a home computer and who want to enhance their children's reading, math, and other learning skills can find information on programs right for their children's ages, interests, and capabilities in this directory.

The TESS database is maintained by the Educational Products Information Exchange, better known as EPIE, an independent, not-for-profit, consumer-oriented organization, funded primarily by school systems, educational agencies, and foundations. It was founded in 1967 to provide independent evaluation of educational products in general, originally focusing on print textbooks and audiovisual materials, but in recent years also including computer software. (For more information, contact: EPIE Institute, 103-3 West Montauk Highway, Hampton Bays, NY 11946; 516-728-9100.)

Another source of information about computer programs is *Only the Best: Annual Guide to Highest-Rated Education Software-Multimedia for Preschool–Grade 12*, Shirley B. Neill and George W. Neill, eds., published by Educational News Service. In addition to annual volumes, a cumulative volume, published in 1989, covers 1985–1989.

For information on specific computer programs covered in this book, see the index on page 227.

Something New Under the SAT

Today's parents grew up under the sign of the SAT, the dreaded Scholastic Aptitude Test, the "gatekeeper" exam that largely makes or breaks college entrance and scholarship offerings for most students. Today's students still face the SAT, but some changes are taking place.

For starters, many school systems have established SAT review classes to help students prepare for the exams, openly acknowledging what has long been clear: that students who prepare intensively for the SAT do better than those who do not. Such SAT preparation and review programs vary widely. Some are offered for a low fee as a series of Saturday, late afternoon, or evening classes; some are informal lunchtime tutoring sessions; some are free, semester-long courses, often for credit; some are courses offered on a cable television channel (sometimes for a fee, sometimes not); and some are centered on computer programs or self-help videotapes, often made available through the school. Some schools even routinely offer practice SATs as "warm-ups" in English and mathematics classes.

A student may, for example, take a course in "developmental reading," in which the textbook is an SAT preparation guide, and the course includes instruction on how to approach SAT questions, as by narrowing choices on the multiple-choice exam. Another student may spend a certain part of weekly class time studying vocabulary such as "propitious" or "querulous," drawn directly from previous SAT exams. The object is not only to prepare students on the content and approach, but also to make them so familiar with the SAT format as to ease the test-phobia that has hindered so many SAT-takers in the past.

Such SAT preparation is being provided partly in response to a demand from parents, as an alternative to the costly commercial preparation courses affordable only to some. But school systems also have a stake in test scores: In this era of school choice, parents deciding which school their child should attend often base their judgments to a large extent on how well the school's students have been doing on such exams.

All this is a sharp break from the times when students were told there was no way they could prepare for the SAT because it was an "aptitude," not an "achievement," test. Schools have in years past been reluctant to "teach to the test," but even the College Entrance Examination Board, which sponsors the SAT, now acknowledges that studies show organized review can affect a student's performance.

For years, students have been preparing themselves for the SAT in a different way: by taking the shorter Preliminary Scholastic Aptitude Test (PSAT) in their freshman or sophomore years. But now the SAT itself is being taken by many far younger students. By 1991, over 100,000 of the students taking the SAT were seventh and eighth graders, making up a surprising 6 percent of the students taking the exam annually. Some are taking it as early preparation for the tests they will take at college-application time, or as an overview of the kind of material they will be learning in the coming years. But many are taking the SATs as entrance exams for college-based special summer programs for academically gifted children, such as the Johns Hopkins University's Center for Talented Youth program, started in 1972, and others modeled on it.

Many parents and educators sharply criticize the giving of SATs to children who have not even been taught the algebra and geometry that form much of the content of the mathematical portion. Critics are also concerned that the stress of taking such exams further diminishes the years of childhood. Educators who run programs for the gifted generally acknowledge such problems but say they have no better way to evaluate prospective entrants. They also note that many bright young people are able to solve mathematical problems or understand words they have never seen before by using their general knowledge and intelligence. The College Board, which administers the SAT, does not encourage use of the test with such young students, but has not attempted to bar it. Recognizing the need, however, an advisory panel has recommended that the College Board develop new tests of college potential to be used with seventh and eighth graders—though many people object to yet *another* standardized test for America's already overtested students.

Meanwhile, the Scholastic Aptitude Test itself is undergoing some changes. In late 1990, the College Board announced that it would be revising the test significantly, with a preliminary revised test being offered for the first time as the PSAT in the fall of 1993, and scheduled for full introduction in the SAT itself in the spring of 1994. The main changes will be:

- Increased emphasis on reading, including longer reading passages.
- Elimination of verbal questions involving antonyms, word opposites such as "scarce" and "plentiful." Such questions have been frequently criticized because the material is not directly taught in high schools, though it is drawn from general reading.
- More emphasis on problem-solving ability in the mathematics section, with 20 percent of the multiple-choice questions being replaced by questions calling for students to work out and show their solutions with pencil on paper.
- Allowing the optional use of hand-held calculators. Some critics

are concerned, however, that low-income students, who may be unfamiliar with using calculators, will be at a disadvantage.

• Addition of a separate, optional 20-minute writing exam. Various groups, including some civil rights activists and politicians from heavily immigrant areas, have fought against the inclusion of a writing exam in the SAT itself, as posing an undue hardship for recent immigrants for whom English is a second language. Others say that making the writing exam optional sends the wrong message—that writing is a skill of peripheral importance—when decline in writing skills is a major and widespread concern.

• The addition of language proficiency exams in Japanese and Chinese.

• Provision of an English exam for people for whom English is a second language.

Some educators have hailed the changes as the most sweeping in decades, and as likely to encourage schools to focus less on teaching toward multiple-choice tests, and more on building thinking, analysis, writing, and problem-solving techniques. Critics have charged that the changes are merely superficial, and that they will not improve the SAT's ability to predict student success in college—the purported aim of the test. The College Board has also announced long-term plans to employ computers for mass test taking (see "Testing by Computer—In Your Child's Future?" below). (For more information, contact: The College Board, 45 Columbus Avenue, New York, NY 10023; 212-713-8000.)

Some students do not do well on any traditional tests, SATs or otherwise. For them and their parents, a new book may be helpful: *The Other Route into College: Alternative Admission*, by Stacy Needle (Random, 1991). This is a catalog of colleges that have alternative entrance policies or programs, for students who do not meet the usual admissions standards for high school grades and test scores, for whatever reason, but can in other ways demonstrate the potential to succeed in college.

Testing by Computer—In Your Child's Future?

Maybe so. Starting in October 1992, the Graduate Record Examination (GRE), given to college students for postgraduate entrance, is being given by computer. This may be the wave of the future for standardized testing at all educational levels. The earliest versions tested and used were essentially the old paper-and-pencil tests transferred to computer. But from October 1992, the computer's capacities are being used to make a customized test; in what is called *adaptive testing*, the sequence of questions presented will depend on the answers to previous questions, making the test interactive in the manner of a video or computer game, or a children's mystery, where the story is individualized by the reader's choices. As a student answers correctly, the questions get progressively more difficult; an incorrect answer will lead to an easier line of questions, designed more clearly to demonstrate the student's skills, abilities, and limitations. Questions are weighted according to their difficulty. The actual number of questions asked will depend on the student's performance, but test designers anticipate that—because of the customization—the tests will be considerably shorter, allowing students to complete in one day or less the testing that currently takes several days.

According to students who have taken early versions, the new computer test is much easier to take. It could theoretically be given at an infinite variety of times and places (rather than in a few restricted days and sites, as now) and produce scores immediately on completion. The customized nature of the test is also expected to give a more accurate and reliable test result.

However, at least in the early years, students unfamiliar with computers may be at a disadvantage. Another difficulty with computer testing, at least in early versions, is that students do not have available to them some basic working methods they have been used to in paper-and-pencil tests: They can't scratch out wrong answers before deciding on the final answer in a multiple choice; they can't underline key words or sentences in text passages; and they can't go back to review previous problems, as many students are helped by doing. Some of these problems are being corrected for later versions, however.

The Scholastic Aptitude Test (SAT) is developing a computerized version to appear sometime in the 1990s. As an intermediate stage, starting in the spring of 1994, students will be able to use hand-held calculators (see "Something New Under the SAT" on page 182). By the end of the 1990s, when most of today's preschoolers will be facing precollege examination hurdles, computerized testing may be standard. (For more information, contact: The College Board, 45 Columbus Avenue, New York, NY 10023; 212-713-8000.)

Off to College

While much of parents' and students' attention is focused on getting *into* college, the question of what happens after entrance has received much less attention. However, two new books partly remedy that lack. One is *The Truth about College: How to Survive and Succeed as a Student in the 90's*, by Scott Edelstein (Carol/Lyle Stuart, 1991). This is a straightforward guide to problems and concerns of students in or heading for college, including coping with classes and obtaining financial aid. Another is *College Survival: A Crash Course for Students by Students*, 2d ed., by Greg Gottesman and friends (Arco/Prentice Hall, 1990), which offers the "inside story on college life" and loads of practical tips, on everything from pulling the all-nighter to conquering laundry and taking tests to joining a fraternity or sorority.

And, recognizing that once the student is indeed off to college the family dynamics change, there is *When Kids Go to College: A Parent's Guide to Changing Relationships*, by Barbara M. Newman and Phillip R. Newman (Ohio State University Press, 1992). This work, by a pair of psychologist/professors, discusses how family relationships alter when a child leaves for college, stressing how parents can ease the adjustment and help their child deal with the problems encountered in the college setting.

What's *New* in Parenting Resources

Kids Do Not Come with Instructions

That's the message of the Parents' Resource Center, USA (PRCUSA), which bills itself as "the original 900 guidance and information resource for parents." This nationwide "900" telephone service is the Parents' Advice and Information Network, popularly dubbed the Parents' Advice Line, started in September 1991. It is designed to provide parents with "affordable expert guidance, support," including both traditional and new or alternative ideas on parenting and child-raising issues, to help with the "questions, problems, fears, and anxieties of parenting . . . from infancy through adolescence."

PRCUSA is a New York–based group of psychologists, social workers, and child-development and parenting experts, all with master's or doctor's degrees in their fields and with clinical experience with children and families. Callers to the 900 number can speak directly with a parenting specialist about their problem, in total confidentiality and (if desired) anonymity. PRCUSA notes that "there are no pre-recorded messages, voice mailboxes, or computerized phone menus directing your call." Rather, the PRCUSA staff member listens to each caller's specific situation or problem and provides the guidance or information they seek; this can include recommendations of appropriate local or national services and agencies, as well as written or other materials related to the caller's concerns. The service's hours are 7 A.M. to 11 P.M. EST, seven days a week. The cost (as of 1992) is $2.99 per minute, which is charged automatically to the caller's regular telephone bill; the average call lasts 7 to 10 minutes.

Topics on which PRCUSA staff members can provide guidance and information cover the whole range of parental concerns, "from general developmental questions to specific behavioral and discipline techniques," and include concerns such as "bedwetting, the emotional impact of divorce upon children, sleeping problems, teenage alcohol use, emotional development concerns, eating concerns, coping with colic, the birth of a second child, conflicts over the types of discipline to use, dealing with tantrums, shoplifting, learning disabilities, children feeling bad about themselves, problems with school and/or learning, the encouragement of the parent during a difficult period, and more. . . ." However, founder Meri Lacon—herself a school social worker and mother of two young children—stresses that PRCUSA is "not a substitute for therapy, psychological counseling, medical advice, or for seeing a pediatrician"; rather it aims to offer immediate, affordable information and guidance in the privacy and convenience of a caller's home. (For more information, contact: Parents' Resource Center, USA, P.O. Box 158, New Paltz, NY 12561; 914-255-8119; to use the service, call 900-976-4646.)

Parents may also want to consult reference books designed for parents, among them:

◆ *The Parent's Desk Reference*, by Irene Franck and David Brownstone (Prentice Hall, 1991), which includes discussions of all the major medical, educational, legal, and social questions and issues relating to parents and children, describing organizations offering help and information, as well as related written works for parents and children, and a separate index of hotlines and helplines.

◆ *Help for Children From Infancy to Adulthood*, 5th ed., by Miriam J. Williams Wilson (Rocky River Publishers, 1991), a directory that offers information on hotlines or organizations providing help and information to parents or others working with children; It also includes appendixes of regional poison control centers and state child-abuse and missing-children organizations. (For more information, contact: Rocky River Publishers, P.O. Box 1679, Shepherdstown, WV 25443.)

For some other sources of parenting support, see the parenting support-and-activity groups in "Getting a Move On: The Gymboree® Way" on page 17 and the parenting columns and clubs on computer in "Is There a Prodigy in Your Future?" on page 39.

Children's Problems—When to Get Help

As their children go from stage to stage, from infancy to adulthood, parents are often confused and unsure about when a child's difficulty in transition or problems in coping are expected and in the normal range, and when professional intervention may be advisable. A new book that focuses on just those questions is *When Your Child Needs Help: A Parent's Guide to Therapy for Children*, by Norma Doft with Barbara Aria (Harmony, 1992). Doft offers parents some guidelines for assessing the severity of a child's "growing pains," suggestions on how to choose the therapist best suited to their child, and discussions of what both parents and children should expect from therapy, and how they can aid in its success.

Both child and parent can be curious, unsure, and anxious when a young child is just starting play therapy. A new book has been written for families in this situation: *A Child's First Book About Play Therapy*, by Marc Nemiroff, Ph.D., and Jane Annunziata, Psy.D. (American Psychological Association, 1991). Using simple language and illustrations appropriate for children ages 4 to 7, the book answers questions such as: What is play therapy? Who goes to play therapy, and why? What happens in a session? (For more information, contact: APA, Order Department, P.O. Box 2710, Hyattsville, MD 20784-0710; 703-247-7705.)

A more professionally oriented book is Ann Cattanach's *Play Therapy with Abused Children* (Jessica Kingsley Publishers, 1992), which explores how use of play therapy can help abused children heal their distress and make sense of their experiences through their own creativity, the underlying idea being that play is a developmental activity. (For more information, contact: Taylor & Francis Group, 1900 Frost Road, Suite 101, Bristol, PA 19007-1598; 800-821-8312.)

For a wider look at child psychology and normal development, there is *Family Encyclopedia of Child Psychology and Development: An Easy-to-Understand Parent's Guide*, by Frank J. Bruno (Wiley, 1992).

Other recent books about children with psychological or emotional problems are:

* *A Child Like That*, by Rikva Walburg (Philipp Feldheim, 1992). A young mother's struggle to come to terms with her child's mental disability.
* *Portrait of the Artist as a Young Patient: Psychodynamic Studies of the Creative Personality*, by Gerald Alper (Plenum, 1992).
* *There's a Boy in Here*, by Judy Barron and Sean Barron (Simon & Schuster, 1992). A mother and son tell the story of their experience with his autism, from the difficulties of learning about the disease and trying to obtain a proper diagnosis to coping with it and gradually overcoming the characteristic inability to communicate.
* *Ghost Girl: The Story of a Child Who Refused to Talk*, by Torrey L. Hayden (Little, Brown, 1991). The true story of a teacher's efforts to help a severely disturbed child, emotionally neglected, sexually abused, and possibly a victim of a satanic cult.

Parents will also want to look at "Putting Child Abuse in the Past" on page 206 and "Kids Do Not Come with Instructions" on page 188.

Buying Best—and Smart—for Kids

Parents want the best for their kids. In this economic climate, they also want to get the best *buys* for their kids. Several books are designed to help parents pick the safest, best-designed, most convenient, and most reliable products, and to buy them at a modest price. Among them are:

* *Guide to Baby Products*, 3d ed., by Sandy Jones with Werner Freitag and the editors of Consumer Reports Books (Consumer Reports Books, 1991). Helps parents in "buying the best for your baby," evaluating safety, convenience, and durability of baby products, including brand-name ratings and recommendations, and gives buying advice and product recall information. Product types covered include backpacks and soft carriers; bassinets, carrycots, and cradles; bathtub and bathing accessories; breast-feeding and bottle-feeding equipment and pacifiers; changing tables; child restraints and booster seats for traveling in cars; clothing and footwear; cribs and mattresses; diapers

and accessories; baby foods; gates; health and safety devices; high chairs and booster seats; infant seats; nursery decor and accessories; playpens; portable cribs; portable hook-on chairs; strollers; swings; toilet-training aids; toys; and walkers and jumpers.

 • *The Childwise Catalog*, rev. ed., by Jack Gillis and Mary Ellen R. Fise, Consumer Federation of America (HarperCollins, 1990). A brand-specific "consumer guide to buying the safest and best products" for newborns through children age 5. The first part of the book is organized by age group (newborn to 6 months, 6 months to 2 years, and 2 to 5 years), and includes shopping lists and checklists of items appropriate for children in those age groups. The second part of the book covers services purchased for children, including child care, preschool, and baby-sitting; health matters; and traveling. The third part focuses on safety inside and outside the home, and protection (as from abduction or abuse), and also offers resources for parents.

 • *Bargains-by-Mail for Baby and You: Where to Buy for Your Baby, Nursery, Playroom, and Yourself at Mail-Order Discount Prices*, by Dawn Hardy (Prima, 1991). A book describing mail-order houses and catalogs from which parents can buy children's and other products, noting also which provide special incentives or discounts to *Bargains-by-Mail* users.

 • *Great Buys for Kids: How to Save Money on Everything for Children and Teens*, by Sue Goldstein (Penguin, 1992).

What About Me?

That's the deeply felt but often unspoken question for young children when another baby is on the way. Parents concerned about how to handle such questions may find guidance and help in some new books, such as:

 • *Will There Be a Lap for Me?*, by Dorothy Corey (Albert Whitman, 1992). A story about a young child who can no longer sit on his mother's lap when she becomes pregnant, but is reassured by once again being able to do so after the birth (for ages 2 to 5).

 • *Bigger Than a Baby*, by Harriet Ziefert (HarperCollins, 1991). Outlines early childhood development—physical, social, intellectual, and emotional—for young children themselves, placing it in the context of the growth of all living things. Using anatomically correct drawings and incorporating various ethnic groups, this book may be especially useful for children adjusting to new siblings.

• *Don't Wake the Baby*, by Jonathan Franklin (Farrar, Straus and Giroux, 1991). A picture book for children ages 3 to 6; shows young Marvin acting out imaginative roles—matador, magician, and the like—around the crib, despite parents' cautions not to disturb the infant.

• *The Book of Babies: A First Picture Book of All the Things That Babies Do*, photographs by Jo Ford (Random House, 1991). For children ages 6 months to 3 years.

• *My Baby Brother*, by Harriet Haims (Dorling Kindersley, 1992). For children in preschool through grade 3.

Has Parenting Been Taken Over by Professionals?

That's the thesis of Sonia Taitz's *Mothering Heights: Reclaiming Motherhood from the Experts* (Morrow, 1992). Recognizing that parents are bombarded with often-contradictory, supposedly scientific advice from all quarters, on everything from prenatal care to the "right" toys to how to get a child into the "right" preschool for a fast-track education, Taitz urges parents to follow their own instincts. A columnist for *Child* magazine, she uses wit as well as commonsense wisdom in poking fun at advice overload on topics from labor to day care to overvigilance (as in her "The Everything Can Kill Him Chapter"), in the process providing some practical parenting advice of her own, drawing on her own mothering experiences.

Meanwhile, parents continue to seek enlightenment, guidance, support, information, and comfort from among the host of parenting and child-raising works published each year. Here are a selection of recent offerings on a wide range of parent/child–related topics:

On Parenting in General

• *The Parent's License* (1991), produced by Brenda Reiswerg and directed by Nancy Malone. This film/video (for purchase or rental) illuminates the responsibility of parenting by presenting a fictional tale based on the fanciful notion that people must pass inspection and be licensed before becoming parents. (For more information, contact: Pyramid Film & Video, Box 1048, Santa Monica, CA 90406.)

• *When Partners Become Parents: The Big Life Change for Couples*, by Carolyn Pape Cowan and Philip A. Cowan (Basic, 1992). Analyzes how a baby's arrival changes a marriage, based on a 10-year-study of 100 California couples having their first baby, by the co-directors of the Becoming a Family Project; it reviews the parents' relationship before and after the birth, including the decision to have the child.

• *Dr. Mom's Parenting Guide: Commonsense Guidance for the Life of Your Child*, by Marianne E. Neifert (Dutton, 1991). A comforting, motherly guide by a pediatrician and mother of five. Neifert also is the author of *Dr. Mom: A Guide to Baby and Child Care* (Putnam, 1986).

• *Mothering: The Complete Guide to Mothers of All Ages*, by Dr. Grace Ketterman (Thomas Nelson, 1991). Gives advice on successful mothering and grandmothering in every area of life—physical, emotional, spiritual.

• *Your 30-Day Journey to Being a World-Class Mother* and *Your 30-Day Journey to Being a World-Class Father*, by C. W. Neal (Thomas Nelson, 1992). Offers day-by-day pointers to becoming more nurturing parents.

• *Raising Your Spirited Child: A Guide for Parents Whose Child Is More Intense, Sensitive, Perceptive, Persistent, Energetic*, by Mary Sheedy Kurcinka (HarperCollins, 1991).

• The "Parenting Keys" series from Barron's includes *Keys to Parenting Your One-Year-Old* (1992) and *Keys to Preparing for Your Second Child* (1991) by Meg Zweibach; *Keys to Child Safety and Care of Minor Childhood Injuries* (1992), by Robert J. Vinci; *Keys to Parenting Your Teenager* (1992), by Don H. Fontenelle; *Keys to Dealing with Childhood Allergies* (1992), by Judy L. Bachman; *Keys to Comforting the Fussy Baby* (1991), *Keys to Becoming a Father* (1991), *Keys to Caring and Preparing for Your Newborn* (1991), and *Keys to Breast Feeding* (1991), all by William Sears; *Keys to Children's Nutrition* (1991), by Carolyn E. Moore and others; and *Keys to Choosing Child Care* (1991), by Stevanne Auerbach.

• *Parents' Guide to Raising Responsible Kids: Preschool through Teen Years*, by Karyn Feiden (Prentice Hall, 1991). Takes a developmental view of child rearing, especially stressing how parental responsibility and discipline change as children themselves grow and change. Topics covered include "Building a Child's Self-Esteem," "Praise and

Criticism: The Art of Providing Feedback," and "Education Begins at Home." Part of the "Children's Television Workshop Family Living" series.

♦ *Familyhood: Nurturing the Values That Matter*, by Dr. Lee Salk (Simon & Schuster, 1992). This new work by the well-known late child psychologist focuses on identifying the prime family values and how to nurture them in an age of upheaval for family life.

♦ *Parenting by Heart*, by Ron Taffel with Melinda Blau (Addison-Wesley, 1991). Aims to help parents "connect" with their kids.

♦ *Fathers and Sons: One of the Most Challenging of Family Relationships*, by Lewis Yablonsky (Gardner, 1990).

♦ *Tough-Minded Parenting*, by Joe Batten and others (Broadman, 1991). Batten, an author of business management books, applies management and leadership techniques to the job of parenting, aiming to help parents give their children strength and stability, while allowing them breathing and growing room, in an atmosphere of firm fairness. The work also stresses how to create a family environment that develops children's value systems.

♦ *Connections: Using Personality Types to Draw Parents and Kids Closer*, by Jim Brawner with Duncan Naenicke (Moody Press, 1991). Advises parents on how to understand and deal with the unique personality of each family member.

♦ *Spoiled Rotten: Today's Children and How to Change Them*, by Fred G. Gosman (Villard, 1992). This light-handed book explores the unhappiness that has resulted from children having and being given too much, and calls for a return to child-rearing basics, including appropriate discipline and children's accountability for their own actions.

♦ *Positive Parenting Fitness: A Parent's Resource Guide to Nutrition, Stress Reduction, Total Exercise, and Practical Information*, by Sylvia Klein Olkin (Avery, 1991). Offers a holistic approach to parenting, based on the theory that parenting fitness is a state of body as well as of positive attitude; the book focuses on natural nutrition, relaxation skills, stretching and breathing exercises, and interaction with the new infant.

♦ *Different and Wonderful—Raising Black Children in a Race-Conscious Society*, by Darlene Powell Hopson and Derek Hopson (Prentice Hall Press, 1992).

♦ *The Hadassah Book of Jewish Parenting*, Roselyn Bell, ed. (Avon, 1991).

♦ *Raising Jewish Children in a Contemporary World: The Modern*

Parent's Guide to Creating a Jewish Home, by Steven Carr Reuben (Prima, 1992). A rabbi's approach to Judaism as a religion "not of creed but of deed," addressing both Jewish and interfaith parents.

On Parenting Babies and Young Children

* *Raising Baby Right: A Guide to Avoiding the 20 Most Common Mistakes New Parents Make,* by Charles Schaefer and Theresa Di-Geronimo (Prince, 1992).
* *The Complete Baby Check List: A Total Organizing System for Parents,* by Elyse Karlin and others (Avon, 1992).
* *Baby Tactics: Parenting Tips That Really Work,* by Barbara Albers Hill (Avery, 1991).
* *Caring for Your Baby and Young Child: Birth to Age Five,* Stephen P. Shelov and others, eds. (Bantam, 1991).
* *Caring for Your Baby and Young Child: Birth Through 5,* by American Academy of Pediatrics Staff (American Academy of Pediatrics/Bantam, 1991).
* *The Parenting Challenge: Your Child's Behavior from 6 to 12,* by Arnold Rincover (Pocket, 1991).
* *Kid Think,* by Dr. William Lee Carter (Word, 1992). Advises on how to deal with "the six most common behavioral problems of children," partly by learning how to think from the child's point of view.
* *I Wanna Do It Myself: A Radical Three-Tiered Approach to Helping Your Child Achieve Independence,* by William Sammons, M.D. (Hyperion, 1992). A pediatrician, Sammons suggests how to help a child become calm and controlled and provide her or his own entertainment.
* *The Little Girl Book,* by David Laskin and Kathleen O'Neill (Ballantine, 1992). A guide to parents on how to raise their female children, from birth to age 8, in a difficult world.
* *Raising Your Type A Child: How to Help Your Child Make the Most of an Achievement Oriented Personality,* by Steven Shelov and John Kelly (Pocket, 1992). Shares a pediatrician's advice for parents of ambitious, aggressive children.
* *How to Raise a Healthy Achiever: Escaping the Type A Treadmill,* by Laurel Hughes (Abingdon, 1992). Suggests ways to encourage achievement without unhealthy distortion of life.
* *Stress and Your Child: Its Causes, Dangers and Prevention,* by Dr. Archibald D. Hart (Word, 1992). Examines causes for moods,

resentments, and insecurities, and emphasizes development of positive coping habits in children.

• *The Importance of Being Baby*, by Bertrand G. Cramer (Addison-Wesley, 1992). A Swiss psychiatrist and mother-infant psychotherapist, Cramer believes that infant problems, such as fussiness or failure to thrive, stem largely from conscious or unconscious messages parents are sending the baby. Reviewers felt that the work had a new perspective but took insufficient consideration of other causes, such as physical problems.

See also "Sleep—The Impossible Dream" on page 208.

On Parenting Teens

• *Caring for Your Adolescent: Ages 12–21*, Donald E. Greydanus, ed. (Bantam, 1991). Presents a series of advisory essays by specialists in adolescent medicine, on physical, psychological, sexual, and social growth and development; education; and "care and feeding" questions, problems, and solutions relating to adolescents, emphasizing especially medical concerns.

• *When Love Is Not Enough: Parenting Through Tough Times*, by Stephen Arterburn and Jim Burns (Focus on the Family, 1992). Helps parents help their teenagers through the major crises of adolescence.

• *Decoding Your Teenager: How to Understand Each Other During the Turbulent Years*, by Michael DeSisto (Morrow, 1991). This parents' survival guide explores teenage behaviors and suggests how parents can help their children through adolescent difficulties, stressing patience and communication, especially with troubled teens. DeSisto operates two schools for teenagers.

• *You Can Say No to Your Teenager: And Other Strategies for Effective Parenting in the 1990's*, by Jeannette Shalov and others (Addison-Wesley, 1991). Stresses how parents can best deal with the inevitable problems of teens, and how to avoid some of them, if only by focusing on what is truly important and ignoring the rest, with many real-life examples.

• *Parent/Teen Breakthrough: The Relationship Approach*, by Mira Kirshenbaum and Charles Foster (NAL/Plume, 1991). Posits that during the "5,000 days of adolescence," as a child is preparing to leave home, parents must make the crucial shift from being caretakers to being a resource.

• *"Get Out of My Life, but First Could You Drive Me and Cheryl to the Mall?": A Parent's Guide to the New Teenager*, by Anthony E. Wolf (Farrar/Noonday, 1991). This question-and-answer guide for parents of teenagers, with its light-handed, often humorous look at teen-centered concerns (including the difficult questions of sex, drugs, drinking, and suicide), offers parents alternative methods and approaches. Wolf is a practicing child and adolescent psychologist who has raised two of his own teens.

• *How to Live with Your Kids When You've Already Lost Your Mind*, by Ken Davis (Zondervan, 1992). A companion to the author's earlier *How to Live with Your Parents Without Losing Your Mind* (Zondervan, 1988).

• *When Good Kids Do Bad Things: A Survival Guide for Parents*, by Katherine Gordy Levine (Norton, 1991). Seeks to help parents in dealing with troubled adolescents, such as those with drug abuse or violent behavior problems.

• *The Teenage Book of Manners . . . Please!*, by Fred Hartley and family (Barbour & Co., 1991). An illustrated book of practical advice.

Parents will also want to see "I'll Never Do That to *My* Children!" on page 204, "It's a Tough World Out There" below, "Parents in Training for Discipline" on page 202, and "Putting Child Abuse in the Past" on page 206.

It's a Tough World Out There

Ask any parent. Ask any child. One of the most difficult parenting issues revolves around preparing children to meet the problems and dangers that surround them—that surround us all. Several new works have been published to help parents deal with this formidable task.

Talking with Your Child about a Troubled World, by Lynne S. Dumas (Ballantine/Fawcett, 1992), is a guide to help parents help their young children (preschool to preteen) understand and deal with the key social issues they face, including homelessness, racism, unemployment, war, divorce, ageism, and natural disasters. In each case, the book focuses on children's most common questions and fears, and provides references to organizations and other books for parents and children. Perhaps of most use, Dumas offers general guidance on how to communicate with children on such subjects—specifically, how to listen, respect children's feelings, be open and honest, and talk with children in different age groups.

Tough Questions: Talking Straight with Your Kids About the Real World, by Sheila Kitzinger and Celia Kitzinger (Harvard Common, 1991), explores how to prepare children to deal with difficult areas such as death, prejudice, aggression, violence, and the complexities of friendship. The work was written by an English mother and daughter, with multicultural experiences and case histories.

Parents' Guide to Raising Kids in a Changing World: Preschool through Teen Years, by Dian G. Smith (Prentice Hall, 1991), focuses on the nature of today's families and the social pressures on them, including drugs, changing sexual patterns, and single-parent homes. Part of the "Children's Television Workshop" series, the work especially urges parents to consider carefully which values they are passing along to their children and the importance of role models for them.

Among other recent parenting works in a similar vein are:

♦ *What Worries Parents Most: Help Parents Need to Protect Their Kids*, by Marlin Maddoux (Harvest House, 1992). A guide for parents on the major challenges children face.

♦ *Who Are My Real Friends? Peer Pressure: A Teen Survival Guide*, by Joe White (Questar, 1992). Offers "strong yet tender" advice for parents to give their children.

♦ *Please Don't Tell My Parents*, by Dawson McAllister (Word, 1992). Explores "questions parents never hear from their kids."

Among recent works on related topics meant for kids themselves are:

♦ *Say No and Mean It* (Sunburst Communications, 1991). This video aims at helping youngsters (grades 2 through 4) learn how to say no in difficult situations, using assertiveness-training techniques to build children's confidence and help prepare them for handling peer pressure now and later in life. (For more information, contact: Sunburst Communications, 39 Washington Avenue, Pleasantville, NY 10570.)

♦ *But Everyone Else Looks So Sure of Themselves: A Guide to Surviving the Teen Years*, by Denise V. Lang (Betterway, 1991). For children in grades 7 through 9, this work compares adolescence to scuba diving, in which most waters explored are both new and unfamiliar, and offers teens advice on navigating through the shoals.

♦ *What, Me Worry? How to Hang in When Your Problems Stress You Out*, by Alice Fleming (Scribner's, 1992). This gently humorous book advises children ages 12 and up on how to deal with worries, problems, and anxieties, using pertinent real-life examples.

• *Social Savvy: A Teenager's Guide to Feeling Confident in Any Situation*, by Judith Ré with Meg Schneider (Summit, 1991). Offers general guidelines as well as specifics on social skills, such as how to build a friendship or how to ask for a bigger allowance. For grades 7 through 12.

• The "Lifeskills Library" (Rosen Publishing, 1992). A new series of books focusing on the practical skills that adolescents need to develop as they prepare to live independently. Designed for grades 7 through 12, and especially useful for "reluctant readers," the series includes: *Setting Goals, Independent Living, Shopping Savvy, The World of Work, Great Grooming for Guys, Great Grooming for Girls, Staying Healthy*, and *Money Smarts*. (For more information, contact: Rosen Publishing, 29 East 21st Street, New York, NY 10010; 800-237-9932.)

• *Surviving after High School: Overcoming Life's Hurdles*, by Arthur J. Heine (J-Mart Press, 1991). A guide for young people going out on their own, from high school straight into independence, though it is also useful to those heading toward college, with its practical advice on topics such as managing money, finding an apartment, arranging for insurance, searching for a job, eating right, and being careful about sex. (For more information, contact: J-Mart Press, P.O. Box 8884, Virginia Beach, VA 23450-8884.)

• *Straight Answers for Kids About Life, God, and Growing Up*, by William Coleman (David C. Cook, 1992). Answers questions of interest to children ages 8 to 12.

• *Greetings from High School*, by Marian Salzman, Teresa Reisgies, and many teenage contributors (Peterson's Guides, 1991).

• *Cults*, by Sarah Stevens (Crestwood/Macmillan, 1992). Part of the "Facts About" series, for grades 5 and 6.

See also "On Parenting Teens," under "Has Parenting Been Taken Over by Professionals?" on page 193.

Help in the Fight Against Drugs

The spread of drugs and their effects on both individuals and society continue to be high on the list of parental concerns. And because the drug culture threatens to influence younger and younger children, parents must start very early to educate their children about the dangers that may face them. A series of three recent books from Troll Associates is designed to help them do just that: *What Are Drugs?* (1990), *Drugs and Our World* (1990), and *You Can Say No to Drugs* (1990; Spanish version, 1991), all by Gretchen Super. Written for children in preschool through grade 3, these works explain what drugs are, what they do in the body, the consequences of drug abuse, the differences between medicines and illegal drugs (an especially important question for very young children to get straight, right at the start), and from whom they should—and should not—take medicines. In the process, the books also describe the most commonly abused drugs and discuss how to deal with peer pressure.

For parents themselves, there is *Straight Talk with Kids: Improving Communication, Building Trust, and Keeping Your Children Drug Free* (Bantam, 1991). This work stresses prevention of drug involvement, giving solid parenting advice on communication, self-esteem, and peer pressure, and also emphasizes the need for intervention with children who have become drug users, offering advice on how to confront the child, where to get help, and how to go on from there. *Straight Talk with Kids* is a project of the nonprofit Scott Newman Center, which seeks to reach kids before they experiment with drugs; the center is named after Paul Newman's son, whose death was drug-related. TAB Books has also recently published two helpful books: *Drug Free Zone: Keeping Drugs Out of Your Child's School* (1991), by Carol Sager, and *Keep Your Kids Straight: What Parents Need to Know about Drugs and Alcohol* (1991), by Ronald Main and Judy Zervas. Note also that *The Parent's Desk Reference*, by Irene Franck and David Brownstone (Prentice Hall, 1991), contains a substantial section of organizations, agencies, and other helping resources related to substance abuse.

Because of the urgency of the problem, many firms have been producing publications designed to help educate children as to the danger of drugs. Among the recent works are:

◆ *Say No and Know Why: Kids Learn About Drugs*, by Wendy Wax (Walker, 1991). For ages 7 to 10.

◆ The "Drug Abuse Prevention Library" from Rosen Publishing, a series for grades 4 through 12. Titles include *Marijuana, Crack, Cocaine, Heroin, Drugs on Your Streets, Drugs and Your Brothers and Sisters, Drugs and Your Parents*, and *Drugs and Your Friends*.

◆ The "Drug-Alert" series, published by Twenty-First Century

Books, for children ages 8 to 12. Titles include *Focus on Opiates* (1991) and *Focus on Medicines* (1991), by Susan DeStefano; *Focus on Steroids* (1991), by Katherine Talmadge; and *Focus on Hallucinogens* (1991) and *The Drug-Alert Dictionary and Resource Guide* (1991), by Jeffrey Shulman. The latter offers a guide to the main terms, concepts, and issues relating to drugs, along with key hotlines and drug agencies.

♦ The "Social Impact" series, also from Twenty-First Century Books, explores the effects of drug abuse on society, for children in grades 4 through 7. It includes *Drugs and the Family* (1991), by Susan DeStefano, about living with a parent or sibling who abuses drugs or alcohol, exploring short- and long-term effects, outlining ways to cope, and suggesting ways to find help; *Drugs and Crime* (1991), by Jeffrey Shulman, which details the relationship between the growers, sellers, and users of drugs; and *Drugs and Sports*, by Katherine S. Talmadge (1991), which relates true stories of athletes whose lives have been affected by drug use.

♦ *Drugs in the Body: Effects of Abuse*, by Mark Yoslow (Watts, 1992). This takes quite a different approach, tracing the minute-by-minute effects of cocaine, crack, opium, morphine, heroin, marijuana, hashish, LSD and other psychedelics, amphetamines, and PCP, as well as their long-term effects.

♦ *Chemical Dependency: Opposing Viewpoints*, Charles P. Cozic and Karin Swicher, eds. (Greenhaven Press, 1991). For grades 7 through 12, part of the "Opposing Viewpoints" series.

♦ *Early Warning: Recognizing the Signs of Addiction*, produced by Advanced American Communications (1991). A video for sale or rental, for ages 12 and up, this shows through flashbacks how families and teens themselves often deny drug problems. (For more information, contact: MTI Film & Video, 108 Wilmot Road, Deerfield, IL 60015.)

Parents will also want to read "Anabolic Steroids and Their Substitutes: Controlled Substances" on page 110.

Parents in Training for Discipline

New research has been showing that discipline is more effective when first applied to *parents*, then to children. Several studies have shown that parents rely heavily on their instincts, which are not always useful; respond emotionally, often ending up feeling guilty; and also have difficulty recognizing when their children have behavior problems. The studies suggest that parents can become better disciplinarians— in general, better parents—if they first learn how to manage their own anger and frustration, develop creative problem-solving techniques, and give and accept support from others. Among the findings are that:

* In general, when parents are sensitive to their children's needs, the children are more obedient;
* Praise and love are important, but should be coupled with limits, since too much permissiveness fails to help children develop self-control and is, in the words of one psychologist, "a disaster in the hands of most parents";
* Behavior problems are best dealt with early, rather than waiting until the "problem years" of adolescence, when the child may be at risk;
* Spanking is not only ineffective but also damaging to the child's self-esteem and to the overall parent-child relationship.

Various programs around the country are geared toward training parents in the "tricks" of discipline, showing them how best to communicate with their children, praise and reward them, set limits for them, and handle behavior problems. Several recent works also have the same aim, among them:

* *Discipline: A Sourcebook of 50 Failsafe Techniques for Parents*, by James Windell (Collier, 1991). A guidebook by a psychotherapist who works with parents and children on behavior and family problems, with chapters on specific areas of concern—such as encouraging desired behavior or teaching lessons—and discussion of various techniques appropriate to children's ages and situations.
* *Time-Out for Toddlers: Positive Solutions to Typical Problems in Children*, by Dr. James W. Varni and Donna G. Corwin (Berkley, 1991). Offers tips on how to use the "time-out" technique—a brief period in an isolated or dull place—to deal with familiar toddler problems, such as tantrums and whining.
* *Stop Struggling with Your Child: Quick-Tip Parenting Solutions That Will Work for You—and Your Kids Ages 4–12*, by Evonne Weinhaus and Karen Friedman (HarperCollins, 1991). This is based on the authors' parenting workshops, which are centered around five

simple rules: "Don't use your mouth, use your routine; if you can't change the child, change the environment; follow up with follow-through; stay grounded with ground rules; and go for negotiation." Weinhaus and Friedman, with Judy Meyer, also wrote *Stop Struggling with Your Teen* (Speck, 1984; Viking Penguin, 1988).

* *How to Discipline Your 6 to 12 Year Old without Losing Your Mind*, by Jerry L. Wyckoff and Barbara C. Unell (Doubleday, 1991). Focuses on how parents can help shape their children's behavior, in such areas of usual parent-child conflict as table manners but also in dealing with such problems as shyness and building self-confidence.

* *1–2–3 Magic* (Child Management, 1990). This video featuring child psychologist and parent Thomas Phelan uses a workshop format to present his approach to disciplining children 2 to 12 years old, by minimizing or eliminating undesirable behavior and encouraging desirable conduct, with many practical situations. (For more information, contact: Child Management, 800 Roosevelt Road, Building B, Suite 309, Glen Ellyn, IL 60137.)

* *Positively Rewarding: An Effective Program for Reinforcing Positive Behavior* (1989). A computer software program for parents or teachers to use with children in building positive behavior. The adult develops a customized chart that clearly specifies the desired behavior (doing homework or cleaning up a room, for example), assigns "point values" to the behavior, and—by agreement with the child—makes a contract to give a reward when the behavioral goal is met, with the child often selecting the reward from a list onscreen. The program is written for an Apple computer (128K), for use with children ages 7 to 12. (For more information, contact: Tom Snyder Productions, 90 Sherman Street, Cambridge, MA 02140-9923.)

Parents will also want to check out "I'll Never Do That to *My* Children!" below, "Putting Child Abuse in the Past" on page 206, and "Has Parenting Been Taken Over by Professionals?" on page 193.

I'll Never Do That to *My* Children!

Most parents start out with the best intentions, conceiving of themselves as ideal parents and their children as ideal offspring. But the distance between the real and the ideal is often great, and many parents find themselves looking for help in understanding the destructive baggage they have brought from their own past, so that they won't unwittingly pass it on to their own children. Several recent works focus on the weight of the past, stressing that parents must understand how their past has shaped them and come to terms with it before they can be the whole adults and parents they wish to be. Among these new works are:

♦ *I'll Never Do to My Kids What My Parents Did to Me: A Guide to Conscious Parenting*, by Thomas Paris and Eileen Paris (Lowell House, 1992). Helps parents to recognize how their own family legacies—unconscious, negative compulsions learned during their own childhoods—may affect their relationship with their own children, and to make conscious decisions about discipline, rather than acting reflexively. The book includes a questionnaire to help parents identify these legacies and tools for dealing with them.

♦ *How to Avoid Your Parents' Mistakes When You Raise Your Children*, by Claudette Wassil-Grimm (Pocket, 1992). A guide to breaking the cycle of family dysfunction.

♦ *How to Raise the Children You Wish Your Parents Had Raised*, by Carol Marsh (Gallopade, 1991).

♦ *Fathers and Mothers*, by Robert Bly and others (Spring Publications, 1992). A series of 12 chapters on breaking old habits in thinking about family.

♦ *Family Mirrors: What Our Children's Lives Reveal About Ourselves*, by Elizabeth Fishel (Houghton Mifflin, 1991). Examines how family patterns of family-child interaction recur through generations.

♦ *Forgiving Our Parents, Forgiving Ourselves*, by David Stoop and James Masteller (Servant Publications, 1991). Focuses on moving beyond failures to forgiveness and healing.

♦ *Like Father, Like Son: Healing the Father-Son Wound in Men's Lives*, by Gregory M. Vogt and Stephen T. Tirridge (Plenum, 1991).

♦ *About Sibling Rivalry: Understanding the Legacy of Childhood*, by Jane Greer with Edward Myers (Crown, 1992). Gives a clinical social worker's overview of the state of siblinghood, including patterns of sibling relationships that are passed on from parents to children and that may be transferred to surrogate siblings in other relationships.

♦ *Brothers and Sisters: How They Shape Our Lives*, by Jane Mersky Leder (St. Martin's, 1991). Explores sibling relationships at every stage of life, with many anecdotes and case histories, and suggests that sibling rivalry may *not* be inevitable.

Parents may also want to check out "Putting Child Abuse in the Past" on page 206 and "Parents in Training for Discipline" on page 202.

Putting Child Abuse in the Past

For many parents, their own history of being abused as children puts them at risk of becoming abusers themselves. Adult survivors of abuse have become much more vocal and active in recent years, bringing their personal experiences out into the open to share with others, and working in small groups or larger organizations to provide mutual support in healing the hurts of the past and moving beyond them. A number of new books have come out of this process, aimed at helping abused adults understand and accept the past, and heal themselves. Among these recent works are:

On Healing

• *Transcending Turmoil: Survivors of Dysfunctional Families*, by Donna F. La Mar (Plenum/Insight, 1992). A Michigan psychologist's study of case histories of the healing process, as "transcenders" distance themselves from their families and become close to others.

• *Reach for the Rainbow: Advanced Healing for Survivors of Sexual Abuse*, rev. ed., by Lynne D. Finney (Perigee, 1992). Intended for "survivors of sexual abuse and incest, their loved ones, and their therapists."

• *Beyond the Darkness: Healing for Victims of Sexual Abuse*, by Cindy Kubetin and Dr. James Mallory, Jr. (Word, 1992). Explores false beliefs about and effects of sexual abuse.

• *The Sexual Healing Journey: A Guide for Survivors of Sexual Abuse*, by Wendy Maltz (HarperCollins, 1991). A self-help guide by a sex therapist, family counselor, and date-rape victim, discussing the symptoms of sexual abuse, providing various case histories, checklists, and questions.

On the Effects of Child Abuse

• *Too Scared to Cry: Psychic Trauma in Childhood*, by Lenore Terr, M.D. (Basic Books, 1992). A psychiatrist details the effects of psychic trauma.

• *The Kasper Hauser Syndrome of "Psychosocial Dwarfism": Deficient Statural, Intellectual, and Social Growth Induced by Child Abuse*, by John Money (Prometheus, 1992).

+ *When a Child Kills: Abused Children Who Kill Their Parents*, by Paul A. Mones (Pocket, 1991). Explores case studies of children who kill one or both parents, or hire others to do so. A children's rights advocate, Mones notes that in many such cases the child was severely abused; he calls for more effective intervention strategies in his concluding essay, "The Legacy of Child Abuse."

+ *On Trial: America's Courts and their Treatment of Sexually Abused Children*, by Billie Wright Dziech and Charles B. Schudson (Beacon, 1991). Explores ways of communicating with sexually abused children in a courtroom, as through anatomically correct dolls and questioning over closed-circuit television, seeking to balance concern for children's fears against the rights of innocent-until-proven-guilty defendants.

Personal Accounts

+ *Daddy, Please Say You're Sorry*, by Amber (CompCare, 1992). A handwritten, self-illustrated book by a woman survivor of incest.

+ *Dancing with Daddy: A Childhood Lost and a Life Regained*, by Betsy Petersen (Bantam, 1991). Gives a personal account of childhood incest and efforts to break the cycle of abuse in the next generation.

+ *Please, Somebody Love Me! Surviving Abuse and Becoming Whole*, by Jillian Ryan (Baker Book House, 1991). Relates Ryan's personal story of abuse and recovery.

The recent new openness has also led to the understanding that child abuse is far more common than was previously thought, though hysteria or malice sometimes leads to unfounded charges of abuse. Alert parents will want to be aware of the possible signs of child abuse. A checklist of such possible signs, along with a general discussion of the subject and a list of resources, is given in the *Parent's Desk Reference*, by Irene Franck and David Brownstone (Prentice Hall, 1991). Parents seeking to help their young children understand about abuse will find a reading list there as well. They may also want to explore these works:

Works by or for Children

+ *Love Letters: Responding to Children in Pain*, by Doris Sanford and Graci Evans (Multnomah, 1991). Contains responses to letters from children and adults who have written about their abuse or trauma in childhood. Sanford and Evans are also the authors of the "Hurts of Childhood" and "In Our Neighborhood" series.

 • *Don't Make Me Go Back, Mommy,* by Doris Sanford (Multnomah, 1990). Part of the "Hurts of Childhood" series, for children in grades 1 through 4. A young girl reveals to her parents the sexual, physical, and psychological abuse carried on in her day-care center, disguised as religious ritual. The book includes an appendix to help parents handle their own feelings in such a crisis. It is also useful for others who work with children.

Parents will also want to look at "I'll Never Do That to *My* Children!" on page 204, "Parents in Training for Discipline" on page 202, and "Children's Problems—When to Get Help" on page 190.

Sleep—The Impossible Dream

No one can make children magically sleep through the night, but a few recent books may help new parents fighting loss of sleep—or parents of older children tired of fighting *about* sleep—by showing what's normal and what's not, and discussing what can be done about it:

 • *The Sleep Book for Tired Parents,* by Becky Huntley (Parenting Press, 1991). Describes the normal patterns of sleep, various kinds of sleep disorders, and approaches to sleep problems, with real-life examples. (For more information, contact: Parenting Press, P.O. Box 75267, Seattle, WA 98125.)
 • *Getting Your Child to Sleep—and Back to Sleep,* by Vicki Lansky (Book Peddlers, 1991). A useful, reassuring primer for parents facing sleep problems for the first time, progressing from tried-and-true basics through discussion of more serious problems, such as night terrors.
 • *"I'm Not Sleepy,"* by Denys Cazet (Orchard/Jackson, 1992). A story about a patient father devising a tale to lull his son to sleep. For ages 3 to 6.

Parents may also want to look at *Crying Baby, Sleepless Nights,* by Sandy Jones (Harvard Common Press, 1992), a revised edition of *Why Your Baby Is Crying and What You Can Do About It,* which encompasses current research in the rapidly evolving field of infant discomfort.

Splitting and Coming Together Again

Questions of divorce and remarriage are all around us, if not in our own families, then in our communities. Approximately two children in five now grow up in families where there has been a divorce. Although marital splits may be widespread, reducing the traditional social stigma of divorce, the pain and trauma for children shows no sign of abating.

A 1991 national survey of over 1,400 children from divorced families found that an astonishing 23 percent of the fathers had had no contact with their children for the previous five years, and another 20 percent had not seen their children at all during the preceding year. Many fathers fail to maintain child-support payments; even when they do, the level of support for the mother and children is generally lower than when the family was together. Many children of divorce also feel abandoned when the support payments stop at age 18, with many fathers— even professionals with comfortable incomes—failing to contribute to their children's college education.

One surprising result of the fallout from divorce, seen in several recent studies summarized by Judith S. Wallerstein (see *Second Chances*), is that, when parents are in long-term sharp conflict, many children in intact families suffer effects similar to those of children in divorced families. And if significant conflict continues after the divorce, especially over custody arrangements, so does the damage. In fact, where parental conflict persists, some studies indicate that the pattern of switching children back and forth from one parent's residence to another may do more harm than good.

Many young children mistakenly assume that they have somehow caused the parental conflict and separation. Both younger and older children often experience behavioral and academic problems, and difficulty in establishing lasting relationships themselves. Contrary to earlier assumptions, there is some evidence that older children are most affected in the long run; some suggest that that is because they are caught in the battleground longer. Remarriage of one or both parents adds even more complicating elements to the equation; for children, the success and stability of the new "blended" families depends greatly on the level of continuing conflict among the adults.

Because children are so vulnerable to the trauma of a family breakup, courts in some parts of the country are requiring divorcing parents to attend seminars about the effects their children may face and ways to avoid them. Since late 1988, a four-hour program called "Children Cope with Divorce: Seminar for Divorcing Parents" has been mandated for divorcing parents in Cobb County, Georgia. Using a mix of lectures, films, and role-playing by paired leaders, the seminar offers a child's-eye view of divorce, often through dramatizations of parental-conflict scenarios, in the hope that parents will think about how their actions affect their children. This program has served as a model for similar ones around the United States.

For the children themselves, some schools are running special support groups and counseling programs. The prototype was established in Ballston Spa, New York, in 1978. In a program called "Banana Splits," children from divorced families gather together weekly, under the leadership of school psychologists, to share their experiences and to provide support and encouragement for each other. Many such programs have now been established across the United States; most are in elementary schools, with different age groups meeting separately, but the approach is spreading to high schools as well. Programs are voluntary and often require parental consent. Matters discussed are generally confidential, but the adult leader may ask a child's permission to discuss with a parent a particular matter that warrants special attention.

But in the end, it is up to parents themselves to help children deal with the myriad questions surrounding divorce, remarriage, and single parenting. Among the recently released materials that may help parents do so are:

For Young Children

• *Living with Divorce*, by Elizabeth Garigan and Michael Urbanski (Good Apple, 1991). Comes in a Primary version for children in grades 1 through 4 and a Middle School version for children in grades 5 through 9.

• *D Is for Divorce*, by Lori Peters Norris (Health Communications, 1991). Part of the "Little Books for Big Feelings" series of pocket-size minibooks for children ages 5 to 9.

• *About Divorce*, by Joy Berry (Childrens, 1990). Part of the "Good Answers to Tough Questions" series, for children in grades 3 and up.

• *When is Daddy Coming Home?: A Workbook for Children of Divorce*, by Darlene Weyborne (Aronson, 1992).

• *At Daddy's on Saturdays*, by Linda Walvoord Girard (Albert Whitman, 1991). For children ages 5 to 8.

• The "Your Family Album" series, from Twenty-First Century Books, by Gretchen Super, for children in kindergarten through grade 2. Titles include *What Is A Family?* (1991), *What Kind of Family Do You Have?* (1991), *Traditions* (1992), and *Sisters and Brothers* (1992). The series stresses the diversity of families—nuclear, single-parent, extended, blended, adoptive, and foster, as well as those differing in race, ethnicity, socioeconomic class, and traditions—and looking at families from the child's point of view, using homey snapshots of families from various backgrounds.

• *Talking About Stepfamilies*, by Maxine B. Rosenberg (Bradbury, 1990). This series of interviews with stepchildren (mostly ages 10 to 13) gives an overview of common feelings, problems, and solutions, with hints for success, sources of help, and bibliographies (for children in grades 4 through 7).

For Older Children

• *Boys and Girls Book about Divorce*, by Richard A. Gardner (Aronson, 1992). A reprint of a 1983 book, for children in grades 7 and up.

• *Understanding Child Custody*, by Susan N. Terkel (Watts, 1991). For children in grades 7 through 12; describes the different types of custody and such problems as parental abduction and court-shopping (seeking a place that will give a different custody ruling), and explains *children's* rights and responsibilities regarding custody. It includes toll-free numbers for teens needing help.

Note: Many other recent or older books on divorce and related concerns, for children of various ages, can be found in reference books such as those listed under "Best Reading for Kids" on page 133.

Guides for Parents

• *Long-Distance Parenting: A Guide for Divorced Parents*, by Miriam G. Cohen (NAL-Dutton, 1991).

• *Child Support: How to Get What Your Child Needs and Deserves*, by Carole A. Chambers (Summit, 1991).

• *Stepmothers: Keeping It Together with Your Husband and His Kids*, by Merry Bloch Jones and Jo Ann Schiller (Carol/Birch Lane, 1992).

◆ *Re-Married with Children: A Blended Couple's Journey to Harmony*, by Don Houck and Ladean Houck (Here's Life Publishers, 1991).

◆ *Practical Parenting—Blended Families: (Yours, Mine and Ours)* (1991). A video for adults, hosted by actor Dick Van Patten, that discusses the myths and realities of stepfamilies today, including such issues as divided loyalties, periods of adjustment, dealing with absent parents, maintaining family continuity, and handling discipline. (For more information, contact: United Learning, 6633 West Howard, Niles, IL 60648.)

Background Works

◆ *Second Chances: Men, Women and Children a Decade after Divorce*, by Judith S. Wallerstein with Sandra Blakeslee (Ticknor & Fields, 1990).

◆ *Growing Up with Divorce*, by Neil M. Kalter (Fawcett/Ballantine, 1991).

◆ *Caught in the Crossfire: The Impact of Divorce on Young People*, by Lorraine Henricks (PIA Press, 1991).

Free Information for Parents

Many parents are unaware that the government offers numerous free or low-cost publications containing information of consumer interest. Many of these are offered through the Consumer Information Center of the U.S. General Services Administration. Brochures, booklets, pamphlets, and other materials on consumer concerns from any branch of government are offered through the *Consumer Information Catalog*, with each quarterly issue listing approximately 200 free or low-cost booklets. Among the offerings in a recent issue were:

◆ *Children + Parents + Arts* (1992). A series of pamphlets with creative ideas to help children develop their artistic skills in theater, writing, music, dance, and the visual arts. From the National Endowment for the Arts (NEA).

◆ *Books for Children #7* (1991). A list of over 100 of the best children's books recently published for preschool through junior high school readers, providing helpful descriptions of the books, which are divided into appropriate age groups for easy reference. Published annually by the Library of Congress (LC).

♦ *Timeless Classics* (1991). A list of nearly 400 books published before 1960 for children of all ages. From the National Endowment for the Humanities (NEH).

♦ *Food Irradiation—Toxic to Bacteria, Safe for Humans* (1991). How irradiation kills harmful organisms and is especially useful in certain foods. From the Food and Drug Administration (FDA).

♦ *Get Hooked on Seafood Safety* (1991). How to select, store, and prepare seafood to eliminate or avoid the viruses and bacteria that cause illness. From the Food and Drug Administration (FDA).

♦ *Is That Newfangled Cookware Safe?* (1991). The advantages of and safety concerns about seven popular types of cookware from aluminum to nonstick coated to cast iron. From the Food and Drug Administration (FDA).

♦ *Preventing Food-Borne Illness* (1991). A discussion of symptoms, prevention tips, and safety storage, with charts on common disease-causing organisms and where they come from. From the Food and Drug Administration (FDA).

♦ *Contact Lenses: The Better the Care the Safer the Wear* (1991). Discusses the risks of infection and provides a step-by-step chart for proper care of lenses, including hard, gas-permeable, and extended-wear soft lenses. From the Food and Drug Administration (FDA).

♦ *Seal Out Dental Decay* (1991). How dental sealants can prevent tooth decay in young children. From the National Institutes of Health (NIH).

♦ *Acne: Taming that Age-Old Adolescent Affliction* (1991). A discussion of the myths, causes, and most effective treatment for both mild and severe acne. From the Food and Drug Administration (FDA).

♦ *More Than Snuffles: Childhood Asthma* (1991). Examines causes, symptoms, and treatments of this common chronic disease: From the Food and Drug Administration (FDA).

♦ *Panic Disorder* (1991). Discusses what to do when anxiety or sudden fear seems to be too much to handle, providing lists of symptoms, treatments, and sources of help. From the National Institute of Mental Health (NIHM).

♦ *Access Travel: Airports* (1991). Lists design features, facilities, and services at 553 airport terminals worldwide for people with disabilities and provides tips for easier travel. From the Office of Consumer Affairs.

* *Staying Healthy and Whole: A Consumer Guide to Product Safety Recalls* (1991). Lists products regulated by eight federal agencies, with addresses and phone numbers. From the Office of Consumer Affairs.

* *Consumer's Resource Handbook* (1992). Lists contacts for help with consumer problems or complaints, including corporate consumer representatives, private resolution programs, automobile manufacturers, and government agencies; tells how to write an effective complaint; and also offers tips on a wide range of topics, such as selecting child care and choosing a school. From the Office of Consumer Affairs.

To receive a free copy of the *Consumer Information Catalog* offering these and other such free or low-cost publications of interest to consumers, send your request (along with your name and address) to S. James, Consumer Information Center-2B, P.O. Box 100, Pueblo, CO 81002. When you place an order, you can ask to receive the next quarterly catalog, containing additional publications.

Many books of consumer interest are also published by the government, on topics that include children, families, education, and health. For a copy of the catalog listing such books, write to: Free Catalog, P.O. Box 37000, Washington, DC 20013. Request the *U.S. Government Books Catalog*, publication #5045, and be sure to include your name and address.

To keep current on food news and on health and safety issues, parents may also want to subscribe (also through the Consumer Information Center) to two inexpensive publications: *The FDA Consumer*, a magazine published 10 times a year, containing articles discussing the consumer implications of recent developments in the regulation of foods, drugs, and cosmetics, from the Food and Drug Administration; and *Food News for Consumers*, a quarterly that discusses food safety, health and nutrition, and recent findings on various food concerns, from the U.S. Department of Agriculture (USDA). The USDA also offers free food safety information over the telephone on its Meat and Poultry Hotline, 800-535-4555, or in Washington, DC, 202-720-3333, available 10 A.M. to 4 P.M. EST.

Families with access to a personal computer and a modem (a device to connect the computer to a database) can now hook into the Food and Drug Administration's Electronic Bulletin Board Service (FDA BBS)—for free. The service contains information for a wide range of users, from consumers to health professionals. Among the materials most interesting to parents are the contents of FDA news releases,

Consumer Information Catalog
(CONSUMER INFORMATION CENTER, U.S.
GENERAL SERVICES ADMINISTRATION)

The FDA Consumer (FOOD
AND DRUG ADMINISTRATION)

Food News for Consumers
(U.S. DEPARTMENT OF
AGRICULTURE)

answers to questions arising from news stories, indexes to both news and answers, and the full text of current and past issues of *The FDA Consumer*. The FDA BBS also contains material of interest primarily to professionals and parents with special concerns, such as the text of enforcement reports; information on drug and device product approvals; bulletins on drugs and on devices and radiological health; current AIDS information; indexes and summaries of FDA stories in the *Federal Register*, by subject and by date; the text of testimony at FDA Congressional hearings; speeches given by the FDA Commissioner and Deputy Commissioner; veterinary medicine news; import alerts; and news of coming FDA meetings. The FDA BBS was formerly a commercial service but has been enhanced and simplified for ease of use by the general public, from spring 1992. For the brief setup and sign-on instructions, contact: Parklawn Computer Center (BBS), 5600 Fishers Lane, Room 2B59, Rockville, MD 20857; 301-443-7318, or see the April 1992 issue of *FDA Consumer*.

Many branches of the federal government also provide information over the telephone. On child or maternal health matters, for example, there is the National Maternal and Child Health Clearinghouse (NMCHC), 202-625-8410; on drugs there is the National Institute on Drug Abuse (NIDA), 800-HELP [4357], in Spanish, 800-66A-YUDA [662-9832], 9 A.M. to 3 A.M., Monday to Friday, and noon to 3 A.M. Saturday and Sunday. To find the right government arm for a particular question, call the Federal Information Center, 800-347-1997, 9 A.M. to 10:30 P.M. EST. On health questions, call the National Institutes of Health (NIH), 301-496-4000, for referral to the proper agency.

Many private organizations also offer hotlines and helplines, some of them toll-free. For example, starting in late 1991, the National Center for Nutrition and Dietetics, a service of the American Dietetic Association, began offering a hotline to answer consumers' questions about food and nutrition. From 10 A.M. to 5 P.M. Eastern Standard Time, Monday through Friday, parents can call 800-366-1655 and talk directly to a registered dietitian on anything from lowering cholesterol to feeding a finicky two-year-old. Pre-recorded messages on topics such as healthy holiday eating, food safety, fat, cholesterol, and weight control are available 24 hours a day on the same hotline, with messages updated monthly to reflect timely nutrition information. To find hotlines or helplines for your particular question, you can call the National Health Information Clearinghouse, 800-336-4797, or AT&T's Toll-free Number Directory, 800-555-1212. Some reference books for parents (including our own; see under "Kids Do Not Come with Instructions" on page 188) also provide information on helpful organizations and hot-lines, listed and grouped under topics of interest.

Social Security, Baby

Even before they're able to walk, today's infants need a Social Security number—that is, if the parents wish to receive the deduction allowed for dependents (as of April 1992, $2,150 each). Since 1991, each child must be registered for a Social Security number. Parents can do this by visiting their local Social Security Administration or Internal Revenue Service (IRS) office, bringing with them the child's birth certificate (the original, with raised seal, not a photocopy) and another piece of identification. At the office, they should ask for the Application for a Social Security Number (Form SS-5); to get the form ahead of time, call 800-772-1213. Processing of the application takes about two weeks. Parents will be given an application receipt; if the infant's Social Security number does not arrive before the parents' tax return needs to be filed, a copy of the receipt should be attached with the notation "applied for" on the return. **Note**: Some parents have been receiving official-looking mail offers to obtain an infant's Social Security number for a $15 "administration fee." This should be ignored. It is totally unofficial and unnecessary. Some hospitals provide the forms for a child's Social Security number and send it in, even before the mother is released after childbirth.

Low-income families—those earning below $21,250 before taxes—also need Social Security numbers for their children so they can receive Earned Income Credits from the IRS when they file their tax returns. As of April 1992, the basic credit for one child was $1,192, with an additional $828 for two or more children, for a maximum of $2,020. In addition, if parents paid health insurance premiums for one or more children during the tax year, they may be able to claim as much as $428 in credits, depending on the amount they actually paid. If money is owed on the tax return, these credits can be subtracted from the amount due; but if no taxes are owed, parents will receive these credits as payments. Credits may also be available for a child born during that tax year. Details of such programs vary from year to year. (For more information, contact the Internal Revenue Service, 800-829-1040, and ask for Publication 596, *Earned Income Credit*, or any successor publication in a later year.)

Appendix: Building
A Home Library

Note: This list is reprinted by permission of the American Library Association. For more information, see page 134.

Building a Home Library: Preschool

• *The Paper Crane*, by Molly Bang. Illus. 1985. Greenwillow, hardcover; Morrow/Mulberry, paper. A quiet restaurant plays host to a mysterious man who pays for his meal with a paper crane that magically comes alive and attracts many customers.

• *Annie and the Wild Animals*, by Jan Brett. Illus. 1985. Houghton. One cold winter day, Annie's cat mysteriously disappears, and, because she misses her pet so much, she attempts to attract other animals. When the cat reappears in the spring, it brings a special surprise.

• *Goldilocks and the Three Bears*, by Jan Brett. Illus. 1987. Putnam. A newly illustrated version of an old favorite; the elaborate illustrations feature borders that help tell the story.

• *Not So Fast, Songololo*, by Niki Daly. Illus. 1986. Macmillan/Margaret K. McElderry, hardcover; Penguin/Puffin, paper. A South African boy desperately wants a pair of red tackies, or sneakers, that he sees in a store window while shopping with his grandmother.

• *Growing Vegetable Soup*, by Lois Ehlert. Illus. 1987. HBJ. The joy of planting and growing vegetables and making vegetable soup, as shared by a father and child and celebrated in electrifyingly bright illustrations.

• *The Seasons of Arnold's Apple Tree*, by Gail Gibbons. Illus. 1984. HBJ. Arnold enjoys every season of the year because of his apple tree.

• *Chester's Way*, by Kevin Henkes. Illus. 1988. Greenwillow, hardcover; Penguin/Puffin, paper. Cautious and conservative, Chester and his best friend, Wilson, are horrified when zany, freewheeling Lilly moves into their neighborhood and shows them new ways of doing most everything.

• *Jessica*, by Kevin Henkes. Illus. 1989. Greenwillow, hardcover; Penguin/Puffin, paper. A humorous story about a girl who has an imaginary friend.

• *The Doorbell Rang*, by Pat Hutchins. Illus. 1986. Greenwillow. The number of their mother's delicious cookies Victoria and Sam have to share keeps decreasing as people continue to arrive at teatime.

• *The Trek*, by Ann Jonas. Illus. 1985. Greenwillow. A young girl's imagination causes her to see many animals—all ingeniously hidden in the pictures—in the street scenes on her way to school.

• *The Wolf's Chicken Stew*, by Keiko Kasza. Illus. 1987. Putnam. In an effort to fatten up some chickens for a tasty dinner, Wolf unwittingly makes many new friends.

• *I Go With My Family to Grandma's*, by Riki Levinson. Illus. by Diane Goode. 1986. Dutton. Grandma's house in Brooklyn gets increasingly busy as five families of cousins arrive, all by different means of transportation.

• *First Snow*, by Emily Arnold McCully. Illus. 1985. HarperCollins. A story without words about a timid mouse child's experiences sledding in the winter's first snowfall.

• *Down by the Bay*, by Raffi. Illus. by Nadine B. Wescott. 1987. Crown. Wescott's bright, cheerful pictures bring this funny story-song to life; the music as well as the lyrics are included.

• *Making Friends*, by Fred Rogers. Photos by Jim Judkis. 1987. Putnam. Reassuring advice from the television personality; full-color photographs picture modern children in everyday situations.

• *Sharon, Lois and Bram's Mother Goose: Songs, Finger Rhymes, Talking Verses, Games and More*, by Sharon, Lois and Bram. Illus. by Mary A. Kovalski. 1986. Atlantic Monthly. Music, lyrics and game instructions for many popular Mother Goose rhymes; the original arrangements echo those from the trio's recording *Mainly Mother Goose*.

• *Pumpkin, Pumpkin*, by Jeanne Titherington. Illus. 1986. Morrow. A boy plants a pumpkin seed and watches it grow until he chooses to carve it into a jack-o'-lantern.

• *Where Does the Brown Bear Go?*, by Niki Weiss. Illus. 1989. Greenwillow, hardcover; Penguin/Puffin, paper. A gentle bedtime story that answers the question of where the animals go when night comes.

• *The Little Old Lady Who Was Not Afraid of Anything*, by Linda Williams. Illus. by Megan Lloyd. 1986. HarperCollins/Crowell. A lady meets odd bits of clothing—one pair of pants, two gloves—as she is walking home; she devises an ingenious solution for all the parts, even the pumpkin head, which become upset when they cannot scare her.

• *Stringbean's Trip to the Shining Sea*, by Vera B. Williams. Illus. by Jennifer and Vera B. Williams. 1988. Greenwillow. A series of postcards that Stringbean Coe and his brother Fred send home tells the story of their long trip across the U.S. one summer in Fred's truck.

• *A Year of Beasts*, by Ashley Wolff. Illus. 1986. Dutton. Ellie and Peter live in rural New England and, throughout the year, see many different animals in the field and forest surrounding their home.

Building a Home Library: Early School-Age

• *Dinosaur Bones*, by Aliki. Illus. 1988. HarperCollins. A brief, clear, engagingly illustrated introduction to the exciting discoveries of fossilized dinosaur bones in the nineteenth century.

• *Desert Giant: The World of the Saguaro Cactus*, by Barbara Bash. Illus. 1989. Little, Brown. Full-color paintings and delicate calligraphy describe the life cycle of this giant cactus and the desert animals it helps to support.

• *Visiting the Art Museum*, by Laurene Krasny Brown and Mark Brown. Illus. 1986. Dutton. A lighthearted, comic book–style introduction to a family visit to an art museum, with a brief overview of some of the types and styles of art likely to be seen.

• *The Wednesday Surprise*, by Eve Bunting. Illus. by Donald Carrick. 1988. Clarion. Anna and Grandma spend every Wednesday night together and plan a special surprise for the whole family.

• *More Stories Julian Tells*, by Ann Cameron. Illus. by Ann Strugnell, 1986. Knopf. Five short stories about Julian, his friend Gloria, and his little brother Huey, who decides to be Superboy.

• *Magic School Bus Inside the Human Body*, by Joanna Cole. Illus. by Bruce Degen. 1989. Scholastic. An exciting, fact-filled, fantastical voyage with the amazing Mrs. Frizzle.

❖ *Aliens for Breakfast*, by Jonathan Etra and Stephanie Spinner. Illus. by Steve Bjorkman. 1988. Random. Richard joins in a fight to save Earth from the Dranes after he finds an intergalactic special agent in his breakfast cereal box.

❖ *Georgia Music*, by Helen V. Griffith. Illus. by James Stevenson. 1986. Greenwillow. An old man and his granddaughter find pleasure in the sounds of a rural Georgia summer and in the music they can make on his harmonica.

❖ *Scaly Babies: Reptiles Growing Up*, by Ginny Johnston and Judy Cutchins. Illus. 1988. Morrow. Color photographs and an informative text describe the birth and early life of all kinds of reptiles: turtles, crocodilians, lizards, and snakes.

❖ *Whiskers and Rhymes*, by Arnold Lobel. Illus. 1985. Greenwillow, hardcover; Morrow/Mulbery, paper. A collection of original, short, humorous poems in the tradition of nursery rhymes.

❖ *Fox on the Job*, by Edward Marshall. Illus. 1988. Dial. Fox wants a new bike but first must earn the money to buy it.

❖ *Knots on a Counting Rope*, by Bill Martin and John Archambault. Illus. by Ted Rand. 1987. Holt. Evocative watercolor illustrations and an emotionally powerful text tell the story of a Native American child who repeatedly asks his grandfather to tell him the exciting story of the boy's birth and childhood and about how—even though he was born blind—his grandfather taught the child to ride a horse.

❖ *I'll Meet You at the Cucumbers*, by Lilian Moore. Illus. by Sharon Wooding. 1988. Atheneum, hardcover; Bantam/Skylark, paper. Adam is afraid he may lose his good friend after the two country mice visit the city and Junius admits he might like to stay.

❖ *The Boston Coffee Party*, by Doreen Rappaport. Illus. by Emily A. McCully, 1988. HarperCollins. A young Boston woman suggests a scheme to get back at a wealthy merchant who consistently over-charges for scarce merchandise during the Revolutionary War. An easy-to-read story based on a true historical incident.

❖ *Keep the Lights Burning, Abbie*, by Peter Roop and Connie Roop. Illus. by Peter E. Hanson. 1985. Carolrhoda, hardcover; Lerner, paper. When the lighthouse keeper is delayed by a severe storm, his daughter must keep the lights burning herself.

❖ *Henry and Mudge: The First Book of Their Adventures*, by Cynthia Rylant. Illus. by Suçie Stevenson. 1987. Bradbury, hardcover; Macmillan/Aladdin, paper. Henry, who has no brothers or sisters, and no other children on his street to play with, finds a very special friend in his dog, Mudge.

• *How Much Is a Million,* by David Schwartz. Illus. by Steven Kellogg. 1985. Lothrop, hardcover; Scholastic, paper. An imaginative way to conceptualize the enormity of abstract numerical concepts. Steven Kellogg's whimsical illustrations help readers see how much a trillion really is.

• *The Sun,* by Seymour Simon. Illus. 1986. Morrow. Stunning color photographs, a clear text, and a clean, fresh design combine to create an inviting book about the nature of the sun.

• *Saying Good-bye to Grandma,* by Jane Resh Thomas. Illus. by Marcia Sewall. 1988. Clarion. A beloved family member dies, and the whole family gathers for her funeral in a realistic, moving view of a time that is especially mysterious to children, as seen through the eyes of spunky seven-year-old Suzie.

• *Oliver, Amanda and Grandmother Pig,* by Jean Van Leeuwen. Illus. by Ann Schweninger. 1987. Dial. Oliver Pig and his sister Amanda discover good and bad things about having a visit from Grandmother.

Building a Home Library: Middle Grade

• *Monster Garden,* by Vivien Alcock. 1988. Delacorte, hardcover; Dell/Yearling, paper. Frances (Frankie) Stein's secret experiment with a glob of goo has monstrous results.

• *Saving the Peregrine Falcon,* by Caroline Arnold. Photos. by Richard R. Hewett. 1985. Carolrhoda, hardcover; Lerner, paper. Full-color photographs and a brief text describe an unusual project to save the peregrine falcon from extinction. Chicks are hatched from eggs taken from the wild and later are released when they are strong enough to survive.

• *The Big Beast Book: Dinosaurs and How They Got That Way,* by Jerry Booth. Illus. by Martha Weston. 1988. Little, Brown. Fascinating facts, directions for projects, and plenty of illustrations in a fun-filled exploration of dinosaurs and fossils.

• *The Burning Questions of Bingo Brown,* by Betsy Byars. 1988. Viking, hardcover; Penguin/Puffin, paper. A humorous look at a middle-school boy's notebook in which he wrestles with some of life's harder problems, such as how he could fall in love with three girls within three minutes.

• *The Village by the Sea,* by Paula Fox. 1988. Orchard, hardcover; Dell/Yearling, paper. Ten-year-old Emma's father is having open-heart surgery, so she is sent to stay with her weird Aunt Bea for two very long and difficult weeks.

♦ *Birches*, by Robert Frost. Illus. by Ed Young. 1988. Holt. Atmospheric paintings by Caldecott Medalist Ed Young illustrate the well-known poem about the pleasures of climbing birch trees.

♦ *The Iron Giant: A Story in Five Nights*, by Ted Hughes. Illus. by Dirk Zimmer. 1988. HarperCollins. Everyone fears the iron giant until he does battle with a huge space monster.

♦ *The Mermaid Summer*, by Mollie Hunter. 1988. HarperCollins. In a story full of sorcery and superstition, a man refuses to believe in the power of mermaids, and the strong love of his grandchildren, Anna and Jon, helps him return from a three-year absence under the control of the mermaid's magic.

♦ *The Adventures of Ali Baba Bernstein*, by Johanna Hurwitz. Illus. by Gail Owens. 1985. Morrow, hardcover; Scholastic/Lucky Star, paper. David is dismayed about the three other Davids in his third-grade class and is impressed by *The Arabian Nights* in his search for a new name.

♦ *Babe: The Gallant Pig*, by Dick King-Smith. Illus. by Mary Rayner. 1985. Crown, hardcover; Dell/Yearling, paper. A pig develops the special dog-like talent of herding sheep and earns the title of sheep-pig.

♦ *Orp*, by Suzy Kline. 1989. Putnam, hardcover; Avon/Camelot, paper. Orville Rudemeyer Pygenski, Jr., forms an "I Hate My Name" club.

♦ *Lost Star: The Story of Amelia Earhart*, by Patricia Lauber. 1988. Scholastic. An exciting, fast-paced biography of the famous aviator who disappeared while attempting to fly around the world.

♦ *Hey World, Here I Am!*, by Jean Little. Illus. by Sue Truesdell. 1989. HarperCollins. Short essays and poems about friendship, growing up, and her family as penned by the always honest and sometimes funny Kate Bloomfield, a character in two of the author's previous books.

♦ *All about Sam*, by Lois Lowry. Illus. by Diane DeGroat. 1988. Houghton, hardcover; Dell/Yearling, paper. A humorous autobiography (fictional, of course) of Anastasia Krupnik's precocious little brother, Sam, from the moment of his birth until he attends nursery school.

♦ *Number the Stars*, by Lois Lowry. 1989. Houghton, hardcover; Dell/Yearling, paper. In Denmark in 1943, 10-year-old Annemarie Johansen and her family must hide Jewish Ellen Rosen from the Nazis until, with the aid of the underground Resistance, they help her escape to safety in Sweden.

♦ *Sarah, Plain and Tall*, by Patricia MacLachlan. 1985. HarperCollins. Caleb and Anna become captivated by their father's mail-order bride and hope Sarah, who describes herself as plain and tall, will choose to stay with them.

• *The Agony of Alice*, by Phyllis Reynolds Naylor. 1985. Atheneum, hardcover; Dell/Yearling, paper. Alice's mother died long ago, and now she's worried that she won't be a normal teenager since she has no one to help her with the hard parts of growing up.

• *Ramona: Behind the Scenes of a Television Show*, by Elaine Scott. Photos by Margaret Miller. 1988. Morrow, hardcover; Dell/Yearling, paper. A lively photo-essay about the making of the Public Broadcasting System's popular television series.

• *Broccoli Tapes*, by Jan Slepian. 1989. Putnam/Philomel, hardcover; Scholastic, paper. Stuck in Hawaii for five months with her family, Sara sends cassette tapes home to her class in Boston describing her experiences, including her adoption of a wild black cat.

• *The Friendship*, by Mildred D. Taylor. Illus. by Max Ginsburg. 1987. Dial, hardcover.

• *The Gold Cadillac*. Illus. by Michael Hays. 1987. Dial, hardcover. Bantam/Skylark, paper. Two emotionally powerful stories about relations between whites and blacks in the American South.

Building a Home Library: Young Adult

• *A Girl from Yamhill: A Memoir*, by Beverly Cleary. Illus. 1988. Morrow, hardcover; Dell/Yearling, paper. A moving autobiography explores how the popular author for children became a writer.

• *The Goats*, by Brock Cole. 1987. Farrar. A boy and a girl are stripped and marooned on a small island but, through their growing friendship, discover the inner resources to survive this humiliating practical joke.

• *Prairie Songs*, by Pam Conrad. Illus. by Darryl S. Zudeck. 1985. HarperCollins. Louisa loves the Nebraska prairie that is her home, but when she makes friends with the doctor's frail, beautiful wife, Emmeline, Louisa discovers not everyone is able to survive the harsh and lonely pioneer life.

• *Stotan!*, by Chris Crutcher. 1986. Greenwillow, hardcover; Dell/Laurel-Leaf, paper. Four friends from the Frost High swim team are challenged by their coach to a week of intensive training he calls "Stotan Week."

• *Say Goodnight, Gracie*, by Julie R. Deaver. 1988. HarperCollins.

Seventeen-year-old Morgan must find her own way to cope with the sudden death of her best friend, Jimmy.

• *The Honorable Prison*, by Lyll B. De Jenkins. 1988. Dutton/ Lodestar, hardcover; Penguin/Puffin, paper. Teenage Marta and her family are political prisoners because of a moral stand taken by her father, a writer whose newspaper editorials repeatedly attack the military dictator ruling their Latin American country.

• *Eva*, by Peter Dickinson. 1989. Delacorte, hardcover; Dell/Laurel-Leaf, paper. After a serious traffic accident, 13-year-old Eva awakens from a coma in a hospital to discover that an unusual medical technique has been used to keep her alive.

• *Lincoln: A Photobiography*, by Russell Freedman. Illus. 1987. Clarion. Discover the truth about one of our most intriguing presidents in this profusely illustrated biography.

• *Wise Child*, by Monica Furlong. 1987. Knopf. Wise Child is adopted by a local sorceress who tutors her in the healing arts, but the child becomes tempted by promises of a wealthy life when her real mother, a student of the black arts, reappears and tries to lure the child away.

• *The Lives of Christopher Chant*, by Diana Wynne Jones. 1988. Greenwillow, hardcover; Knopf, paper. Because he has nine lives, young Christopher Chant, who is learning to be the next Chrestomanci (the one in charge of the world's magic), finds himself involved in a battle with renegade sorcerers.

• *After the Rain*, by Norma Fox Mazer. 1987. Morrow, hardcover; Avon/Flare, paper. Fifteen-year-old Rachel develops a special relationship with her gruff grandfather after she discovers he is dying.

• *Scorpions*, by Walter Dean Myers. 1988. HarperCollins. Jamal, the reluctant leader of the Harlem gang, the Scorpions, finds he earns new respect from his enemies when he carries a gun.

• *In Summer Light*, by Zibby O'Neal. 1985. Viking, hardcover; Bantam, paper. With the help of a graduate student who has come to work with her artist father, 17-year-old Kate Brewer learns that she doesn't have to do everything exactly the way her famous father wants it, which encourages her to have the courage to pursue her own artistic goals.

• *Hatchet*, by Gary Paulsen. 1987. Bradbury, hardcover; Penguin/ Puffin, paper. Thirteen-year-old Brian spends 54 days in the Canadian wilderness after surviving a plane crash that leaves him stranded— and alone.

• *Remembering the Good Times*, by Richard Peck. 1985. Delacorte, hardcover; Dell/Laurel-Leaf, paper. Three special friends find their relationship in jeopardy when one finds the pressures to succeed too much to bear.

• *Ruby in the Smoke,* by Philip Pullman. 1987. Knopf. Sixteen-year-old Sally Lockhart, an orphan living in nineteenth-century London, finds herself involved in a dangerous search for a mysterious ruby.

• *Strange Attractors,* by William Sleator. 1990. Illus. Dutton, hardcover; Penguin/Puffin, paper. A science fiction novel that explores the scientific theory of chaos, as a teenage science student decides whom he can trust with a powerful time travel device.

• *Libby on Wednesday,* by Zilpha K. Snyder. 1990. Doubleday, hardcover; Dell, paper. Eleven-year-old Libby, who has never before attended school, finds herself a reluctant member of a weekly writers' workshop after winning a writing competition at her new school.

• *Sons from Afar,* by Cynthia Voigt. 1987. Atheneum, hardcover; Fawcett/Juniper, paper. James and Sammy Tillerman begin a quest to learn more about their long-lost father.

• *So Far from the Bamboo Grove,* by Yoko K. Watkins. 1986. Lothrop, hardcover; Penguin/Puffin, paper. Eleven-year-old Yoko has a harrowing escape from Korea to Japan in this true story, which takes place at the end of World War II.

• *Blitzcat,* by Robert Westall. 1989. Scholastic. The black cat, Lord Gort, tries to find her master who has gone to fight for England during World War II.

• *Probably Still Nick Swansen,* by Virginia E. Wolff. 1988. Holt, hardcover; Scholastic, paper. Nick, a "Special Ed" kid, finds that his date for the prom with a former classmate doesn't go exactly as he has planned.

Index

Po bci 2